OLD TESTAMENT MESSAGE

A Biblical-Theological Commentary

Carroll Stuhlmueller, C.P. and Martin McNamara, M.S.C.

EDITORS

Old Testament Message, Volume 9

JEREMIAH 1-25

Lawrence Boadt, C.S.P.

A Michael Glazier Book
THE LITURGICAL PRESS
Collegeville, Minnesota

A Michael Glazier Book published by The Liturgical Press

The Bible text in this publication is from the Revised Standard Version of the
Bible, copyrighted 1946, 1952, © 1971, 1973 by the Division of Christian Education of the National Council of the Churches of Christ in the U.S.A. and used
by permission.

Cartography by Lucille Dragovan
Cover design by Lillian Brulc
Typography by Robert Zerbe/Graphics

ISBN 0-8146-5262-X

CONTENTS

BOOK III
Late Oracles from the Time of Zedekiah
Jeremiah 21-25

Editors' Preface

Old Testament Message brings into our life and religion today the ancient word of God to Israel. This word, according to the book of the prophet Isaiah, had soaked the earth like "rain and snow coming gently down from heaven" and had returned to God fruitfully in all forms of human life (Isa 55:10). The authors of this series remain true to this ancient Israelite heritage and draw us into the home, the temple and the marketplace of God's chosen people. Although they rely upon the tools of modern scholarship to uncover the distant places and culture of the biblical world, yet they also refocus these insights in a language clear and understandable for any interested reader today. They enable us, even if this be our first acquaintance with the Old Testament, to become sister and brother, or at least good neighbor, to our religious ancestors. In this way we begin to hear God's word ever more forcefully in our own times and across our world, within our prayer and worship, in our secular needs and perplexing problems.

Because life is complex and our world includes, at times in a single large city, vastly different styles of living, we have much to learn from the Israelite Scriptures. The Old Testament spans forty-six biblical books and almost nineteen hundred years of life. It extends through desert, agricultural and urban ways of human existence. The literary style embraces a world of literature and human emotions. Its history began with Moses and the birth-pangs of a new people, it came of age politically and economically under David and Solomon, it reeled under the fiery threats of prophets like Amos and Jeremiah. The people despaired and yet were re-created with new hope during the Babylonian exile. Later reconstruction in the homeland and then the trauma of apocalyptic movements prepared for the revelation of "the mystery hidden for ages in God who created all things" (Eph 3:9).

While the Old Testament telescopes twelve to nineteen hundred years of human existence within the small country of Israel, any single moment of time today witnesses to the reenactment of this entire history across the wide expanse of planet earth. Each verse of the Old Testament is being relived somewhere in our world today. We need, therefore, the *entire* Old Testament and all twenty-three volumes of this new set, in order to be totally a "Bible person" within today's widely diverse society.

The subtitle of this series—"A Biblical-Theological Commentary"—clarifies what these twenty-three volumes intend to do.

Their *purpose* is theological: to feel the pulse of God's word for its *religious* impact and direction.

Their *method* is biblical: to establish the scriptural word firmly within the life and culture of ancient Israel.

Their *style* is commentary: not to explain verse by verse but to follow a presentation of the message that is easily understandable to any serious reader, even if this person is untrained in ancient history and biblical languages.

Old Testament Message—like its predecessor, *New Testament Message*—is aimed at the entire English-speaking world and so is a collaborative effort of an international team. The twenty-one contributors are women and men drawn from North America, Ireland, Britain and Australia. They are scholars who have published in scientific journals, but they have been chosen equally as well for their proven ability to communicate on a popular level. This twenty-three book set comes from Roman Catholic writers, yet, like the Bible itself, it reaches beyond interpretations restricted to an individual church and so enables men and women rooted in biblical faith to unite and so to appreciate their own traditions more fully and more adequately.

Most of all, through the word of God, we seek the blessedness and joy of those

who walk in the law of the Lord!...

who seek God with their whole heart (Ps. 119:1-2).

Carroll Stuhlmueller, C.P.   *Martin McNamara, M.S.C.*

TABLE OF ABBREVIATIONS

ANET   James Pritchard, *Ancient Near Eastern Texts relating to the Old Testament* (3rd edition; Princeton, 1969)

Jer   Jeremiah

NT   New Testament .

OT   Old Testament

RSV   Revised Standard Version (National Council of Churches, 1952)

CHRONOLOGY OF THE TIMES OF JEREMIAH

c. 645   The birth of Jeremiah.

640   Josiah becomes king of Judah at the age of 8.

629   Assurbanipal makes his son Sin-shar-ushkin coregent.

628   Josiah begins his first reforms (2 Chr 34:3ff).

627   King Assurbanipal dies. Jeremiah begins his ministry.

626   Nabopolassar of Babylonia revolts against Assyria.

622   The "Lawbook" is found in the Temple.

612   The Babylonians and Medes capture Nineveh.

609   The final collapse of Assyria. Josiah dies in battle; Jehoahaz king (3 months) followed by Jehoiakim.

605   The Babylonians drive the Egyptians from Asia in the Battle of Carchemesh.

601   King Jehoiakim revolts against Babylon.

598   Babylonians besiege Jerusalem in December. City falls in March, 597.

597   Zedekiah becomes king (or regent) until 587.

593   Ezekiel called to be a prophet in Babylon.

589   Zedekiah revolts. The Babylonians attack immediately.

587   Jerusalem falls the second time in July, 587; the city and temple are destroyed.

586   Gedeliah acts as governor and is assassinated before 583.

c. 583   Jeremiah forced to go to Egypt in exile.

582   The Babylonians make a 3rd deportation of Judeans.

c. 581   Jeremiah dies in exile.

INTRODUCTION TO JEREMIAH

1. *Reading Jeremiah*

In order to appreciate the Book of Jeremiah and get the most out of its message, we need to understand something about the prophet's life and about the complexity of the book under his name. This book, one of the richest in the Old Testament, is filled with poetry, sermons and stories, sometimes by the prophet, at other times about the prophet, or again building upon the prophet's words. His life, too, was rich, filled with political events of great consequence for Israel: the destruction of Jerusalem, the exile to Babylon, and personal rejection and suffering at the hands of his own people. To simply sit down and read Jeremiah through as though it were a novel or an exciting adventure would be quickly disappointing. Many of the oracles and events are not arranged chronologically, even more are not labeled as to time and place, and sometimes not even to subject matter. What does stand out is the vision of a man who saw the hand of God so clearly in the events of his day. Because of this vision, Jeremiah was recognized by his own contemporaries as a prophet whose words were worth saving and handing on and even expanding and reusing in new situations of danger and discouragement. But before we read the book as a whole, we will need a brief discussion of his life and times, some guides to understanding how the book came together, and a few remarks on the most important themes of Jeremiah's message.

2. *Jeremiah and His World*

The first notice of the prophet Jeremiah records his call to be a prophet in 627 B.C., the 13th year of King Josiah's reign. At the time he was probably a young man somewhere between 16 and 20 years old. This information from the opening verses of the book set Jeremiah right into the middle of Israel's most crucial moment. The seventh century in the ancient Near East was the century of Assyria. From its heartland in upper Mesopotamia, what is now northern Iraq, this powerful nation had gained control over the entire Near Eastern world from the borders of Iran to the Mediterranean, and from central Turkey down to the middle of Egypt. It had expanded slowly throughout the ninth and eighth centuries in an ever-westward direction, using military conquest, terror, and mass exile of conquered peoples to make the small city-states submit. Two hundred years before Jeremiah's birth, about 840 B.C., Assyrian armies had forced King Jehu of northern Israel to be a vassal who paid tribute in gold and fine garments to the Assyrian king each year. This was recorded for ages to come on the famous "Black Stele" of King Shalmanezer, now found in the British Museum. A hundred years before Jeremiah's call, the Assyrians had attacked and destroyed Samaria, the northern capital, in 722, deporting most of the people to distant countries and putting an end to the northern ten tribes forever. The southern kingdom, made up mostly of the tribe of Judah, with its capital in Jerusalem, had escaped the same fate only because her kings, Ahaz, his son Hezekiah and the latter's son Manasseh, had made themselves vassals and held off Assyrian invasion with the promise of faithful obedience. Much of this eighth century drama is reflected in the books of the prophets Amos, Hosea, Micah and Isaiah.

Naturally, the political battles for independence were not the only acts in a growing tragedy. There was religious drama as well. The ninth century prophets Elijah and Elisha had demanded faithful service to Yahweh and the rejection of any loyalty to the Canaanite God Baal. The eighth century prophets challenged an Israel and its leaders who constantly committed injustice and oppression of the poor for political gains, and who would quickly desert Yahweh if it meant a secure political treaty with Assyria or another neighbor Hosea and Amos stressed that God would punish and abandon his own people if they did not return to the commands of the covenant and practice justice, honesty and true worship. Isaiah went further in demanding no political treaties or decisions be made for purely political reasons, but that the people return to obedience to God's law and wait in trust for God to care for them.

The struggle between the prophets and the kings was intense. The reign of King Hezekiah at the end of the eighth century reveals this clearly. When he began to rule, he also inaugurated a great reform of the religious practices in the temple to return them to their original purity. This led him in turn to attempt a political fight for freedom from Assyria against the advice of Isaiah. In 701, the Assyrian king Sennacherib attacked in force and wiped out all of Judah's cities except Jerusalem, where he set up a siege to starve it into surrender. Only some unexpected disaster forced the Assyrians to return home before leveling Jerusalem and deporting all of its people, but Hezekiah was still made to hand over all of the wealth of the city, pay annual tribute, and remain a faithful vassal, quiet and docile, for the rest of his reign until his death in 688 B.C.

Thus the seventh century began with Judah firmly under the control of Assyria. Hezekiah's son Manasseh reigned for over forty years (687 to 643) and, according to the Book of Kings, was not only faithful to Assyrian control, but even encouraged or at least officially tolerated all sorts of pagan rituals. 2 Kgs 21 records how he cancelled Hezekiah's reforms, allowed the fertility cult of Baal with its sacred prostitution to invade the Temple itself, and even permitted child sacrifices. All of this went far beyond the Assyrian demands for a statue of their god Assur to be placed in the royal chapel; it violated the most basic demand of Israelite faith that no god but Yahweh be worshipped. As a result the authors of the Book of Kings judged Manasseh to have been the worst of all the kings of Israel.

Manasseh died when Jeremiah was a boy. His son Amon ruled for two years, apparently following in his father's footsteps, but was assassinated by a people dissatisfied with the growing situation of violence, injustice and political weakness. This brought Amon's eight year old son Josiah to power in 641-640 B.C. While so young he could do little, but it seems that as soon as he gained the right to rule in his own name, he began a new reform of Israel's religion, eliminating many of the pagan shrines and rites. This would have been in his 12th year as king, about 628 or 627 B.C. In his 18th year, workmen repairing the temple found a "Book of the Law" hidden away. When they brought it to the king he was overwhelmed by its call for reform and fidelity to Yahweh, and he immediately began a major effort to implement its words. Most scholars believe this lawbook to be some form of the Book of Deuteronomy. Its basic message declared that Israel had constantly turned away from its God during its long history despite his promises and love for them; and that if the people persisted, God would hand them over to their enemies. Only if they "loved the Lord their God with all their heart and soul and strength" (Deut 6:5) would he bless them in their land.

Meanwhile Josiah also played politics. The seventh century had begun with a Near Eastern world solidly in the grip of Assyria but in the long reign of King Ashurbanipal (668-627), it both reached the heights of its empire and at the same time began to fall apart. After 650, the king had to fight his own brother who tried to set up a new kingdom centered in Babylon to the South. At Ashurbanipal's death in 627, a local Babylonian prince, Nabopolassar, did successfully revolt and win freedom. With the help of the Medes from Iran, he attacked Assyrian forces every year until he had driven to the very heart of their nation. in 614, the Medes captured and burned to the ground Assur, their ancient citadel, and by 612 the Babylonians and Medes together attacked and destroyed Nineveh the capital. Assyria was for all intents gone forever.

King Josiah of Judah took advantage of this period of Assyrian decline to make his nation as independent as possible. His religious reform was part of his overall plan to give Israel its own identity and restore its former glory under David and Solomon. To this end he moved into Samaria and the northern area of Israel and rejoined the two parts of the country. But in the aftermath of the fall of Nineveh, he was caught in the struggle of the big powers for their pieces of the former Assyrian empire. Babylon pushed westwards under Nabopolassar and his energetic son Nebuchadnezzar. Egypt pushed North through Israel to stop the Babylonians. In 609, Josiah tried to prevent Egyptian aid to the remnant of the Assyrians by attacking the pharaoh's army at the pass of Megiddo in the northern part of Israel but was killed in the battle.

The years from the death of Josiah up to the final collapse of the city of Jerusalem in 587-86 saw a succession of kings often mentioned in the prophecies of Jeremiah. All of them were deeply involved in playing off the balance of power between Egypt and Babylon. At first Egypt took control of Palestine (609 to 605) and replaced Josiah's son and successor Jehoahaz with another son, Jehoiakim. In 605, Nebuchadnezzar defeated the Egyptians at the battle of Carchemesh in Syria and drove them out of the Palestine. Jehoiakim then changed and sided with the Babylonians. When Babylon looked weak in 599, he rebelled but guessed wrong. The Babylonian army besieged Jerusalem in 598 and in the midst of the crisis, Jehoiakim died. His son

Jehoiachin was proclaimed king and immediately surrendered. Nebuchadnezzar deported this young man to
Babylon as a prisoner along with many leading citizens
and put his uncle Zedekiah on the throne as regent. This was
undoubtedly intended to keep the Judeans quiet while their
king remained captive. Yet Zedekiah himself finally gave
into the temptation to revolt in 589. This fateful action
led to the second and final assault on Judah and Jerusalem
by the Babylonian army. This time they did not spare the
city but totally tore it down, deported most of the educated
people, removed all the religious vessels and objects from
the temple, and made the broken land into a Babylonian
province.

It is against this background of reform that Jeremiah
began his ministry. In the very year after Josiah began his
efforts, Jeremiah appears as a proclaimer of warning, an
announcer of the evils of people, priests, and political
leaders, and a caller to repentance. He preached on and off
for the next 42 years, until after 585 B.C. As we shall see in
what remains of his words and in the stories about his life
collected in our present Book of Jeremiah, he was a complex
person. He worked through periods of reform, political
shifts of power, failure, destruction and exile. He had
moments of hope and many more of despair. He agonized in
private over his mission, but in public was sternly faithful
to the difficult and very severe words that God gave him to
say. He was respected by many in high places, but also
suffered greatly from others who considered him a traitor
and an enemy of his own people. Yet, in the end, his
prophecy became the key tradition by which Israel interpreted and understood its own failure and exile, and so
Jeremiah was preserved—but not without the explanations,
additions and interpretations that made him usable for
generations to follow. The result is that it will be difficult
to find the man Jeremiah easily. He has become a legend;
but more than that, a model and a prophet par excellence
for all times. Thus what his book preserves is the Jeremiah

who interprets the covenant, the Law, as a permanent gift to Israel. After Jerusalem fell for the last time in 587, Jeremiah was allowed to stay in Judah by the Babylonians. In the political chaos that followed, however, he was forcibly taken to Egypt by a group of fellow Israelites. There he ended his ministry; the last recorded message shows him at odds with his people.

During all these difficult periods, Jeremiah spoke firmly. He rebuked the political intrigues of the kings, called for repentance and a return to the covenant with God, and rejected all attempts to gain independence from the Babylonians. This naturally made him unpopular, even a threat, to the policies of both Jehoiakim and Zedekiah. Jehoiakim hated and opposed him strongly—and Jeremiah clearly disliked the king in return. Zedekiah in the last and more trying period had mixed feelings. He secretly admired the prophet and even spared his life on occasion but would not accept his message nor permit Jeremiah freedom to speak as he would have liked.

As we read the Book of Jeremiah, we shall become more and more aware of how deeply the prophet combined his religious proclamation with political insight.

3. *The Composition of the Book of Jeremiah*

The Book of Jeremiah confronts the reader with major textual difficulties. Even a casual reader notes an apparent lack of unity and direction in the book. Some of the more obvious examples include the combination of poetic oracles with prose oracles, the mixture of Jeremiah's own words with stories about his life, the repetition of some oracles in different places (the most important example being the Temple sermon recorded in chaps. 7 and 26), and the lack of chronological order. Oracles from the time of Jehoiakim, for instance, can be found scattered in different places throughout the book.

For years scholars have wrestled with these problems. They usually centered their attention on two questions: Why are some of the passages composed in poetic oracle style and others in long prose stories or sermons? They asked if we could detect a series of rewritings or additions that would show us how the book was put together? No one denies that earlier collections contributed to our present Biblical book. We can see a hint of such a division in chap. 25 where the prophet's words from his first 23 years are said to be written down (v. 13). In chap. 36, Jeremiah dictates a scroll containing all of his earlier prophecies to his assistant Baruch to be read to the king. Besides these mentions of an early collection of his words by the prophet himself, we detect other clustering of material: chaps. 46-51 prophesy against foreign nations; chaps. 30 to 33 contain oracles of hope; chaps. 36-45 form a biographical account of Jeremiah's ministry under Jehoiakim and Zedekiah.

Another group of oracles in chaps. 11-12, 15, 18 and 20 form a special type of personal complaint of the prophet and are seen together as "Jeremiah's Confessions."

The greatest puzzle occurs in chaps. 1-25 in which prose and poetry are mixed together. Many commentators have felt that only the poetic oracles are originally from Jeremiah while the biographical details were added by his scribe Baruch or another disciple. The most heated discussion of this type involves the long speeches in prose throughout chaps. 1-25. Some hold that they are the work of later religious leaders who adapted Jeremiah's message to the time of the exile or after. Others see a close relationship between these sermons and the language of the Book of Deuteronomy. Since Deuteronomy is closely tied to the reform of King Josiah, some connection with Jeremiah and his ministry should be expected. Thus this second group of scholars pictures the priests and other members of the school of Deuteronomy editing and saving Jeremiah's words while at the same time expanding and interpreting them within the framework of their own thought. Jeremiah becomes the hero of the deuteronomic reformers because his prophetic word helps explain why Israel fell to the Babylonians. Many factors commend this interpretation. The similarity of language and the concern of Jeremiah with ideas such as the covenant, repentance, and infidelity to Yahweh as a kind of adultery, are all noted individually in the commentary below. The addition of chapter 52, taken from the Second Book of Kings, is also a deuteronomic touch, since the Books of Kings are part of the larger Deuteronomic history of Israel.

Studies of Jeremiah commonly distinguish between the different types of material as simply "A," "B" and "C" where "A" represents the poetic oracles spoken by Jeremiah, "B" the narrative biography of the prophet written by Baruch or someone else close to the scene, and "C" marks the prose sermons that resemble Deuteronomy.

It may come as a new and even surprising idea to us that so much of the book of Jeremiah is not attributed to the prophet himself. If we accept only "A" texts as Jeremiah's original words, the prophet was immediately responsible for only about a third of the present text. But this should not shock us. Old Testament books usually evolved this way. They include not only writings and sayings *of* a person, but also those *about* the person, and normally at some point the editors add even later oracles and writings from disciples to show how the prophet (or Moses or David, etc.) was to be understood and applied in the years after his death. Deuteronomy itself forms the prime example. It is entirely written as a speech of Moses yet dates to nearly 600 years after his death! It took this particular form to show how the covenant given through Moses could be lived and kept in the seventh century, i.e., by the Israelites of Jeremiah's time. We are dealing as much with an inspired tradition as with an inspired book.

If we do not have problems enough dealing with the growth of the Hebrew text of Jeremiah, more questions arise when we examine the earliest Greek translation of Jeremiah, the Septuagint, which dates to pre-Christian times. It is not only quite a bit shorter than our current Hebrew Text but also has several sections in a different order. The major rearrangement involves all of chaps. 46-51 which are placed after 25:13 and in a different sequence. Small pieces of the Hebrew text of Jeremiah were found in the Qumran caves dating to the first century, in which some follow our present Hebrew order and some follow the order known in the Greek text. We must conclude that in the time before Christ there were at least two versions of Jeremiah. One was shorter and probably more original; the other was longer and reflects later reediting. Jews in Egypt used the shorter one, while Jews in Palestine, and perhaps even those in Babylon, began to follow also the later and longer edition. Such is the inspired history and the growth of a biblical book through the years.

Only when a book became accepted as "sacred" by Israel—that is, when it was canonized—was it considered totally closed and not to be updated nor adapted to new questions.

As far as we know the Pentateuch and the Prophets were "canonized" sometime between the end of the exile in 540 B.C. and 200 B.C., with a higher probability that it took place earlier rather than later. The canon, especially for the Pentateuch, has been associated with the reform and reorganization of Israel's religion by Ezra about 450 B.C. But since the Prophets were viewed as interpreters of the Law of Moses, it seems that they too were canonized soon after the time of the Pentateuch. At least the major prophets would have been. It always remains a possibility that other prophets were added to the list of sacred authors at a later date.

In a book such as Isaiah which contains the words of a prophet of the eighth century, the final canonized form contains his oracles, plus those of his disciples at the time, plus an entirely new series uttered by a follower two hundred years later during the Exile who brought his message in an updated form to an Israel in despair (chaps. 40-55), plus some chapters from the first years of the return to Jerusalem after the Exile (539-516 B.C.) which renewed Isaiah's message of hope (chaps. 56-66). In the Book of Jeremiah, written much closer to its time of canonizing, almost all of the materials deal with the prophet's times and the period of exile. We do not have to assume that the editors, whether they were followers of Deuteronomy or not, wanted to change the meaning of Jeremiah's words in order to face different times and new problems. Instead, they were careful to preserve his words and to add much material about his life (something which no other prophetic book has!) because they believed he had been right on target, and that his experience and his revelation from God about the covenant would stand the test of time as a model for all ages. The editors added a framework of speeches built on the authentic words of Jeremiah or on small incidents from his life (such as his images of the potter's shop in chaps. 18-19) that would not detract from or change his message, but sharpen its focus for a new time and place, namely for the Israelites in Exile and their brothers and sisters left in the devastated countryside of Judea. In the following commentary, some of the important theological and religious points made by these prose sermons will be discussed as models even for today.

A small example of the complex nature of the Book of Jeremiah is the question of what constituted the original scroll that Jeremiah dictated to Baruch as reported in chap. 36. Almost all scholars agree that the bulk of this scroll can still be found today as poetic oracles of type "A" in chaps. 1-25. This would include almost all of chaps. 2-6 and 8-10. It would not include much of chap. 1 or of chap. 7 which are in prose. In chaps. 11-18, the original oracles are now mixed in with a large number of later prose sermons. And it would include very little of chaps. 19-25; these chapters, as we shall see, must be dated later than the time of the first scroll. To make matters worse, chap. 36 also notes that this first scroll contained words against "all the nations." Should we then think that many of the oracles against foreign nations, found in chaps. 46-51, were also part of that original work? We cannot say for sure. What we do know from the end of chap. 36 is that when Jeremiah had to dictate the scroll a second time, he added still more oracles to it (v. 32).

This example is important for its uniqueness. Very rarely can we follow the process of how biblical documents were edited. This incident from Jeremiah's life tells us first of all that the prophets themselves often had a hand in compiling and collecting their words into writing, and secondly that the process could be done again and again, always adding to and changing the earlier collection. Not only did Jeremiah expand his body of spoken oracles, but disciples added stories and sermons to it at later times. And they did not just attach the new materials to the end of the book. They inserted them inside the work, placing like topics near like (e.g., gathering the images of the potter in chaps. 18 and 19), or placing images and sermons where they will have the most impact (Jeremiah's anguished "confessions" beside his most pessimistic oracles in chaps. 11, 15, 18 and 20). This makes the book read like a very disorganized history, but it does create a rhythm of dramatic points. It is no easy task to figure out the structure and outline of all the pieces in the Book of Jeremiah, even though many scholars have tried their hands at it. Yet, structure there is, and throughout this commentary we shall see how effectively one oracle of Jeremiah leads into the next and sharpens the color or drama.

4. *The Message of Jeremiah*

To understand the message of Jeremiah most fully, we need to be acquainted not only with his life and times, but also with the sources of his thought. The comments on individual passages will bring out similarities to other Old Testament books, but some general trends might be best noted before we start.

Jeremiah owes the most to prophets who went before him. A tradition of prophecy had grown up in Israel dating back to at least the time of Samuel and David. According to this understanding, a prophet held a special commission from Yahweh to be his spokesperson. As practiced and developed by earlier prophets, this role was more than that of a messenger, it was the role of a vicar, a delegate of God, who would not only speak in God's name, but be willing to offer some practical applications on his or her own. The prophet was also portrayed praying for the people or interceding with God for mercy when the prophetic word seemed too devastating. The prophet was seen primarily as a guardian over Israel, a warning voice against their sins. The element of hope was held out but only in a guarded way, sometimes after conversion, often after punishment, as part of God's long-range program of renewal and fidelity. The prophets saw themselves as protectors of the Mosaic covenant and defenders of the worship of Yahweh. In this sense they were also the sermon-givers of Israel, exhorting people to moral behavior and to true fidelity. Jeremiah was no different. He embodied all of these characteristics and preached on all of these themes.

More particularly, Jeremiah followed in the footsteps of Hosea and other nothern Israelite thinkers such as the authors of Deuteronomy and of the Elohist source in the Pentateuch. He stressed Israel's infidelity to God as a kind of adultery. For Hosea and Jeremiah breaking the covenant was not just violating a contract; it was a personal rejection of a loving God and all that God had done for Israel. Because of this, the language of these two prophets becomes highly emotional and even passionately wounded at times. It explains the extraordinary amount of feeling that Jeremiah expresses in his oracles. But it also allows the prophet great trust in God's mercy and forgiveness if the nation will only repent. As a loving spouse would welcome back the wayward partner, or a parent the prodigal child, so God would always be waiting for Israel to turn back in conversion. For Jeremiah, God becomes above all else a God of compassionate love, what in Hebrew is called *hesed*, an idea most difficult to translate into English because it includes faithfulness, uprightness, loyalty, generosity, love and forgiveness, among people usually united by blood, or at least by treaty.

A second critique of Israel shared with Hosea is the people's lack of knowledge of God. Despite God's many acts of mercy throughout their history, and despite his divine word through the prophets and his faithful loyalty to his side of the covenant, the people often acted as if they could simply discard Yahweh for another god or follow their own whims rather than his commandments. This "knowledge" is not the kind learned in school but more like the "experience" we have of relatives and friends. If Israel fails to know God it is because she failed to follow his demands and to experience his presence.

Still another side to the message of Jeremiah is his intensely personal manner of speaking. Readers have long identified certain passages as his "confessions" — 11:18-12:6; 15:10-21; 17:12-18; 18:18-23; 20:7-18 — these poems record his internal struggle with God about the task asked of him. They picture a prophet in anguish, abandoned by God while everyone mocked him, faced with failure as no one listened to him or took his words seriously. Even though we know from the study of ancient style that much of this vocabulary is traditional and was used almost automatically to show how deep was the national blindness, we can still confidently believe that we are discovering a part of the real Jeremiah. Throughout his life, the prophet saw disaster coming. The combination of religious failure and political opportunism would end in the loss of the nation. He saw the people excited by Josiah and his reforms, by Jehoiakim and his cunning way of playing off Egyptians and Babylonians, by Zedekiah and his break for independence. They jumped at every new hope and political shift. If only they could see where it all led.

Jeremiah put most of the blame on the kings. For his part he somewhat accepted the Babylonian rule—all as part of God's overall plan. It is quite probable that Jeremiah was not altogether pleased with the religious reforms of King Josiah. He never makes any mention of them as such. This can be due to one of two reasons: either he was displeased because they became so closely connected with political power plays by Josiah, an aspect of his policy which led to his own early death on the battlefield in a hopeless attempt to stop Egypt from helping Assyria against the Babylonians; or else he noted how little effect the reforming zeal of the priests and king had on the lives of the ordinary Israelite. Jeremiah found little sign of true conversion in the land.

Jeremiah suffered on behalf of his people as each new chance for turning back to God or reversing their course came and went. Despite his bitterness, at times even anger with God, he never lost sight of his own role to intercede for them, to beg for them, to warn and call them back.

Although Jeremiah owes a great deal to the prophets before him, he was perceived as somewhat unconventional in his own day. We can see from his biography in chaps. 26 to 44 that the leaders mistrusted him as a traitor who called for the nation to surrender. He did not make the priests very happy either when he denounced the temple as a superstitious source of hope and support, and predicted its collapse. Even when he offered hope, he included very little comfort. He wrote the exiles in Babylon to settle in for a long seventy year period and give up the dream of early freedom (chap. 29). He did believe that religious life could go on even under the Babylonians. His attempt to buy a field in his hometown right in the middle of the last battle for Jerusalem was meant to show this. But if we leave aside the very hopeful words of chaps. 30 to 31 as possibly expanded after his death into a new vision, the few positive signs that Jeremiah offered are usually overwhelmed by his pessimism that the people's blindness will never change until God has dealt the final blow to the land.

This negative attitude put Jeremiah into opposition with many other prophets of his day who saw their chief role to comfort a people in distress. The famous confrontation between Jeremiah and Hananiah in chap. 28 must be understood in this way. Hananiah was sincerely prophesying out of a sense of compassion, but it led him to misunderstand the depth of God's hurt and the extent of Israel's hardheartedness. Jeremiah could prove his point, as unpopular as it was, only by calling for a sign from God that would vindicate his position against Hananiah - nothing less than the other prophet's death.

Jeremiah used signs and symbolic actions often. These are generally of two different types. One is the dramatic gesture that he acts out, such as when he refused to take a wife or when he went down to the *Tophet* dump to smash a pot. Others are more like comments on his everyday observations of life. Thus in chap. 18 he creates an oracle about God's power to rebuild and refashion Israel after watching a potter at work in his shop. Both types are well-known among earlier prophets, especially Amos and Isaiah. Both dramatize the power of the prophetic word and signify that God's word always ends in action.

Often in opposition to the hopes and beliefs of both the leaders and the people, Jeremiah needed to be not only a man of courage and conviction, but also a visionary. As it became clearer that Judah's days were numbered and that disaster would overtake the institutions most central to her religious faith—the temple, the freedom of the nation, the possession of the land, the dynasty of David—he looked ahead to a new time. He stressed that God would not act in the same way but make the covenant more personal and more inward (chap. 31). His own personal struggles and sense of personal responsibility became the model of the faithful Israelite of the future. There could no longer be safety in national identity nor any security in living in the Promised Land. The theme of conversion in Jeremiah became extremely prominent and was highlighted even more by those who edited his oracles in the spirit of Deuteronomy. The watchword for true loyalty to Yahweh centered in personal decision-making to obey and accept the covenant. This dimension profoundly influenced Ezekiel after him and laid the foundation for the new community of Israel that emerged when the exile was over, a community of faith and careful practice that has flowered into modern Judaism.

5. *Reading This Commentary*

In order to make this commentary more useful and manageable for study and reflection, only part of the text of Jeremiah is actually printed for each section under discussion. For chaps. 1-25, roughly half of the entire book, 35 individual passages are printed, which represent the most important and the most typical sections of the prophet's message. They have been chosen in part because they allow us to move from their words to the wider context in which they stand. That permits us to explore the whole range of Jeremiah while focusing on key texts or on those most suggestive for theological reflection.

It will certainly be important to have the Old Testament open to Jeremiah so that you can read the entire chapter or section under discussion. It is always painful to have to choose just so many passages of a biblical book, because in no way can we do justice to the richness of its whole structure and the interrelationship of its parts. Besides, the selection that one scholar makes may leave aside much that appears most beautiful to others or seems especially relevant to our particular situations. So this volume must serve to lead us into the Book of Jeremiah and to introduce us to his thought, until we become familiar enough to explore the prophecy on our own.

Book I
Jeremiah's Early Oracles
Jeremiah 1-10

I. THE CALL TO BE A PROPHET
JEREMIAH 1:1-19

The first chapter of Jeremiah forms an introduction to the entire collection of oracles and stories about the prophet. It gives us some information about the life of the prophet and provides a background for better appreciating his ministry. The most important clue comes from the models of prophetic achievement in Israel's past history hinted at in the description of Jeremiah's call to office: Moses and Samuel.

THE INITIAL LABEL
1:1-3

1 The words of Jeremiah, the son of Hilkiah, of the priests who were in Anathoth in the land of Benjamin, ²to whom the word of the LORD came in the days of Josiah the son of Amon, king of Judah, in the thirteenth year of his reign. ³It came also in the days of Jehoiakim the son of Josiah, king of Judah, and until the end of the eleventh year of Zedekiah, the son of Josiah, king of Judah, until the captivity of Jerusalem in the fifth month.

Verses 1-3 make up a small label at the beginning of Jeremiah's collection to tell us the book's contents. In this way, the editors explain what they consider important for the reader to understand about what follows. Labels reveal much, but they are so brief that they often leave unanswered many questions we moderns would ask. This certainly holds true here. We learn of Jeremiah's roots and the major periods of his preaching task, but we are left to wonder whether he actually did perform any of the priestly roles his family background permitted, and more significantly, to wonder about years when he was silent.

Jeremiah was the son of a priest of Anathoth, a small village just three miles north of Jerusalem. Even today, a small Arab village named Anata still exists in the area, although there are no traces of the ancient ruins within its boundaries. We can feel secure, however, that Jeremiah's home was nearby, and can imagine the prophet making the trip to Jerusalem on foot in little more than an hour. Anathoth once before entered Israelite history—when Solomon banished Abiathar, the high priest of King David, to live there in exile from Jerusalem (1 Kgs 2:26-27). We do not know whether Jeremiah was a descendant of Abiathar or not, but the village probably still kept an image of being a place foreign in spirit to the priestly traditions of the capital city. Though geographically close to Jerusalem, the capital of Judah, Anathoth was part of the tribal area of Benjamin which had always been more akin in thought and spirit to the northern tribes than to the southern people of Judah. If Jeremiah grew up and studied here, it explains why his message has so many echoes of Hosea and other northern prophets.

King Josiah, as part of his reform movement occasioned by the discovery of the lawbook in the temple, closed down almost all of the local priestly shrines outside of Jerusalem in his eighteenth year, about 622 B.C. (1 Kgs 22:8; 23:4-20). This would mean that Hilkiah and his son Jeremiah may have been out of a job as priests after that time. Possibly

Jeremiah never functioned as a priest at all. Certainly very little in his prophecies points to priestly concerns nor do any of his opponents ever make any reference to his priestly background.

Verse 2 says that Jeremiah began to preach in the 13th year of King Josiah, or about 627 B.C. Many scholars find this hard to believe since almost none of the following oracles make any reference to the major reforms started by the king only five years later. Also, the combination of vss. 2 and 3 make an awkward sequence. It suggests that Jeremiah had a spurt of activity early in the reign of Josiah, and then a long period of inactivity before he prophesied somewhat continuously from the beginning of Jehoiakim's reign down to the time of the fall of Jerusalem, a period of some twenty-five years, from 609 to 586. One possible explanation for this lies in the nature of Josiah's program. Many of Jeremiah's early words call for reform. After Josiah began to respond and carry out serious religious changes, Jeremiah did not need to preach. But at the death of Josiah and the coming of his son who had little interest in religious reform, the atmosphere of the nation changed, and Jeremiah's message became vitally necessary once again.

But because of the natural difficulty involved in imagining Jeremiah's long silence, commentators have offered several other possible answers to the problem. Some think that the word "thirteenth" is a mistake in copying and should really read "twenty-third" year (616 B.C.). Others would interpret the phrase to mean that God chose Jeremiah *from his birth* in the thirteenth year of Josiah. These scholars propose that he did not actually begin his preaching until he was eighteen in 609 B.C., the year when Jehoiakim became king. This is an attractive idea. Jeremiah insisted all along that God called him from birth. At the same time, his mission would not include preaching about the reform of Josiah, but rather about Jehoiakim's rejection of the reform after the young king took the throne. If, as many believe, Jeremiah was strongly influenced by the thought of Deuteronomy in his prophecies, a beginning in 609 makes much more sense since it would be well after the finding of the lawbook (Deuteronomy) in the temple and its use by Josiah. In the next section, vss. 4-10, the call of Jeremiah has many similarities to the story of Moses, and Jeremiah probably saw himself as the prophet who would come after Moses just as Deut. 18:18 predicted. This too suggests that Jeremiah did not begin his ministry until well after 622. We cannot be absolutely sure, however, since the phrase "the word of the Lord came to me in the days of Josiah," would be a very unusual way of talking about someone's birth in Hebrew usage. It is better then to keep the traditional birthdate around 645 B.C.

The final words of the label suggest that Jeremiah ended his preaching shortly after the actual fall of the city. Material in chaps 40-44 refer to words and actions of the prophet after this date. These may form an appendix added somewhat later to the chapters covered by the original label, or the label may consider only oracles delivered in Judah to be "official." In any case, the events described in chaps. 40-44 all take place soon after the fall of the city, and the few words of Jeremiah that come from his forced exile to Egypt lead to the conclusion that he must have died there shortly afterwards, an old and perhaps very brokenhearted man.

JEREMIAH'S COMMISSION
1:4-10

4Now the word of the LORD came to me saying,
5"Before I formed you in the womb I knew you,
    and before you were born I consecrated you;
    I appointed you a prophet to the nations."
6Then I said, "Ah, Lord GOD! Behold, I do not know how to speak, for I am only a youth." 7But the LORD said to me,
    "Do not say, 'I am only a youth';
    for to all to whom I send you you shall go,

and whatever I command you you shall speak.
⁸Be not afraid of them,
  for I am with you to deliver you,
                              says the LORD."
⁹Then the LORD put forth his hand and touched my
mouth; and the LORD said to me,
  "Behold I have put my words in your mouth.
¹⁰See, I have set you this day over nations and
    over kingdoms,
  to pluck up and to break down,
  to destroy and to overthrow,
  to build and to plant."

Verses 4-10 describe the call of Jeremiah to be a prophet. The passage begins with a standard formula. When a prophet says "the word of the Lord," he is not just making conversation or giving his opinion, but is fulfilling his office as prophet—he is speaking on behalf of God. Since our Bibles normally translate Yahweh as "the Lord" following the Jewish practice of reverently avoiding God's proper name, we lose some of the power of the original, "the word of no earthly lord or monarch but Yahweh, the God of Israel." This particular phrase, "the word of Yahweh," occurs often in the prophets Jeremiah and Ezekiel but somewhat rarely elsewhere. It may have been favored in the century in which they lived, or it may express the urgency of the message when disaster was so imminent: "this is not *my* message but Yahweh's."

The call of Jeremiah contains a striking dialogue between God and the prophet. God lists the initial job description in vs. 4: he has known Jeremiah even before he was conceived by his parents; he has set him aside for a special mission before he was born; and he has appointed him to the enormous task of prophet to all the nations. These three parts of his office focus our attention on the fact that God has taken the initiative, not Jeremiah, and that the task cannot be understood in any other category except what fits into God's plans. It also implies that God will take care of Jeremiah, that his special love for him runs deep, deeper than even that of the parents who conceived and gave birth to their son. This piety echoes the trust expressed by the psalmist in Ps. 22:10-11 that God had watched over him and cared for him since his conception in the womb. In Hebrew, *knowing* carries the sense of experiencing intimate friendship and strong loyalty. *Consecration* comes from the same Hebrew word that expresses holiness. It will not just be dedication, it will be religious commitment of a special kind. The *appointment* places Jeremiah beside Abraham, whom God appointed father of Israel in Genesis 17, and beside Moses, whom God appointed like a god for his people against the power of pharaoh in Exodus 7.

Jeremiah's role might seem to be even greater than theirs since it involves other nations and not just Israel. Yet, only a small part of the prophet's words were ever actually addressed to foreign nations. Jeremiah, it seems, conceived his mission to be directed primarily toward summoning Judah and the former northern kingdom of Israel to hear and return to the national covenant with Yahweh. But at the same time, he knew that the power struggles of Assyria, Babylonia and Egypt constantly tempted Israel to play by their rules and subject Yahweh's covenant to their foreign policies. Because these nations now pressed in on Israel as they never had before, Jeremiah must take his stand against them. From now on, no word of the Lord would stand without its international political implications.

Jeremiah objects at this point that he is only a youth. He may well be thinking of the story of Samuel, the greatest of the prophets who had to face political choices. In I Sam 1-3, the young Samuel's birth comes as a special gift from God to his previously barren mother, and she in turn dedicates him as a "youth" to the service of Yahweh's temple. Since the Hebrew idea of a *na'ar*, a "youth," can cover from infancy to young adulthood, we would better understand it in Jeremiah's case to mean a young man rather than a boy. The meaning lies in the realm of education and experience. Jeremiah had likely received no training in public speaking nor studied the books of wise sayings and proverbs that went along with a profession as an ambassador or messenger. Yet God's reply makes clear that a prophet does not require these skills. God gives the word, marks out the audience to whom it is directed, and provides the strength to carry through the task. Just how this happens remains somewhat obscure. But there is a definite theology of the prophetic office here, one which clearly downplays the personal opinions and insightful genius of the person called and stresses the divine origin of the message.

The dialogue continues with God's reassurance. "Be not afraid" occurs frequently among Israelite prophecies of hope and salvation. It is particularly common in the second part of Isaiah (chaps. 40-55) which addresses the exiles in Babylon and tries to bolster their spirits and confidence that God will act on their behalf. See Isa 41:8-13 or 44:1-5 as examples. In Jeremiah, it prepares the prophet for the difficulties ahead. In the case of a modern audience the command to fear not may have lost the impact it had on an ancient one. The phrase summed up all the hopes of people that the gods really did hear their prayer and respond. It is well-known even in the few Assyrian prophecies that have been preserved. In one, directed to King Esarhaddon (680-668), a few years earlier than the time of Jeremiah, we read: "Esarhaddon, king of countries, fear not! Notice the wind which blows over you; I speak of it . . . your enemies, like a wild boar in the month of Sivan, will flee from before your feet. I am the great divine lady, I am the goddess Ishtar of Arbela who will destroy your enemies from before your feet."

Then the Lord touches the mouth of the prophet and consecrates his lips to the task of proclaiming the word. This gesture purifies him for a speaking mission just as in the parallel story told about the call of Isaiah an angel burned his lips with a live coal to make him worthy of preaching God's word (Isa 6). But the touch also serves to transform the human thoughts of Jeremiah into God's way of thinking. Another incident from the call of a prophet, this time Ezekiel, makes the picture clearer. God puts a scroll, inscribed with a divine message, into the mouth of the prophet and tells him to eat it. Ezekiel finds it sweet to the taste, but the message turns out to be one of lamentation and woe, one that will bring bitterness to the prophet as he performs his task. Above all, this act of touching the lips accents the verbal role of a prophet as a spokesperson and as an interpreter of the divine message. But it also brings out the personal union between God and prophet, between the speaker and the message. The sense of healing and purifying the mouth stresses that the prophet must share in the holiness of God.

Verse 10 describes the nature of these divine words more fully. God gives a double task: one of destroying, the other of rebuilding. "To uproot and destroy, to build and to plant," can be found throughout the Jeremiah tradition, said in many different ways to many different audiences: see 12:14-17; 18:7-9; 24:6; 31:28; 31:40; 42:10; 45:4. It represents a central idea for the editors who gathered Jeremiah's oracles together. They place it in key spots to reveal the complex nature of the message—sometimes judgment, sometimes words of hope; sometimes for Israel, sometimes for other nations.

The whole unit of vv. 4-10 requires two final comments. First, scholars have noted a strong resemblance between this call of Jeremiah and the call stories of other prophets, notably Isaiah and Ezekiel, and these in turn resemble the calls of early heroes such as Moses and Gideon. They share a common pattern which can be illustrated from the story of Gideon in Judg 6:11-17: 1) the divine confrontation when an angel appears to Gideon while he threshes his grain; 2) the word of the angel announcing that this is a divine message; 3) the commission to rescue Israel from her enemies; 4) Gideon's objection that he is a nobody and without power; 5) the angel's reassuring word that God will be with him; and 6) a divine sign to back up the commission, in Gideon's case making dew fall on the ground but not on a fleece in its midst.

The force of such a pattern comes from the formal repetition of traditional phrases, which identify the prophet in a long line of leaders who have been specifically called by Yahweh. Because the pattern seemed so important to biblical authors, its regular use adds weight to the belief that the prophets did see themselves as part of an ongoing office within Israel. They were not eccentric oddities but shared in a permanent and important role in society. Especially, since the account of Moses stands first in the series and follows the pattern very closely, the idea must have grown through the centuries that the prophets really stood in the shoes of Moses as spokespersons on behalf of God and as defenders of the covenant. The following chart shows how closely the calls of the major prophets parallel that of Moses:

	Exodus 3	*Isaiah* 6	*Jeremiah* 1	*Ezekiel* 1-3
Divine Meeting:	3:1-4a	6:1-2	1:4	1:1-28
Word of Identification:	3:4b-9	6:3-4	1:5a	1:29-2:2
Commission:	3:10	6:7b-10	1:5b	2:3-5
Objection:	3:11	6:5, 11a	1:6	2:6, 2:8
Reassurance:	3:12a	6:11b-13	1:7-8	2:7-8
Sign:	3:12b	6:6-7a	1:9-10	2:8-3:11

Our second comment strengthens this connection of Jeremiah with Moses. The unusual features of Jeremiah's call, such as God's knowing him since his birth or Jeremiah's objections that he cannot speak well and is only a youth, resemble incidents from the life of Moses. Exodus 2 records how Moses was rescued at birth in a miraculous fashion so that God could use him to deliver Israel from Egypt, while Exodus 3 and 4 repeatedly mention Moses' timidity and smallness and his protest that he did not know how to speak well. Anyone familiar with the Exodus adventures could hardly miss how closely Jeremiah resembles Moses in his youth. But another passage sharpens the point even more. In Deut 18:1-20, according to the Deuteronomist redactor, Moses promises that a new prophet like himself will arise in later years to speak to the people. In v. 18, the Lord says: "I will raise up a prophet like you from among their kinsmen, and will put my words into his mouth; he shall tell them all that I command him." In Jeremiah, God repeats almost exactly the same words in vv. 7 and 9. Because Deuteronomy was written in the same century that Jeremiah lived, we cannot be sure which passage came first. Most scholars believe, however, that the call of Jeremiah was modeled on the words of Deuteronomy so that the entire passage in vv. 4-10 reflects the opinion of the disciples and editors of the Book of Jeremiah that the prophet had fulfilled the hopes and ideals spelled out in Deuteronomy better than had any previous prophet. In his love for the covenant, his fearless preaching in the face of anger, his insistence on loyalty only to Yahweh, Jeremiah had walked in the footsteps of the founding father of the people. In this view, then, although Jeremiah experienced some kind of call, we can only know that the editors who collected his oracles chose to word his call in such a way that he became a true follower of Deuteronomy's program of reform and religious repentance. Since it is placed first as a kind of prologue to the whole book, readers will naturally interpret all of the oracles that follow in the light of Deuteronomy.

On the other hand, it is not impossible that Jeremiah saw himself as a new Moses and worked at being worthy of the master. Jeremiah could easily have thought this way in light of the suffering and misunderstanding he had to endure, much as Moses had to put up with the murmuring and threats of the Israelites in the desert. As Moses had continued to pray for the people and to ward off God's anger against them, so Jeremiah kept speaking his message and praying for an Israel on the edge of self-destruction. If Jeremiah had meditated on the meaning of Ps 22 and its picture of the psalmist persecuted by his enemies, the story of Samuel and his dedication to God's service as a prophet from his youth, and the early life of Moses, he may well have seen the promise of a new prophet in Deuteronomy 18 pointing to himself.

In either case, Jeremiah and the authors of Deuteronomy shared a similar outlook and struggled with the same conviction that only a true return to Yahweh and his commandments could save Israel from losing its land. Both experienced how difficult it is to change a nation once it has set itself on a course of action that locks its decisions and policies to those of other nations. Both challenged Israel to discover its own roots and unique values, to recover its own special character, and then to make its decisions. These included the possibility of submission to foreign powers, in order to be purified and disciplined. But very few, including the leaders, saw the issues in such terms.

VISIONS AND SUPPORT
1:11-19

11And the word of the LORD came to me, saying, "Jeremiah, what do you see?" And I said, "I see a rod of almond." 12Then the LORD said to me, "You have seen well, for I am watching over my word to perform it."

13The word of the LORD came to me a second time, saying, "What do you see?" And I said, "I see a boiling pot, facing away from the north." 14Then the LORD said to me, "Out of the north evil shall break forth upon all the inhabitants of the land."

The rest of chapter one consists of two visions of the prophet and a renewal of his commission by God. The first vision turns a little joke and a play on words into a serious point. Jeremiah sees the early blooming almond tree with its flowers open like hundreds of eyes while the other trees still sleep. Its name, *shaqed*, means a "watching tree," and it reminds Jeremiah that he must be on the watch or lookout (*shoqed*) for Israel. The event may be unusual, but the job description is not. Two other prophets also see themselves as watchmen for the nation, Habakkuk (Hab 2:1) and Ezekiel (Ezek 3:17-21). Especially from the latter we learn that the title means that a prophet must be ready to warn the people of their sins and of the coming judgment of God. Because the image occurs so commonly, it probably represents the standard idea of the prophetic office among prophets of the seventh century. Two hundred years earlier, King Ahab referred to the prophet Elijah as "the disturber of Israel" (1 Kgs 18:17). Although said as an insult, it described the same task of warning the people.

The second vision of the boiling pot tipping over from the north and burning the people of Judah describes in metaphor the coming attack of the Babylonians. Jerusalem was always invaded from the north; the mountainous gullies to the east and west were too dangerous a trap for armies to brave. The explanations of this vision, found in vv. 15 and 16, foresees that foreign nations will conquer Jerusalem because of the nation's idolatry.

Possibly the two visions come from different stages of Jeremiah's ministry. The first probably happened early, perhaps shortly after his call to be a prophet. It captures the need to speak out against the sins of the people, particularly their infidelity to the covenant. The vision of the pot, however, must come from a period when the Babylonians were active in the area of Syria and Palestine. This could only take place after their series of victories over Assyria gave them control of Mesopotamia and northern Syria. Beginning in 614, the armies of Nabopolassar, king of Babylon, joined with the Medes from the northern part of modern Iran to attack and capture the major cities of the Assyrian state: Assur, Nineveh, and finally Haran. When Nebuchadnezzar, the Babylonian crown prince, took Haran in 609 Assyria passed from the stage of world history except as legend. King Josiah of Judah had died that year in the battle of Megiddo trying to prevent the Egyptians from coming to the aid of the Assyrian remnant. Egypt could not stop the final defeat of Assyria, but did try to grab Palestine and lower Syria for itself. Nebuchadnezzar pressed his attack west and south until in 605 he crushed the Egyptian army at Carchemesh and took possession of the Mediterranean coast including Palestine. At the same time, his father died and he became king of Babylon. He did not send his armies to occupy the small kingdoms such as Judah that fell within his control. He was content to allow them to govern themselves as long as they were loyal and sent money and goods in tribute each year.

From this sequence of events, it seems reasonable to suppose that Jeremiah received his vision of the threat from the North sometime between 609 and 605, while Babylon already held control of northern Syria but before it moved south in force. Jeremiah had little use for worry about Egypt even when it was seemingly calling the shots. The real power and the ultimate danger to Israel came from the empire now strengthening its position above them to the North and East. Jeremiah's prophetic call was joined to keen political and military insight.

Verses 17-19 return to the thought of the call narrative in vv. 4-10. God reassures the prophet once more not to be afraid for "I am with you." The Lord promises to strengthen and defend Jeremiah against his own people. The battle imagery stands out here: the leaders, priests and even the people, the whole land, will become an attacking army, but Jeremiah will be an impregnable city fortified to withstand their siege no matter how bitter and violent.

II. JUDGMENT ON ISRAEL'S SIN
JEREMIAH 2:1-3:5

Chapters 2 to 6 contain a bloc of Jeremiah's early oracles, perhaps the entire body of his first scroll dictated to Baruch (chap. 36). This would be a much smaller scroll than that projected by most critics who include large amounts from all of chaps. 1-25, but it would be a more consistent and more unified document. Its theme of harsh judgment certainly could explain the anger of the king as he heard it read.

This large section opens with a lawsuit of Yahweh against his own people in 2:1-13, followed by a number of shorter descriptions that develop the theme in terms of the experience of the people. Altogether this unit which extends from 2:1 to 2:37 makes an impressive opening summary of Jeremiah's message of warning. It can be divided into two parts for discussion: vv. 1-13, the lawsuit, and vv. 14-37, the fuller development. The section closes with a shorter unit, 3:1-5, in which the imagery reflects the procedures for divorce as the legitimate sentence which the people deserve for their harlotry and infidelity to Yahweh.

A. 2:1-13, THE PEOPLE ON TRIAL

2 The word of the LORD came to me, saying, ²"Go and proclaim in the hearing of Jerusalem, Thus says the LORD,

I remember the devotion of your youth,
   your love as a bride,
how you followed me in the wilderness,
   in a land not sown.
³Israel was holy to the LORD,
   the first fruits of his harvest,
All who ate of it became guilty;
   evil came upon them,

                      says the LORD."

⁴Hear the word of the LORD, O house of Jacob, and all the families of the house of Israel. ⁵Thus says the LORD:
   "What wrong did your fathers find in me
      that they went far from me,
and went after worthlessness, and became worthless?
⁶They did not say, 'Where is the LORD
   who brought us up from the land of Egypt,
who led us in the wilderness,
   in a land of deserts and pits,
in a land of drought and deep darkness,
   in a land that none passes through,
   where no man dwells?'
⁷And I brought you into a plentiful land
   to enjoy its fruits and its good things.
But when you came in you defiled my land,
   and made my heritage an abomination.
⁸The priests did not say, 'Where is the LORD?'
   Those who handle the law did not know me;
the rulers transgressed against me;
   the prophets prophesied by Baal,
   and went after things that do not profit.

⁹"Therefore I still contend with you,
               says the LORD,
   and with your children's children I will contend,
¹⁰For cross to the coasts of Cyprus and see,
   or send to Kedar and examine with care;
   see if there has been such a thing.

> [11]Has a nation changed its god,
>   even though they are no gods?
> But my people have changed their glory
>   for that which does not profit.
> [12]Be appalled, O heavens, at this,
>   be shocked, be utterly desolate,
>
>   says the LORD,
> [13]for my people have committed two evils:
>   they have forsaken me,
> the fountain of living waters,
>   and hewed out cisterns for themselves,
> broken cisterns,
>   that can hold no water."

God presents his case against his own people in these verses, and the violation of the Sinai covenant clearly represents the grounds for the accusation. The passage is filled with covenant language and reference to the solemn union that bound God to lead Israel to a promised land in freedom and bound Israel to obey God and worship him alone. Jeremiah's thought offers a sharp contrast between the time in the desert when the covenant was made and the later behavior of Israel after they received the land and forgot the Lord who had given it to them.

2:1-3 addresses the people of Jerusalem, while vv. 4-13 expand the audience to all Israel, including the northern tribes who had been sent into exile in 722 when the Assyrians took Samaria and had gradually lost the practice of their faith while subject to a foreign power. The double address may be a sign that originally the two parts were spoken separately. But it may also be a rhetorical flourish that sharpens the dramatic flair: "not only you, Jerusalem, but all you, O Israel . . ." The interest in both the South and the North suggests that Jeremiah uttered these oracles soon after Josiah began to recover parts of the northern kingdom as the Assyrians grew weaker and withdrew. According to the Second Book of Chronicles 34:6-7, this took place shortly after 628 B.C., very early in the career of Jeremiah.

The images in vv. 2-3 draw heavily on Hosea. Israel's "devotion" (i.e., her *hesed*, the loving loyalty of a covenant partner) and her "bridal love" (her *'ahab*, the intense love of a husband and wife used often in Deuteronomy when speaking of the covenant) picture a golden time in the desert similar to that given by Hos 2:14-16, 11:1-4 and 13:4. Jeremiah also borrows Hosea's double image of Israel as God's beloved child and as his bride. But Jeremiah adds a new note of his own when he compares an Israel under the covenant to the first fruits of each year's harvest, set aside and made holy only for Yahweh's enjoyment. Anyone who would eat these became guilty of a sin. Grammatically, a present sense seems best, but the RSV puts the last sentence into the past tense as though Jeremiah had in mind some very concrete cases of enemies whom God had punished for attacking his people. As a great king in the covenant arrangement, God would have been duty-bound to respond against any nation that set upon his vassal. Possibly the prophet had in mind the Canaanites defeated by Joshua in the conquest or the nations of Edom, Moab and Ammon conquered by David.

The reference to the First Fruits in describing the covenant loyalty of Yahweh recalls the famous passage in Deut 26:1-11 in which every Israelite must bring the first fruits to the priest and recite a creed praising God for the Exodus and the giving of the Holy Land. Once again, Jeremiah stands closer to the thought of Deuteronomy than to the priestly description of first fruits in Lev 23.

In v. 4, Jeremiah moves to the accusation. He no longer speaks of Israel in the feminine singular, the spouse of Yahweh, but now uses the masculine plural: "all of you!" The basic charge contends that God kept his part of the bargain, but the Israelites did not keep theirs. Why did they abandon the covenant? Not because God had failed in any of his obligations, but because of their own lust. In v. 6, the prophet calls it a search after nothingness; in v. 7, a defilement of the land, meaning here sexual abuses associated with the worship of Baal and its fertility cult. In contrast, God rescued them from the Egyptians, guided them through the wilderness and its dangers, brought them into a land as rich as a garden. The catalog of God's deeds again resembles the list in Deut 26. Jeremiah may have known this very form of the ritual. He certainly wants to show that Israel's actual practice had little in common with their pious recital of the creed on the Feast of Weeks.

No class of people is left out. He names four: the priests, the teachers of the Torah (which may include both priests and levites), the shepherds of the people, a term for the rulers which accented how little civic care for the citizens they really had, and the prophets. The fact that even the prophets had turned to Baal must have stung Jeremiah deeply. Later on, he strongly condemns prophets who speak God's word while living immoral lives (23:9-12) and preaching empty words in the name of Baal (23:13-15). Jeremiah however spares no one from the judgment of Yahweh in light of his covenant—neither privileged priestly leader nor political power. Everyone must hear the prophetic word and apply it to his or her life. Especially the modern church can find a source of reflection in these words of Jeremiah, not only to be willing to hear criticism but to be fearless in addressing the evils of nations and power groups everywhere.

Verse 9 makes the lawsuit explicit. God brings not only the present generation to court to insist on the fulfillment of the covenant terms, but generations to come. This echoes the treaty language found throughout the Ancient Near East. Esarhaddon in his treaties with vassals, drawn up to guarantee their loyalty to his son Ashurbanipal when he succeeded to the throne, addresses the individual kings with the formula, "The treaty of Esarhaddon, king of the world, king of Assyria . . . with Ramataya, city ruler of Urakazabanu, with his sons, grandsons, with all the people of Urakazabanu" (ANET 534). The choice of standard treaty language has a point as the prophet goes on to show that no other nation would abandon their god as Israel had done. One could travel from the far West (Cyprus) to the remote Arab tribes of the East (Kedar) without finding such an abomination. Even the divine witnesses of such pagan treaties would be horrified. The reference to the heavens in v. 12 recalls the god-list of Esarhaddon's treaty: "you are adjured by all the gods of every land, you are adjured by the gods of heaven and earth" (ANET 535). Even the Hebrews could take over the idea in their poetry, as in the beautiful opening to the Song of Moses in Deut 32: "Give ear, O heavens, and I will speak; and let the earth hear the words of my mouth."

The charge is finally brought to a climax in the last verse of the section. Israel has a double sin: she forsook Yahweh to whom she was bound in covenant, she gave loyalty to Baal who was an empty idol. The comparison between God as a bountiful spring of water always flowing and the cracked and broken cistern which cannot even hold the little water it collects captured all the fears and struggles and needs that Israel had experienced as dwellers in a desert climate where every drop of water was precious.

B. 2:14-37; 3:1-5 FURTHER ACCUSATIONS

14"Is Israel a slave? Is he a homeborn servant?
  Why then has he become a prey?
15The lions have roared against him,
  they have roared loudly.
They have made his land a waste;
  his cities are in ruins, without inhabitant.
16Moreover, the men of Memphis and Tahpanhes
  have broken the crown of your head.
17Have you not brought this upon yourself
  by forsaking the LORD your God,
  when he led you in the way?

¹⁸And now what do you gain by going to Egypt,
   to drink the waters of the Nile?
Or what do you gain by going to Assyria,
   to drink the waters of the Euphrates?
¹⁹Your wickedness will chasten you,
   and your apostasy will reprove you.
Know and see that it is evil and bitter
   for you to forsake the LORD your God;
   the fear of me is not in you,
                              says the Lord GOD of hosts.

²⁰"For long ago you broke your yoke and burst
   your bonds;
   and you said, 'I will not serve.'
Yea, upon every high hill
   and under every green tree
   you bowed down as a harlot.
²¹Yet I planted you a choice vine,
   wholly of pure seed.
How then have you turned degenerate
   and become a wild vine?
²²Though you wash yourself with lye
   and use much soap,
   the stain of your guilt is still before me,
                              says the Lord GOD.

²³How can you say, 'I am not defiled,
   I have not gone after the Baals'?
Look at your way in the valley;
   know what you have done—
a restive young camel interlacing her tracks,
²⁴a wild ass used to the wilderness,
   in her heat sniffing the wind!
   Who can restrain her lust?
None who seek her need weary themselves;
   in her month they will find her.
²⁵Keep your feet from going unshod
   and your throat from thirst.

But you said, 'It is hopeless,
   for I have loved strangers,
   and after them I will go.'

26"As a thief is shamed when caught,
   so the house of Israel shall be shamed:
they, their kings, their princes,
   their priests, and their prophets,
27who say to a tree, 'You are my father,'
   and to a stone, 'You gave me birth.'
For they have turned their back to me,
   and not their face.
But in the time of their trouble they say,
   'Arise and save us!'
28But where are your gods
   that you made for yourself?
Let them arise, if they can save you,
   in your time of trouble;
for as many as your cities
   are your gods, O Judah.

29"Why do you complain against me?
   You have all rebelled against me,
                    says the LORD.
30In vain have I smitten your children,
   they took no correction;
your own sword devoured your prophets
   like a ravening lion.
31And you, O generation, heed the word
   of the LORD.
Have I been a wilderness to Israel,
   or a land of thick darkness?
Why then do my people say, 'We are free,
   we will come no more to thee'?
32Can a maiden forget her ornaments,
   or a bride her attire?
Yet my people have forgotten me
   days without number.

³³"How well you direct your course
    to seek lovers!
So that even to wicked women
    you have taught your ways.
³⁴Also on your skirts is found
    the lifeblood of guiltless poor;
you did not find them breaking in.
    Yet in spite of all these things
³⁵you say, 'I am innocent;
    surely his anger has turned from me.'
Behold, I will bring you to judgment
    for saying, 'I have not sinned.'
³⁶How lightly you gad about,
    changing your way!
You shall be put to shame by Egypt
    as you were put to shame by Assyria.
³⁷From it too you will come away
    with your hands upon your head,
for the LORD has rejected those in whom you trust,
    and you will not prosper by them.

3 "If a man divorces his wife
    and she goes from him
and becomes another man's wife,
    will he return to her?
Would not that land be greatly polluted?
You have played the harlot with many lovers;
    and would you return to me?
                    says the LORD.
²Lift up your eyes to the bare heights, and see!
    Where have you not been lain with?
By the waysides you have sat awaiting lovers
    like an Arab in the wilderness.
You have polluted the land
    with your vile harlotry.
³Therefore the showers have been withheld,
    and the spring rain has not come;

yet you have a harlot's brow,
　　you refuse to be ashamed.
4Have you not just now called to me,
　　'My father, thou art the friend of my youth—
5will he be angry for ever,
　　will he be indignant to the end?'
Behold, you have spoken,
　　but you have done all the evil that you could."

The lawsuit in 2:1-13 is followed by a new series of accusations brought by Yahweh against his people. We may divide these remaining verses into six short scenes, each of which brings out a different aspect of the charges.

(1) Verses 14-19 point out that the nation's fortunes have been anything but good despite their playing Egypt against Assyria, always seeking the best political alliance for themselves. Although Yahweh has promised them the status of a son or of a full wife within the family, they have experienced nothing but the lot of a slave. Yet they never see the connection between their sinful ambitions and the suffering of the land as one army or another marches over it. Loyalty has not played a part in their decisions with the result that they in turn have been treated only as pawns in the ambitions of larger nations. A true sense of God's covenant would have prevented them from fawning over one or the other large nation as the moment seemed opportune.

(2) Verses 20-22 describe the passion with which Israel had taken to the ritual of Canaanite religion. Jeremiah calls the worship of Yahweh a yoke or bond because it stresses strong ethical demands and total attachment to one God. Emphasis was placed as much on what you avoided as on what you did. For many this proved too hard and too unattractive. They turned instead to the innumerable shrines of Baal and Asherah and Astarte that capped

prominent hills and were set in large groves of trees—anywhere that a spot seemed particularly sacred.

(3) Verses 23-25 pictures two desert animals in heat. The image of the young female camel wandering around somewhat haphazardly during her period contrasts sharply with the female ass who chases after the male, locating him by the trail of urine that he leaves behind. But both are driven by bold sexual lust and cannot be turned aside easily. Jeremiah in v. 25 warns Israel not to wear herself out lusting after the pagan Baals, but the people answer that they cannot control themselves. The strong sexual aspect of this and other descriptions of the cult of Baal and Asherah reveals how deeply disgusted the prophets of Israel felt toward the sexual license permitted in the pagan religions for the purpose of obtaining fertility and blessing from the gods. Throughout the Old Testament Yahweh demands that sexual behavior be subject to the order and proper social restraints imposed by obedience to the covenant. The Israelites had their share of sin in this matter, but the prophets constantly called them back to fidelity in their marriages as well as in their union with God. The worship of Yahweh had no place for a passion directed mostly to sensual pleasure for the individual while responsibility lay forgotten.

(4) Verses 26-28 mock the devotion of the Israelites to their new gods. They address the mother goddess Asherah and her "tree" as "my father" and the stone pillar that stood for the male god Baal as "you who gave me birth!" Not only do they get the devotions backwards, confusing the male and female imagery, but when the gods prove useless in times of trouble, Israel runs back to Yahweh and expects him to come to their aid. Like Elijah on Mount Carmel, Jeremiah tells them to call louder to their new gods if they want help (1 Kgs 18:27-29). He makes the point that they had better not hope for God to answer them or save them while this indecent foolishness goes on. The shame he sees ahead is nothing less than their own defeat, as they are marched naked into exile.

(5) Verses 29-32 return to the scene of the lawcourt. Now the people are suing Yahweh for deserting them. But he defends himself boldly, turning the accusation back on their own deeds. They rebelled, they even received punishment but refused to accept it. They killed the prophets sent to call them back. They knew that God had never been like a desert or black night when they called, yet they left him to wander into their own darkness. Jeremiah contrasts Israel to the example of the new bride so excited and proud to be married that she shows off her wedding gifts—the silver, the gold, the jewels that form her dowry and her own personal bank account as a wife, and her wedding sash that marks her forever among the married women of the village or town. Yahweh had taken Israel as such a bride and yet she has simply turned her back on him. Worse perhaps, she has *forgotten* him.

Remembering forms the heart of Israel's confession of faith. God has done great and wonderful deeds for his people, deeds that must be recalled and taught to each generation. He has established his covenant which must be learned and passed on. Nowhere is this expressed more firmly than in Deuteronomy's command to "love the Lord your God with all your heart, and with all your soul and with all your might," and "put these words on your heart and teach them diligently to your children and talk of them when sitting, walking, lying down and getting up" (Deut 6:4-7). Many earlier prophets condemned Israel because they forgot what God had done and did not know him. Hosea and Isaiah in particular thunder against this lack of knowledge of Yahweh among the people of the eighth century. Jeremiah is walking in their footsteps.

(6) Verses 33-37 return to the picture of Israel as a lustful lover, seeking nothing but one sexual encounter after another and even committing murder if someone gets in the way. Despite the total immorality of her actions, she cannot or will not admit her guilt. The image is tied to a lesson of politics, however. The "lovers" are the world superpowers, Assyria one time, Egypt another. The lust

for foreign gods can be identified with the lust for the
nations which worship those gods. Israel plays power
politics with gusto, giving up Yahweh and his small-time
promises for the hopes of dealing on a one-to-one basis
with nations much larger and stronger. This will not be
Jeremiah's last chance to warn his people of their folly,
but it serves as a timely reminder to all generations that
no pragmatic power politics can rightly replace a deeply-
rooted faith in God's providence and lordship nor a vision
of God's plan in creation and history.

This ends the series of scenes that Jeremiah uses to illustrate God's lawsuit against Israel. The total picture drawn
by the prophet resembles the lawsuit of God found in the
Song of Moses of Deuteronomy 32. In many ways they are
more like lament psalms, in which the writer can describe
both the pitiable state to which the people have fallen and
their soaring hope that God will hear and possibly answer
them. Jeremiah, however, at this stage of his life, was much
more pessimistic than Deuteronomy 32 because he was
convinced of the people's stubborn refusal to listen.

Many scholars think this chapter comes from the earliest
days of Jeremiah's preaching, perhaps even before the
reforms of Josiah. It would fit well with the following
sections in 3:1-10 and 3:11-25; 4:1-4. These passages all
stress the practices of idolatry and Canaanite fertility rites
that flourished in the years before 622. 2 Chr 34:3-7 mentions that Josiah took some steps at reform in his twelfth
year as king, about 627, the year of Jeremiah's call. But
both the authors of Chronicles and those of the Book of
Kings agree that the major reform was connected with the
finding of the lawbook some five years later. 2 Kgs 22-23
show clearly that the primary focus of the king's reforming
zeal centered on getting rid of the pagan cult statues and
shrines. If Jeremiah did begin his actual preaching in the
period between 627 and 622, as most traditional interpreters
believe, he would certainly have approved of the king's
actions, and many of the oracles from chaps 2 and 3 could

well reflect those early days. But note that Jeremiah never addresses the king by name in these oracles, but speaks to the nation, desiring a sincere turning back to Yahweh from the heart of the people as a whole. This theme of "return" and "conversion" marks Jeremiah's message throughout his life.

The entire section, 2:1-3:5, now closes with the accusation that Israel has become a harlot and unfaithful wife and that she deserves to be divorced for this. In vv. 1-5, the prophet cites the law of Deuteronomy that a man may not take back a wife who has left him and married another husband (Deut 24:1-4). This would be an "abomination," a great evil which defiles the proper sanctity of marital relationships. To compound her sin, Israel has not even properly divorced God but simply went after other lovers with a passion that makes the defilement even worse. Nature itself seems to be punishing the people for their evil ways. The drought that came upon the land would naturally have been seen by all ancient peoples as a punishment for sin, yet the residents of Judah do not even worry about it; they continue to call on God tenderly and with great faith pretend that he will not really punish too severely. But Jeremiah once again warns darkly, as he did in 2:26-28, that Yahweh may not easily accept his people back if their cries for help are not joined to real actions of reform. God's anger is a just anger. He must deal with the abomination that the people have created and which now defiles the land.

III. THE CALL TO REPENT
JEREMIAH 3:6-4:4

The second part of chapter 3 and the beginning of chapter 4 continue the theme of faithlessness. Like the preceding sections, it contains a number of small units that have been combined and sometimes added to in order to bring out the key theme. Note how the present text suggests an urgent and breathless quality as it shifts from the image of Israel and Judah as wife to that of children to that of sheep all in the first five verses. Prophetic language was never patient nor resigned about the need to reform. God may delay his actions but because he involved himself so deeply in the life of Israel, one could never be sure. Jeremiah, like most of the other writing prophets, possessed a strong conviction that God would not stand aside from events but would surely intervene in the not-too-distant future. One criterion for a passage that comes from a later and different hand than the prophet's own is a calmer spirit and more far-seeing confidence that a new situation would develop. Verses 15-18 give us an example of such a later reflection in the present context.

IDOLATRY AS ADULTERY
3:6-10

⁶The LORD said to me in the days of King Josiah: "Have you seen what she did, that faithless one, Israel, how she went up on every high hill and under every green tree, and there played the harlot? ⁷And I thought, 'After she has done all this she will return to me'; but she did not return, and her false sister Judah saw it. ⁸She saw that for all the adulteries of that faithless one, Israel, I had sent her away with a decree of divorce; yet her false sister Judah did not fear, but she too went and played the harlot. ⁹Because harlotry was so light to her, she polluted the land, committing adultery with stone and tree. ¹⁰Yet for all this her false sister Judah did not return to me with her whole heart, but in pretence, says the LORD."

Verses 6-10 are in prose and may well be a separate oracle of Jeremiah uttered on another occasion. In spirit it really belongs with the following unit, 3:11-25; 4:1-4 on the theme of "return" (the Hebrew *shub*, "to turn around," "convert"); it describes the occasion and the reason for God's call to return in those verses. Yet it stands after 3:1-5 because it shares the image of divorce. By placing this picture right in the middle between 3:1-5 and 3:11-4:4, the editor of the book sums up the history of idolatry and betrayal for all of Israel, both Judah and the northern kingdom, and prepares for the dramatic summons to repent in the verses ahead. Seen in this way, all of chaps 2:1 to 4:4 form a single bloc announcing Jeremiah's basic accusation against the people as idolatry. They contain a dialogue between God as prosecutor and the people as defendants in the courtroom, and ends in 4:1-4 with the promise to release prisoner Israel from her guilty sentence if she will only take an oath to reform.

We can describe the important message found in vv. 6-10 as the age-old teacher's plea to learn from history. Israel,

meaning here the northern kingdom that had been destroyed by the Assyrians in 722, had already tried the same
sort of infidelity. Jeremiah colorfully describes Israel's
defeat and exile as God's divorce of his people. It is not a
comforting image nor does the prophet intend it to be. But
Judah should have been frightened by what happened to
the northern kingdom and learned reform herself. Instead,
in the 100 years that followed the loss of Israel, Judah has
become worse than the northern kingdom ever was. By an
unspoken but hard logic, Judah's bill of divorce from
Yahweh will result in a darker fate than that of her sister
state Israel (or Samaria, as it is often called after its capital
city).

The same description occurs in even more detail in the
thought of Jeremiah's younger contemporary Ezekiel
(Ezek 16 and 23). Both saw in their times a dangerous
parallel with the earlier history of their people. But Judah
always thought somehow things would be different in a
different age. Jeremiah rejects this reasoning out of hand.
In v. 11 he concludes that the northern kingdom was less
guilty than Judah. After all, Israel had never been punished
so severely before for its crimes and might well have convinced itself that God would put up with anything. Judah
knew better and still did not reform her ways.

The combination of Yahweh as loving but hurt husband,
the unfaithful wife who turns out to be a harlot, and the
possibility of divorce proceedings all reveal that Jeremiah
owed much to the oracles of Hosea. Even the style of
Jeremiah's language borrows from the anguished expression of the earlier prophet. Hosea had captured an important aspect of the covenant in choosing the image of
marriage to stress the personal love involved in being
faithful to the binding relationship between God and Israel
as a whole. Not only did Jeremiah use the same images over
and over again, but so did Ezekiel and the author of Isaiah
62. It became so rooted in Israelite thought that even the
sensual love songs of the Canticle of Canticles were interpreted as a wedding song of Yahweh and Israel. In time,

St. Paul applied the image to the union between Christ and the Church.

RETURN, FAITHLESS ISRAEL
3:11-4:4

> 11And the LORD said to me, "Faithless Israel has shown herself less guilty than false Judah. 12Go, and proclaim these words toward the north, and say,
>> 'Return, faithless Israel,
>>> says the LORD.
>> I will not look on you in anger,
>>> for I am merciful,
>>> says the LORD.
>> I will not be angry for ever.
>> 13Only acknowledge your guilt,
>>> that you rebelled against the LORD your God
>> and scattered your favours among
>>> strangers under every green tree,
>> and that you have not obeyed my voice,
>>> says the LORD.
>> 14Return, O faithless children,
>>> says the LORD;
>>> for I am your master;
>> I will take you, one from a city and
>>> two from a family,
>> and I will bring you to Zion.
>> 15"'And I will give you shepherds after my own heart, who will feed you with knowledge and understanding.

Verses 11-14 make up a short poem addressed to the northern kingdom. Jeremiah maintains his distinction here between Israel and Judah in order to shake the people of Judah from their blind and complacent attitudes. He uses a little pun. "Faithless Israel" in vv. 11-12 literally reads "turned away Israel," so that he calls to them: "turn back, O turned away Israel." He follows this dramatic invitation with a promise: Yahweh will not be angry with them any longer, and he backs it up with the powerfully abrupt statement "for merciful am I." Often God is called a God of mercy (*hesed*) through his covenant, as in the beautiful summary of Exod 34:6-7 that Yahweh is a God rich in mercy, guarding mercy through the centuries, but rarely is the adjective used directly: God is the merciful one! All that his people must do is to admit their sin, a sin that has taken two forms: one, a rejection of the covenant bonds, signified in the rebellion and refusal to listen to his voice; and the other idolatry, signified by the sexual acts with cultic prostitutes at the local pagan shrines. At this point, Jeremiah shifts his address, now calling them children "who turn away." And like children, they need to be disciplined. After a hundred years of exile, destruction of their land and rule by the Assyrians, the faith of the northern tribes lacks backbone. Again, in an abrupt and forceful phrase Yahweh announces: "I am master over you." He will have to use a firm hand with these unruly children. But Jeremiah again uses a pun to bring home the demand for repentance. The word *ba'al*, "to be a master," can also mean "to be the husband." The love affair with foreign gods must stop. If they repent, Yahweh promises to bring them back to Zion as in the glorious days of David and Solomon when the nation was one.

In contrast to the wayward and fickle behavior of Israel, Judah has proven to be treacherous. The same word which the RSV translates as "false" Judah in v. 11 occurs again in 3:20; 5:11; 12:1,6 about the people, always with the sense of underhanded and deceitful actions. Judah does not blunder into evil, she plans it. The whole of vv. 11-14 creates a strong impression. Besides the play on "turning away" and "master and husband," the formula for a direct oracle from Yahweh is repeated four times in such a short space, like hammer blows nailing down the phrase: "says the Lord, says the Lord . . . ."

The RSV sets vv. 15-18 in prose to separate it from the rest of the section, but this unit is more distinctive. It foresees a day when new leaders will arise who will follow God's law better than the present kings have done, and who will rule over a reunited and populous Israel from a Jerusalem without the Ark of the Covenant in the heart of the temple. This reference to the loss of the Ark leads most scholars to hold that the passage was not composed until after Nebuchadnezzar looted the Temple in his attack of 597 B.C. at the earliest. The imagery of the passage resembles the thought of Ezekiel who describes his hoped-for restoration of the nation after exile in terms of new shepherds (Ezek 34) and a temple without the ark (Ezek 40-43), and with the North and South once again united (Ezek 37). The remark that Jerusalem, instead of the ark, will become God's throne shares the vision found in Isa 60-62, a passage describing the hopes of the exiles returning from Babylon in 539 B.C. Probably disciples expanded the promise of restoration in vv. 11-14 to show to a later generation that God still accomplished his prophetic word through Jeremiah.

Verses 19-20 develop the thought of v. 14. Yahweh will bring the exiles of the north back in small numbers. A few from here and there, all that are left of the once prosperous Israel, a remnant that God can work with. Again the prophet mixes his images of Israel as child and wife. There is nothing unusual about this. Hosea could shift his oracles from marriage imagery in chaps. 1-3 to that of father and son in chaps. 11 and 13. And at a later time Ezekiel thought enough of Jeremiah's combination to develop the allegory of an adopted daughter that God raises to adulthood and then marries (Ezek 16). In v. 19, she is set in a place of honor with the sons of the house, and given a share of the inheritance. It would be too much to suggest that at this point Jeremiah makes a bold break with male-dominated custom in his society. The laws generally specified only sons could inherit since daughters would marry men from outside the family and the family treasure would go to strangers. Only two late laws allowed daughters to inherit provided they married within their own tribe (Num 27:8-11 and 36:6-9). Here, the description of the inheritance suggests the land flowing with milk and honey, that is, the promised land, the gift of God's blessing to Israel. In symbolic terms, she was to receive his full inheritance, and in a deep and honest gratitude call him "father" and be a faithful wife. But instead her faithlessness, literally her "treachery," was too deep.

Verses 21-25 from another short dramatic poem. The four-fold repetition of "the Lord our God" together with the opening "Lord their God," set this off from the other units in chapter 3 and emphasizes the deep-felt distress that Israel has gotten itself into. The very mountains on which the shrines to Baal stood and on which the orgies and shouting for the pagan gods took place (3:2) become the scene of agony and pain when their world has fallen in. They cry out and weep helplessly because they have even forgotten who their God is. His enduring mercy doesn't even come to mind until the prophet proclaims it anew. Suddenly they recover themselves and remember all that they have done in their idolatry and also all the kindnesses that Yahweh "our" God has done for Israel. The thought of vv. 24-25 may be mostly a spiritual metaphor about how everything has been corrupted by their sin, but it carries the hint of the depths to which the worship of Baal can go. The "shameful thing" is a scornful name for the statue of the god. The term is found also in Hos 9:10. The fact that the devotion to Baal devours everything, even the sons and daughters, may refer to the practice of child sacrifice done in the name of the god. The OT contains some mention of it already in the time of Manasseh only a few years before Jeremiah (2 Kgs 21:6), and the western outpost of Canaanite culture in Carthage (settled by the Phoenicians from Lebanon) horrified even the Romans with the wide-spread killing of children to fulfill vows. Verse 25 contains a full confession of guilt. Their own shame has led them to the edge of returning to God. They recognize that the essence of their relationship to God is obedience to his word, a theme to which Jeremiah returns repeatedly.

This passage reflects the heart of the Israelite experience. Pagan religion offered little or no lasting meaning. Sometimes we might get the impression that the crucial issues involved only the political gains to be made by going over to the Canaanites, Assyrians or Babylonians and along the way accepting their religious beliefs. But at other times, the stress on sexual license and the consequent sense of shame reveal that Israel remained alive to a greater issue. Their God Yahweh demanded a different way of life and worship from that of other peoples, a way of life that centered on the ethical and social order because it was obedient to a God compassionate towards the poor and the distressed.

Our last unit, 4:1-4, provides an answer to how the people can turn back to Yahweh. It is really two oracles: one to northern Israel and one to Jerusalem and Judah. For Israel the answer is simple: be serious! If their attitude is that they can turn at their own pleasure, God doesn't want them. They must choose for good and be willing to meet the three-fold conditions: to repent, to remove all of their abominable idols, and to swear only by Yahweh. It means a full reacceptance of the covenant with its key concepts of truth, justice and uprightness. These make possible a return to Yahweh, for they are his virtues par excellence. We find them mentioned often at the heart of the Psalms and in the thought of Deuteronomy (Pss 33:4-5; 89:1-2; 92:2-3; 98:2-3; Deut 32:4). If the people willingly return to their God, then they will be able to have the full sense of promise, as once given to Abraham in Gen 12:1-3; 18:18; 22:18 and 26:4. The people must make an oath, the sign of a solemn relationship, just as Yahweh had sworn his promise to the patriarchs. Jeremiah here brings together all the richness of Hebrew religious faith that understood the unbroken history of God's faithfulness through the ages as a motive for trusting God in the present situation of one's life.

Judah should now apply the lesson. Verses 3-4 were originally a separate oracle but fit well the spirit of all that has been said about Israel to the North. It is a warning about applying the lessons learned from the fall of the northern sister-state. The time is short for the planting season but the manner of planting is all important to gain a good harvest. The farmer must plough up a new field and not simply throw his grain seed where weeds already have control. The moral is: begin right if you want results. The second homily example comes from the cult. Circumcision of the body dedicates the Israelite boy to Yahweh and to the practice of the Law, but it doesn't make him faithful in his duty. Instead, an Israelite boy or girl must dedicate his or her will to God. The external rituals of religion are only as good as the interior commitment. The image of the heart represents not the emotions and feelings of love to an Israelite, as it does for us today, but the power of thinking and deciding. In their view of the human body, feeling came from the pit of the stomach, the kidneys or liver, thinking from the heart, and perception from the head. In using the image of circumcision for the heart, Jeremiah follows once more the thought of Deuteronomy (Deut 10:16). So, too, the second image of God's anger as a fire comes from the common stock of prophetic language, e.g., Amos 5:6; Isa 1:31; Ezek 30:13. Jeremiah employs it often (7:20; 15:14; 17:4; 17:21; 21:12).

4:1-4 caps the thought of chaps. 2 and 3. It describes the emotional pain of God caught in the middle. The people cry to him for help; he wishes to show mercy; but he knows their hearts are not sincere.

IV. THE ENEMY FROM THE NORTH
JEREMIAH 4:5 - 6:30

Chaps. 4-6 have often been called the "Foe from the North" cycle because the emphasis in these chapters falls on the threat of foreign invasion as a punishment from Yahweh. But this by no means suggests that we have located a unified booklet here. Many separate oracles are joined together which place descriptions of battle, calls for repentance, and threats of terrible destruction side by side in a kind of breathless urgency. Like the oracles of chaps. 2 and 3, these come almost directly and untouched from the hand of the master himself. Some have suggested that Jeremiah wrote many of these vivid descriptions of siege and destruction from firsthand experience. The identity of the foe from the north has always been controverted. Herodotus, the Greek historian, described a raid of wild Scythian barbarians from Turkey down to the borders of Egypt in the lifetime of Jeremiah (Herodotus, *Histories* I:105). But the Bible makes no mention of these people, and there is no solid evidence that Judah actually suffered from any such an attack. Rather, we need look no further than Jeremiah's deeply felt sense of prophetic tradition.

The theme of the enemy from the north describes the only direction that normal travel from Babylon and Assyria could take. The deserts of Syria and Jordan lacked enough water to support the donkeys and foot soldiers of invading armies, so that the eastern kings were forced to march up across northern Syria and southern Turkey and down the eastern side of the Anti-Lebanon mountains. Along this wide curving route, often called the fertile crescent, grew up some of the important cities of the ancient World: Mari, Haran, Carchemesh, Ebla, Hamath, Damascus, Hazor, Beth Shan. We can be fairly certain that Jeremiah intended one of the traditional major world powers, choosing among the Babylonians, Assyrians, Medes or Hittites. One reason for this identification lies in his coupling of the theme, Foe from the North, with the image of the Day of the Lord, in 4:23-28, a theme used by Amos and Isaiah of the Assyrians, and by Ezekiel, and probably by Jeremiah, of the Babylonians.

THE FEARFUL INVASION
4:5-31

5Declare in Judah, and proclaim in Jerusalem, and say,
"Blow the trumpet through the land;
　　cry aloud and say,
'Assemble, and let us go
　　into the fortified cities!'
6Raise a standard toward Zion,
　　flee for safety, stay not,
for I bring evil from the north,
　　and great destruction.
7A lion has gone up from his thicket,
　　a destroyer of nations has set out;
　　he has gone forth from his place
to make your land a waste;
　　your cities will be ruins
　　without inhabitant.
8For this gird you with sackcloth,
　　lament and wail;
for the fierce anger of the LORD
　　has not turned back from us."

⁹"In that day, says the LORD, courage shall fail both king and princes; the priests shall be appalled and the prophets astounded." ¹⁰Then I said, "Ah, Lord GOD, surely thou hast utterly deceived this people and Jerusalem, saying, 'It shall be well with you'; whereas the sword has reached their very life."

The rest of chapter 4 can be divided into five poems: vv. 5-10 describe preparations for an attack from the North; vv. 11-18 offer a second warning of attack and call for reform; vv. 19-22 are a personal lament of anguish in a siege; vv. 23-28 dramatically depict the coming terror of the Day of the Lord; and vv. 29-31 picture Judah as a prostitute trying to save her life in war by throwing her favors at the enemy although they want only blood.

Jeremiah makes use of earlier prophetic traditions with great skill. In vv. 5-10, he draws on the role of the prophet as a herald, warning his people—he is the watchman described in his call in 1:11-12. He tells the people to seek refuge in the fortress cities, mocking their trust that God will never let Zion fall. He calls the enemy a lion on the hunt, ready to maul and tear its victim's flesh, an image used often in classical prophecy of an enemy: Isa 5:29, Nah 2:12, Ezek 32:2 and Jer 2:15; and sometimes even of Yahweh against his own people (Amos 1:2 and Hos 5:14), as well as against Israel's enemies (Isa 31:4 and Jer 49:19). Jeremiah summons them to their own funeral in mourning (*cf.*, Amos 5:2, Isa 22:12, Ezek 27:31).

The poem ends with the declaration that God has not turned away his anger from Judah (v. 8) and the cause is clearly stated: the political and religious leaders have all failed. Kings, princes, priests and prophets make up Jeremiah's customary list—he has already condemned them in 2:8 and 2:26. He maintains the shocking claim that the priests and prophets are astounded at the events. Has God deceived them and led his people to defeat? It would be better to understand such statements as a dramatic touch. The Israelites had no clearly worked out theology of the causes of good and evil. Everything came about by God's will, evil included. To the ancient mind, no problem arose in saying that people acted out of their own will and yet also insisting that God gave them lying spirits (1 Kgs 22:19-23). Despite many statements in the prophets that God caused blindness or hardness of heart or a stiff neck, the emphasis always falls on the responsibility of the individual. The people are lulled into a sense of safety by prophets who routinely proclaim Yahweh as a God of faithful protection and support for Israel. Note in 6:14 how these "false prophets" declare "peace! peace! when there is no peace." Jeremiah wrestles often with the question of prophets who announce what people desire, not what God intends (chaps. 14:13-16; 23:9-22; and 28:1-17), and here he suggests a part of his answer. They are too accustomed to giving oracles or reassurance! Such at least seemed to be the tradition since the days of Abraham (Gen 12:1-3). As a result they do not know God well enough to perceive his ideals of justice and honor for his chosen people demand more. Their lack of knowledge of God's deep love for Israel, that included both tenderness and anger, lets them see only one side of the picture, and they refuse to admit God's freedom to differ from their self-interested view. In this case, the results are fatal. The danger threatens the very lives of the nation. RSV's "life" in v. 10 comes from the same word as "throat" (*nepesh*) and so the final line could better be read "the sword is at their throat."

The second poem, in vv. 11-18, has an even stronger sense of haste. It begins with the picture of the hot, sand-filled desert windstorm, the sirocco, beating down all before it as it sweeps across the land, burning eyes, choking the breath, and forcing all work to stop as people hide as best they can. God's punishment will come like this, or is it Nebuchadnezzar and his Babylonian army? Jeremiah captures both in his description. The guards pass the message as rapidly as possible from north to south, from Dan at the frontier, across the central hill country of

Ephraim, and down to Jerusalem: prepare for an enemy attack! But side by side with this military report, the prophet warns further that it is not just the Babylonians, it is Yahweh who comes as a warrior, and he will not be stopped except by repentance.

The third poem, in vv. 19-22, exposes the deep involvement of the prophet in his message:

> ¹⁹My anguish, my anguish! I writhe in pain!
>   Oh, the walls of my heart!
> My heart is beating wildly;
>   I cannot keep silent;
> for I hear the sound of the trumphet,
>   the alarm of war.
> ²⁰Disaster follows hard on disaster,
>   the whole land is laid waste.
> Suddenly my tents are destroyed,
>   my curtains in a moment.
> ²¹How long must I see the standard,
>   and hear the sound of the trumpet?
> ²²"For my people are foolish,
>   they know me not;
> they are stupid children,
>   they have no understanding.
> They are skilled in doing evil,
>   but how to do good they know not."

Literally, within his very guts, the wrenching pain and sorrow overcome him. It is not just a vision, it is a certainty that the land will be wiped out. The sudden use of the first person in this passage reveals how completely Jeremiah identifies himself with the suffering of the people. The grammar of the Hebrew text is as confusing as terrified refugees, fleeing before an invading army. The world is collapsing on all sides. Still Jeremiah hammers home his message that only by knowing Yahweh can they save themselves. No point could be more strongly made than does v. 22: they are stupid, foolish, lacking knowledge and understanding in everything important, but well-practiced and expert in evil!

The fourth small poem, in vv. 23-28, paints a scene of cosmic disaster:

> ²³I looked on the earth, and lo, it was waste and void;
>   and to the heavens, and they had no light.
> ²⁴I looked on the mountains, and lo, they were quaking,
>   and all the hills moved to and fro.
> ²⁵I looked, and lo, there was no man,
>   and all the birds of the air had fled
> ²⁶I looked, and lo, the fruitful land was a desert,
>   and all its cities were laid in ruins
>   before the LORD, before his fierce anger.
> ²⁷For thus says the LORD, "The whole land shall be a desolation; yet I will not make a full end.
> ²⁸For this the earth shall mourn,
>   and the heavens above be black;
>   for I have spoken, I have purposed;
>   I have not relented nor will I turn back."

The earth has returned to being waste and void as it was at the beginning of creation before God gave his spirit to make it live. The same words are used in v. 23 as in Gen 1:2: *tohu wabohu:* nothingness, chaos, total emptiness. As a poem, the structure is simple and the lines have great power. It opens with a vision in which the prophet looks four times and sees nothing but collapse: all signs of life and civilization have fled, and even the mountains, those eternal pillars of solidity, are shaking. Yet Jeremiah adds the exquisite touch: the last of the birds has flown across the horizon! It closes in vv. 27 and 28 with a word of judgment: God cannot be turned back from punishment, yet he will not totally destroy, so that nothing can be rebuilt. Many scholars doubt that Jeremiah would have pulled his punch this way. They delete the phrase "I will not make a full end." The RSV has this in prose, which makes it look even more like an addition to the text, but if we print it as poetry, it rings true to the style of Jeremiah: "ravaged will be the entire land/but a total end I will not make of it."

The expression "Day of the Lord" does not appear in this passage but it shares the major outlook of such a "Day," namely that nothing can withstand Yahweh when he goes to battle. As the divine warrior, he conquers everything, humans and nature alike. The description of the mountains' shaking and the world's growing dark and mourning forms part of the earliest war poetry of Israel (*cf.*, Num 10:34-36; Judg 5:4-5; Deut 33:2-3; Hab 3:3-6), and Jeremiah's younger contemporary, Ezekiel, delights in exactly the same imagery when he condemns Egypt in Ezek 30:1-3 and 31:15. Earlier, Isa 13:9-10 had also used this cosmic battle scene against Babylon. Several scholars argue that the language stems from late apocalyptic imagery and that Isaiah, Jeremiah and Ezekiel would not have used such mythical language but would have pictured a specific historical battle in quite earthly terms. This argument has little weight in light of the long and very cosmic traditions that stand behind the idea of the "Day of the Lord" in Hebrew tradition.

The chapter ends with a final sketch of the last stages of a siege. Everybody has fled to hide in the hills as best they can, but prostitutes stay behind thinking they can make money even from the enemy by means of their charms. Many times before Judah and Israel have played the game, selling themselves to every changing world power. But this time it will not work. In a strange shift of imagery, whoring Judah will suffer the pains of giving birth as she falls before her foes. The irony is complete—Yahweh offered daughter Zion the true love of marriage, but she turned away from it; now she perishes and her cries of agony can almost be confused with the short and temporary pain before joyful motherhood.

FALSE TRUST IN THE MIDST OF SIN
5:1-19

> **5** Run to and fro through the streets of Jerusalem,
> look and take note!
> Search her squares to see
> if you can find a man,
> one who does justice
> and seeks truth;
> that I may pardon her.
> ²Though they say, "As the LORD lives,"
> yet they swear falsely.
> ³O LORD, do not thy eyes look for truth?
> Thou hast smitten them,
> but they felt no anguish;
> thou hast consumed them,
> but they refused to take correction.
> They have made their faces harder than rock;
> they have refused to repent.

Chapter 5 follows in the thought of the preceding threat of punishment. It consists of two parts: vv. 1-19 and 20-31, the first of which stresses the nation's disobedience to the practical demands of God's covenant and how God is forced to punish such falsehood, and the second of which stresses their blindness to the love and reverence owed God and how it leads them to perversity and richly deserved punishment. The two oracles belong back to back at this point to underline the reasons for the terrible judgment described in chaps. 4 and 6. The major themes echo one another in both passages: the guilt of the [false] prophets in giving words of comfort rather than condemning evil, the failure to act justly for the poor and powerless, the personal rejection of Yahweh by people high and low, the personal agony of the Lord as he must punish rather than pardon, and finally as a refrain, the promise that he will not destroy everything.

5:1-19 can be subdivided into vv. 1-9 and 10-19. The former centers on the refusal to repent, the latter on the false prophecies so easily spoken. In both, God threatens a destroyer who will swallow Israel up as a victim.

As the chapter opens, we are reminded that God always seeks to forgive. The story of Abraham asking for the life of Sodom if ten good people could be found (Gen 18) comes to mind. But now, Yahweh wants even one good person so that he can forgive. As a sign God asks that such a person pursue justice and seek truth. RSV's "truth" should be translated "faithlessness" (Hebrew *'emunah*) and "justice" rendered as "just demands" to capture the full sense. God looks for one who is steadfast day in and day out to his covenant. This people pays no heed even in moments of crisis. In v. 4, they are described as rocks, completely unyielding. Jeremiah's sense of irony stands out here— Yahweh should be the rock for Israel (Ps 18:3; Deut 32:4, 15,31; Hab 1:12). Jeremiah attempts a little sociology at this point, excusing the ordinary people as perhaps poorly taught in their faith, but expecting that the religious leaders and princes will understand; after all, they are educated. But no, no one high or low can be found who has that "faithfulness the Lord seeks." Verses 4-5 offer another pair of signs to recognize the good person: RSV's "The way of the Lord" and "The law of their God." These stand parallel to one another and the translation hides the real sense. We could better read "the way of Yahweh" and the "just demands of their God," since the sense of obedience to the commandments and laws of the covenant in the concrete actions of life prevails here, not an intellectual commitment of faith alone.

The search proves empty. No one can be found. Borrowing the language of the farm, Jeremiah describes Israel as an ox who has broken away from the plough and run off on its own. Verse 6 draws the results of such freedom—the ox falls victim to lions or wolves waiting for such strays.

Again Jeremiah intends a second level of meaning in his imagery. Ancient practice hurled the bodies of executed criminals out on the highways to be torn up and eaten by wild animals (2 Kgs 9:30-37). In the same way, he moves on to another play on words in v. 7, contrasting Hebrew *shaba'* (to swear) with *saba'* (to feed to the full). Yahweh gives them prosperous times but they give the thanks and praise to other gods and use their renewed strength to commit sexual sins against the Lord's covenant. The Hebrew words for "punishment" and "avenging" in v. 9 are legal and official terms. God will carry out the sentence decreed by the seriousness of their crimes. The oracle of 1-9 ends with the carefully chosen use of *goy*, a foreign nation, rather than of *'am*, a people, to describe Israel. They have sinned so that the Lord can no longer treat them with special favor.

The second oracle in vv. 10-17 also uses a farming metaphor, this time the pruning back of the grape vines in the late fall. They must be cut down to the root in order to bring forth new growth the following year. The old branches cannot be saved, yet despite the severe surgery, the vine should survive. Like the result of this chapter, the development of the thought forms a three-way dialogue between God and the prophet and the people. Jeremiah moves from one image or thought to another with ease, and more than once we can suspect that the editors have joined two striking passages side by side to increase the dramatic effect. In any case, vv. 11-13 suddenly shift to a concern with false prophecy. As in 3:11, the prophet again charges Israel—in the Hebrew—with committing *beged*. In the earlier verse, the RSV translated this word as "false," here as "utterly faithless," but in both uses, the sense of treachery and betrayal is present. Above all, Jeremiah singles out the prophets and their empty words of promise. Their "false" message falls into three levels of intensity: (1) God probably won't act at all against us; (2) he certainly would not bring evil upon his own land; (3) under no condition would be destroy his own people.

Jeremiah's response also has three levels. The first in v. 13 rejects the authority of these prophets of comfort. They have only wind and not the spirit of God. The same word, *ruah*, can mean both wind and spirit, but here the first is meant. Secondly, Yahweh will strengthen the power of Jeremiah's word so that what he proclaims in judgment will surely come about, just as flames eat through dry wood. And thirdly, that word will declare the coming of an enemy nation to destroy the land in fact. From the description of this nation, far away, mighty, and of great age, only Babylon could be intended. Its army will devour the small nation of Judah and overrun all of its cities and their so-called unbreakable walls. No doubt Jeremiah, with the rest of the nation, has been watching the progress of Babylon through the last years of the seventh century as it marched year by year against the great empire of Assyria and demolished and destroyed its strongholds one by one. This oracle may well date from early in the reign of Jehoiakim between 609 and 605 B.C. as the Babylonian armies poised to sweep Egyptian forces out of Palestine and Syria once and for all. The threat was all too real. The RSV places vv. 18-19 in prose, and because the thought centers on the coming exile of the people, it may well have been composed later than the rest of vv. 10-17, either by Jeremiah himself or by a disciple, to indicate that the Babylonian victories of 598 and 586 fulfilled the word spoken earlier to the prophet.

STIFF NECKS AND STUBBORN HEARTS
5:20-31

> 20Declare this in the house of Jacob,
>   proclaim it in Judah:
> 21"Hear this, O foolish and senseless people,

> who have eyes, but see not,
> who have ears, but hear not.
> 22Do you not fear me? says the LORD;
> Do you not tremble before me?
> I placed the sand as the bound for the sea,
> a perpetual barrier which it cannot pass;
> though the waves toss, they cannot prevail,
> though they roar, they cannot pass over it.
> 23But this people has a stubborn and rebellious heart;
> they have turned aside and gone away.
> 24They do not say in their hearts,
> 'Let us fear the LORD our God,
> who gives the rain in its season,
> the autumn rain and the spring rain,
> and keeps for us
> the weeks appointed for the harvest.'
> 25Your iniquities have turned these away,
> and your sins have kept good from you."

The remainder of chap. 5 consists of a loosely-joined pair of oracles, the first of which in vv. 20-25 accuses Israel of foolishness in failing to understand that God's control of nature could mean blessing for them; and the second, in vv. 26-31, details the list of crimes and sins they commit in defiance of God's will and power. The section opens with the same charge found in the call of Isaiah a hundred years before: the people are blind and deaf (Isa 6:9-10). They do not fear the Lord. In Proverbs, in the Psalms, in the Prophets, this reverence for God sums up all that a faithful Israelite does, especially obedience, humility, and worship; see such texts as Isa 11:2-3; Jer 32:40; Pss 19:10 and 34:12; Prov 1:7,29 and 14:26-27. Here Jeremiah draws a sharp contrast between the ideal of Israel's faith and the loyalty due to the pagan gods. Where Yahweh has set the bounds of the sea and the land so that they eternally obey his command, the cult of Baal proclaimed the unending battle between the god and chaotic Sea for control of the earth; where Yahweh has set the proper times for seasons and for feasts, for rains and dry spells, so that they all fall according to his plan, the pagan gods must renew the fight of life against death each year in the cultic ceremonies. The stubborn rejection of Yahweh's order in favor of the precarious cult of blind and deaf gods has resulted in the loss of blessing and the disastrous state of affairs the people now experience.

Verses 26-31 catalog many of the specific evils that violate the covenant and bring down God's punishment. The basic category seems to be the practice of defrauding or cheating others to amass a fortune for oneself. It is described in hunting terms as the snaring of unsuspecting and helpless birds with traps. The little birds filling cages in the hunter's house symbolize the ill-gotten wealth. The methods of capture are then listed: they do injustice to orphans and to the poor, to the powerless in society, and to the very ones for whom the covenant of Moses demands the most protection from society (Pss 68:3; 109:9; 146:9; Jer 7:6; 22:3; Exod 23:6,9). The Temple Sermon in chapter 7 will list even more social abuses. These crimes alone are enough to bring down God's punishment, but Jeremiah can add to these his previous, vehement charge that the false prophets and priests have joined hands to undermine the demands of Yahweh's covenant and are therefore as bad if not worse than the political and economic leaders who carry out this utter disregard for God's justice.

> 30An appalling and horrible thing
>   has happened in the land:
> 31the prophets prophesy falsely,
>   and the priests rule at their direction;
> my people love to have it so,
>   but what will you do when the end comes?

THE FOE APPROACHES
6:1-15

> 6   Flee for safety, O people of Benjamin,
>   from the midst of Jerusalem!

Blow the trumpet in Tekoa,
and raise a signal on Beth-haccherem;
for evil looms out of the north,
and great destruction.
²The comely and delicately bred I will destroy,
the daughter of Zion.
³Shepherds with their flocks shall come against her;
they shall pitch their tents around her,
they shall pasture, each in his place.
⁴"Prepare war against her;
up, and let us attack at noon!"
"Woe to us, for the day declines,
for the shadows of evening lengthen!"
⁵"Up, and let us attack by night,
and destroy her palaces!"

Like chaps. 4 and 5, chapter 6 contains a series of oracles that mix vivid descriptions of the attacking foe whom God will send down on the land with dialogues between Yahweh and his prophet that serve to warn and plead with the people. Five separate units are present: vv. 1-8, 9-15, 16-21, 22-26, 27-30. Jeremiah's love for puns and rural metaphors appears beneath the surface of his message and reveals how deeply involved he himself has become in the proclamation of the word that God has given him.

The opening poem returns to the theme of the Foe from the North. The danger is no longer far away but at the very gates of Jerusalem: Benjamin, Tekoa, Beth-hakkerem all lie within a few miles north and west of the capital city. Which towns are named seems less important than the sense of urgency that the list creates. The commands are shaped into attention-getting puns: *tike'u* ("blow the trumphet") in Tekoa; *se'u* ("lift up") the *mas'et* ("fire signal"). Then Jeremiah develops one of his pastoral metaphors of Zion as a lush meadow suddenly overrun by shepherds and their hungry flocks. This in turn becomes a siege, with troops milling around in hasty preparation to storm the city before the time runs out, even to the unusual tactic of mounting a night attack. We are treated to a vivid picture of ancient battle practice as soldiers prepare the ramps of earth and logs to bring the battering rams against the city gates. Only at the last moment does Jeremiah reveal the city's name: Jerusalem! Verses 6-8 unfold the reasons for this violent attack; it is a city full of oppression, violence and destruction. Suddenly the imagery shifts again, to a comparison between a well filled with fresh water constantly bubbling to the top, and Jerusalem whose wickedness is always rising within her walls. Twice Jeremiah has called her name in these last three verses. Let her heed the frightening warning!

In vv. 9-15, Jeremiah returns again to the picture of a vineyard.

> 9Thus says the LORD of hosts:
>   "Glean thoroughly as a vine the remnant of Israel;
> like a grape-gatherer pass your hand again
>   over its branches.". . .
> 11Therefore I am full of the wrath of the LORD;
>   I am weary of holding it in.
> "Pour it out upon the children in the street,
>   and upon the gatherings of young men, also;
> both husband and wife shall be taken,
>   the old folk and the very aged.
> 12 Their houses shall be turned over to others,
>   their fields and wives together;
> for I will stretch out my hand
>   against the inhabitants of the land,"
>   says the LORD.
> 13"For from the least to the greatest of them,
>   every one is greedy for unjust gain;
> and from prophet to priest,
>   every one deals falsely.
> 14They have healed the wound of my people lightly,
>   saying, 'Peace, peace,'
>   when there is no peace.

¹⁵Were they ashamed when they committed
abomination?
No, they were not at all ashamed;
they did not know how to blush.
Therefore they shall fall among those who fall;
at the time that I punish them,
they shall be overthrown,"

says the LORD.

In v. 9 we see that the pickers miss very few good grapes,
sometimes coming back a second time to search out bunches
they had previously overlooked. In the same way, little will
be left of Israel after divine punishment passes by. Jeremiah
repeats and underlines his constant preaching that the
whole nation shares in the guilt of rebellion against the
covenant. In this passage, as in 2:1-8, 29-32; 5:1-3, 20-29,
the judgment touches all levels of society: children, adults,
the elderly, from the least to the greatest in rank. And as
before, special vehemence is reserved for the priests and
prophets. The charges have not changed. Israel will not
listen to God's word.

This word speaks on many different levels. In v. 11, it
refers to the word of condemnation and threat from the
prophet. It is a word which Jeremiah does not wish to speak
even though he shares the anger and pain of his God at the
evil all around him; but God can wait no longer and orders
his servant to speak out forcefully. They have refused to
listen to warning, now they must hear the sentence. The
legal tone is strong. At another level, some of the ancient
respect for the power of a spoken word also comes through
in this passage. Once uttered, a word lives. It can be compared to an arrow shot toward a target, with a force and
direction of its own. Some years later during the exile,
the author of the second half of the book of Isaiah describes
the word of the Lord's servant as a sharp sword and a
gleaming arrow (Isa 49:2); and Jeremiah quotes Yahweh
forcefully in 4:28: "For I have spoken, I have purposed;
I have not relented nor will I turn back." The order goes

forth now: speak the word! A third level of meaning includes the role of the priests to teach the laws and the torah, Israel's way of life. The prophetic word challenges and summons people to be faithful to that teaching, but they must first learn the demands of the covenant. To Jeremiah, however, the priests and prophets have both failed their duty. They themselves have been so eager for unjust advantage over others and for their own lust that they do not insist on the covenant. Jeremiah describes it well—they cover a gaping wound with a bandaid or piece of gauze and announce: "'Peace, peace!' when there is no peace." See 8:18-21 and especially 30:12-13 for further development of the theme of Israel's rebellion as an incurable wound.

THE PEOPLE'S REFUSAL
6:16-30

¹⁶Thus says the LORD:
"Stands by the roads, and look,
   and ask for the ancient paths,
where the good way is; and walk in it,
   and find rest for your souls.
But they said, 'We will not walk in it.'
¹⁷I set watchmen over you, saying,
   'Give heed to the sound of the trumpet!'
But they said, 'We will not give heed.'
¹⁸Therefore hear, O nations,
   and know, O congregation, what
   will happen to them.
¹⁹Hear, O earth; behold, I am bringing evil upon this
   people,
   the fruit of their devices,
because they have not given heed to my words;
   and as for my law, they have rejected it.
²⁰To what purpose does frankincense come to
   me from Sheba,
   or sweet cane from a distant land?
Your burnt offerings are not acceptable,
   nor your sacrifices pleasing to me.

²¹Therefore thus says the LORD:
'Behold, I will lay before this people
    stumbling blocks against which they shall stumble;
fathers and sons together,
    neighbour and friend shall perish.'"

Verses 16-21 contain a typical prophetic litany. Many
scholars consider this unit to be a prose summary by the
deuteronomic editors of the whole book. Yet, when we look
closely at the text we will find very few phrases repeated
anywhere in Deuteronomy. One exception is the opening
scene of a good "way" in which we may find rest. Deut 9:12,
16; 11:28; 31:29 and other passages refer to the way which
Yahweh has taught his people and warns them not to stray
from it. The metaphor of the watchman in v. 17 occurs often
in Jeremiah, as we have already noted about 1:11-12, as well
as in Habakkuk and Ezekiel, to define their tasks as
prophets (Hab 2:1; Ezek 3:17-21). The verb "to give heed"
never shows up in Deuteronomy, but is common among the
Prophets and in the Book of Proverbs (Hos 5:1, Isa 28:23;
34:1; Prov 4:1,20; 5:1; 7:24) when referring to wisdom or
prophetic teaching. Even the phrase in v. 19, "Hear, O
earth," which might resemble Deut 32:1, makes better
sense in light of Mic 1:2, when the prophet, in calling on
the peoples and the earth to listen to his word, employs the
same two verbs found in Jer 6:18 and 19, "to hear" and "to
hearken." The thought that the religious rites of the temple
and feast days have no worth before God if his law is
rejected echoes the language of Mic 6:6-8, Hos 6:6, and even
of Psalm 51, more than that of Deuteronomy. Finally, the
prophets Jeremiah and Ezekiel favor the vocabulary of
"stumbling" to describe God's method of bringing the
Israelites down from their haughty and proud rebellion
(*cf.*, the verb "to stumble" in Jer 8:12; 20:11, and the noun,
"stumbling block," in Ezek 3:20; 14:3,4,7; 18:30; 21:20).
A century before, Hosea and Isaiah had used the same
language often. But nowhere does Deuteronomy contain
this idea.

In general, vv. 16-21 serve to focus the traditional concerns of the prophets through the generations up to Jeremiah's own day. He does not stand alone as some radical in his preaching. He proclaims the enduring warning of Yahweh's watchmen to the nation. The chief actors and their immediate settings may change, but the blindness and deafness of Israel have taken such deep roots in the national soul that parents pass it on to the children as a way of life. It becomes so much a part of the system that everyone shares in the blame. The economic greed, the social stratification, the privileges of the leadership, the comfort of the temple worship proclaiming "peace, peace" (6:14), all numb any desire or willingness to look at what the prophets point out, and to reject their claims to offer divine guidance and direction. If a connection to Deuteronomy exists in this passage, it is mainly in the shared conviction of both Jeremiah and the deuteronomic writers on this question.

Verses 22-26 offer still one more poem sketching the horrors of a foe from the north.

22Thus says the LORD:
"Behold, a people is coming from the north country,
   a great nation is stirring from the farthest
   parts of the earth.
23They lay hold on bow and spear,
   they are cruel and have no mercy,
   the sound of them is like the roaring sea; . . ."
24We have heard the report of it,
   our hands fall helpless;
anguish has taken hold of us,
   pain as of a woman in travail.
25Go not forth into the field,
   nor walk on the road; . . .
26O daughter of my people, gird on sackcloth,
   and roll in ashes;
make mourning as for an only son,
   most bitter lamentation;
for suddenly the destroyer
   will come upon us.

Interestingly enough, the colorful portrait in vv. 22-24 recurs again in chap. 50:41-43, where it stands against the Babylonians who will suffer their own foe from the north! The original poem fits best here in chap. 6 as part of Jeremiah's series of warnings sometime after 609 B.C. After the fall of Jerusalem for the second time in 586, it could be forcefully repeated in chap. 50 to affirm that Yahweh's justice was even-handed and to give hope to the exiled and wasted nation. "Terror on every side" captures the hopeless attempts of the people to escape their fate. Human efforts cannot stop what God has brought down upon them. In the past Jeremiah had frequently pointed to repentance, change of lifestyle, a sense of trust in Yahweh's mercy. Now it is too late. The only activity left will be mourning at the funeral of the whole nation!

The final small oracle in vv. 27-30 uses still another metaphor to say the same thing. Jeremiah must work like a dealer in precious metals, testing and refining the ores to get the valuable gold and silver he needs for making the bowls and cups and statues that he can sell. He puts the ore into a very hot furnace with some lead, so that in the searing heat, the ore will melt and the silver will separate from other less desirable minerals and metals. The silver will stand free, but the copper and iron will become attached to the melted lead which has oxidized. Yet, after performing all this work, he finds no silver.

The passage brings to an end the first major collection of Jeremiah's words in chaps. 2-6. The charges have been serious, the threats dire, but despite the power of the prophetic word, despite its passion and even anger, none can be found who heeded and separated themselves from the dross and base ore. There is no true silver in this crowd that God can work with.

V. THE TEMPLE SERMON
JEREMIAH 7:1-8:3

Chaps. 2-6 have gathered together many of Jeremiah's earliest oracles from either the days of King Josiah or the very first years of his son King Jehoiakim, that is from 627 at the earliest down to 608 at the latest. The present order has woven the different oracles into a pattern of accusation and vivid threat mixed with the hope of reform and return to Yahweh. If the people persist in both their crimes against justice and in their idolatry, they will bring on themselves a destruction which God will permit by means of their enemies. That series has ended on a note of despair—no silver could be found, no person of sterling quality! At this point, the editors have put into place a sermon that Jeremiah delivered in the winter after Jehoiakim became king. It echoes both of the major themes of injustice and idolatry that make up the meat and potatoes of the prophet's preaching. It was spoken in the gate of the temple according to v. 2, probably meaning in the entrance to the courtyard around the temple building. Worshippers would be coming there either to bring animals to be offered on the outdoor altar of sacrifice, or to speak to the priests, or to pray. It was surely a noisy place, but there seems little reason to believe that quiet and private corners appealed to the ancient mind. A visit to the Western (Wailing) Wall in Jerusalem today gives some idea of the bustle and murmur of voices as crowds try to pray, touch the stones, or just gawk at this surviving part of Solomon's Temple.

Jeremiah was thus assured of a good audience. We might imagine Hyde Park in London or other parks where individuals can command a crowd with a rousing religious oration. Since the same sermon seems to be reported again in chap. 26:1-6, even the editors recognized it as an important summary of Jeremiah's beliefs. In both chaps. 7 and 26, the speech stands in prose not in poetry. Since chap. 7 contains much more material than the second version, we should suppose that the present text does not reflect exactly the way Jeremiah spoke. In fact, the original message lies in vv. 1-15 (=26:2-6). To this the editors added four shorter oracles on the same themes: vv. 16-20, 21-28, 29-34 and 8:1-3. All focus on the question of temple worship and the covenant, and most of the present words probably do not come directly from Jeremiah's mouth but are reported second-hand. Most scholars believe that this sermon has been worked on by the disciples of the school of Deuteronomy—which may mean nothing more than that the religious language of the period just before the exile favored a certain kind of thought and expression, and that both Deuteronomy and Jeremiah, as well as the histories in the books of Joshua, Judges, Samuel and Kings, share the same words because they were written about the same time. Such deuteronomic touches, as they are called, can be seen in such ideas as God placing his name in one place (Deut 12:11; 14:23 and also 1 Kgs 6:12-13), Israel walking after other gods (Deut 30:17; 2 Kgs 22:17), and the need to "hear" God in the sense of obeying him (Deut 3:26; 4:30; 12:28; 27:10; 30:2). But this must not be exaggerated. The heart of chap. 7 is pure Jeremiah with few connections to the Book of Deuteronomy and its language. The mocking of the trust that Israel puts in the foreign gods occurs no more than twice in Deuteronomy but runs continuously through Jeremiah, Ezekiel, Second Isaiah, all from the sixth century, and also through many of the Psalms. The covenant promise that "I will be your God and you shall be my people" in v. 23 comes not from Deuteronomy but from a priestly tradition found in Exod 6:7; Lev 26:12; Jer 7:23; 11:4; 24:7; 30:22; 31:1; 31:33; 32:38; Ezek 11:20, 14:11; 36:28; 37:23 and 37:27. The closest thought in Deuteronomy comes in Deut 14:1-2 and 26:16-19 but that book never uses the whole phrase in one place.

"DO NOT TRUST IN THE TEMPLE"
7:1-8:3

7 The word that came to Jeremiah from the Lord: [2]"Stand in the gate of the LORD'S house, and proclaim there this word, and say, Hear the word of the LORD, all you men of Judah who enter these gates to worship the LORD.[3]Thus says the LORD of hosts, the God of Israel, Amend your ways and your doings, and I will let you dwell in this place. [4]Do not trust in these deceptive words: 'This is the temple of the LORD, the temple of the LORD, the temple of the LORD.'

[5]"For if you truly amend your ways and your doings, if you truly execute justice one with another, [6]if you do not oppress the alien, the fatherless or the widow, or shed innocent blood in this place, and if you do not go after other gods to your own hurt, [7]then I will let you dwell in this place, in the land that I gave of old to your fathers for ever.

[8]"Behold, you trust in deceptive words to no avail. [9]Will you steal, murder, commit adultery, swear falsely, burn incense to Baal, and go after other gods that you have not known,[10] and then come and stand before me in this house, which is called by my name, and say, 'We are delivered!'—only to go on doing all these abominations? [11]Has this house, which is called by my name,

become a den of robbers in your eyes? Behold, I myself have seen it, says the LORD. [12]Go now to my place that was in Shiloh, where I made my name dwell at first, and see what I did to it for the wickedness of my people Israel. [13]And now, because you have done all these things, says the LORD, and when I spoke to you persistently you did not listen, and when I called you, you did not answer, [14]therefore I will do to the house which is called by my name, and in which you trust, and to the place which I gave to you and to your fathers, as I did to Shiloh. [15]And I will cast you out of my sight, as I cast out all your kinsmen, all the offspring of Ephraim.

The temple sermon proper in vv. 1-15 strongly attacks the practices found among faithful worshippers. Jeremiah does not address those who have lost the sense of religious duty and avoid the temple, perhaps content to be nominal followers of Yahweh only. He rather goes after those we would consider as the devout people. By a strange twist, the heart of his threat lies in the very success of religious practice. People do come to the temple; there have never been more offerings than now, the priests might report. But because of this, many think they have done all that needs to be done. The people shared the widespread belief that God dwelt in the Temple hidden from sight, but could almost be felt in the awesome surroundings and the smell of incense and smoke of burned flesh. They also believed that he had promised not to leave Jerusalem unprotected. Possibly such a conviction stemmed from the singing of Psalms 89 and 132 which proclaimed that God had promised to David a dynasty that would not end and had chosen Zion for this divine residence. It must have struck the nation as a divine miracle to realize that David's dynasty had indeed reigned unbroken from the year 1000 B.C. down to their own day, nearly 400 years in all. Similarly, the telling of the astounding story of how Isaiah had prophesied that the Assyrian army would not take Jerusalem in the invasion of 701 B.C. (Isa 37:33-35), and how a plague had then crippled and nearly destroyed the Assyrians, forcing them to leave in haste, must have added to the people's sense of safety.

Jeremiah opens in v. 3 by listing titles of Yahweh, the Lord of the heavenly armies, the God of Israel, to stress his power on a cosmic canvas much greater than the smallness of this "place." The prophet carefully plays on the word "place." According to Deuteronomy, God put his name in that "place," the temple (Deut 12:5,14); but here Jeremiah broadens the idea to mean primarily the whole land. The nation places its hopes in the divine protection of the holy place, but all the while God plans to let the whole land go. Three times he imitates their trusting cry "The Temple of the Lord," in order to show the emptiness of mere words. As in Jesus' words some centuries later about prayerful words without corresponding behavior (*cf.*, the lesson of the gift at the altar in Matt 5:23-24; and the parable of the publican and pharisee in Luke 18:9-14), Jeremiah insists on acting out a way of life that obeys the demands and ideals of the covenant. Verses 5-10 go on to list the covenant commandments. The first group include three examples of absolutely powerless people: foreigners living in the country, orphans and widows—all of them without family to fight for them and protect their interests (*cf.*, Pss 10:14,18; 68:6; 146:9; Isa 1:23 and Deut 10:18). Shedding innocent blood belongs with this class also since the victims are those who were put to death on trumped up charges by the authorities and who had little or no power to defend themselves. The two classic biblical examples that reveal the horror of this crime are the stories of how David put to death Uriah the Hittite, his most loyal vassal, in order to steal his wife (2 Sam 11-12) and how King Ahab executed his poor neighbor Naboth to acquire his vineyard (1 Kgs 21). In both cases, God sent a prophet to condemn the crime.

The following list in v. 9 just about goes through the ten commandments cataloging the common sins of Israel. The addition of such phrases as "gods that you have not known" and the "house which is called by my name," accent the personal bonds of the covenant.

The entire passage from vv. 1 to 15 weaves three key words in and out of the text: *trust*, the *name*, and *other* gods. All of them are used in such a way that they point to Israel's failure to trust God and his name, in stark contrast to the patriarchs of old, Abraham and Jacob, who believed in the promise and acted out of their faith (Gen 13:14-17; 15:18-21; Exod 3:7-8). The unit ends as did the body of oracles in chaps. 4-6 with the threat that God will hand this temple and this place over to destruction just as he had been forced to do on other occasions in the past. First it was with Shiloh in the days of the Judges. At that time the evil of the people and the unfaithfulness of the priestly family of Eli led to the capture of the sacred Ark of the Covenant with the stones of the Ten Commandments. God allowed it to fall into the hands of the Philistines. Moreover, Ps 78:60-61 goes on to tell us at the same time Shiloh was leveled, something clear even in the modern archaeological excavation of the city. Secondly it was the same with Samaria, the capital of the Northern Kingdom, which God allowed the Assyrians to wipe out in 722 B.C. Verse 15 identifies Samaria with Ephraim, the tribal area in which it stood (see 2 Kgs 17).

Verses 16-20 form a separate oracle attacking the widespread worship of foreign gods. The Book of Kings reports that such idolatry was a frequent problem in the seventh century during the reign of King Manasseh and before the reforms of Josiah (2 Kgs 21 and 23). But references in Jeremiah and Ezekiel make it clear that such cults had not been successfully stopped. In Jeremiah's time, at least, the food for the queen of heaven and other gods was not being offered in the temple itself although whole families did take part in the rites. Ezekiel, on the other hand, indicates that some idolatrous services took place directly in the side

chambers of the temple in the last days of the Kingdom—
during the reign of Zedekiah about 590 B.C. (Ezek 8).
Devotees baked cakes and poured out wine before the
statues of the pagan gods and goddesses to beg favors from
them. Although the Psalms frequently express deep trust
and confidence in Yahweh who heals and delivers those
who call on him (see Pss 31, 34, 37, 46, 57, 61), there were
always many people who felt that God did not hear their
prayers nor grant their requests as they would have liked.
Human nature does not change greatly in this regard. Today
many cease to believe in any God at all when they don't get
what they want; in the ancient world, they turned instead
to some other god, hoping for a more favorable response.

God speaks directly to the prophet here, rather than to
the whole people. He commands Jeremiah not to intercede
on their behalf, not to do his expected task. Even in the
founding days of the Exodus wanderings in the wilderness,
Moses had expended much of his energy interceding with
Yahweh not to destroy the people for their rebellion and
lack of gratitude (*cf.*, Exod 32:11-13, 30-32; 33:7-11; 34:8-9,
Num 11:11-15; 14:13-25). And the prophets had conceived
their own mission in terms of filling the shoes of Moses as
they plead with God to remember his compassion (*cf.*,
Amos 7:1-6; Hos 11:1-9). The description of Jeremiah's
call in chap. 1 explicitly compares his mission to the
prophetic role of Moses in the Exodus. The hopelessness of
the present situation stands out in Jeremiah's enforced
silence.

Verses 21-28 add a third element to the list of charges
in this chapter.

> 21Thus says the LORD of hosts, the God of Israel:
> "Add your burnt offerings to your sacrifices, and eat the
> flesh. 22For in the day that I brought them out of the
> land of Egypt, I did not speak to your fathers or com-
> mand them concerning burnt offerings and sacrifices.

23But this command I gave them, 'Obey my voice, and I will be your God, and you shall be my people; and walk in all the way that I command you, that it may be well with you.' 24But they did not obey or incline their ear, but walked in their own counsels and the stubbornness of their evil hearts, and went backward and not forward. 25From the day that your fathers came out of the land of Egypt to this day, I have persistently sent all my servants the prophets to them, day after day; 26yet they did not listen to me, or incline their ear, but stiffened their neck. They did worse than their fathers.

27"So you shall speak all these words . . . 'This is the nation that did not obey the voice of the LORD their God, and did not accept discipline; truth has perished; it is cut off from their lips.' "

Not only does moral evil abound under the mask of pious worship, not only do the cults of Ishtar and other gods and goddesses multiply in the land, but the people have substituted sacrifices for obedience to the covenant and its teaching. Lev 1-9 gives highly detailed directions for all kinds of sacrifices. A clear distinction is made between the burnt offering, given completely to Yahweh and totally consumed by the flames, and the communion sacrifices, which are partly burned for Yahweh and partly eaten by the worshippers and priests. In v. 21, however, God signals his anger with a shallow legalism, by lumping them all together. "Do what you want," he says, "I could care less!" This entire section shows considerable relation to the thought of Deuteronomy in its approach and even in its language. Both trace the theme of disobedience through the entire history of the people and indict the present generation as the worst of the lot. The theme of the "stiff-necked" people recurs in Deut 9:6,13, 10:16 and in the deuteronomic passage of 2 Kgs 17:14 as well as in Jer 17:23; 19:15. It also appears four times in Exod 32-34, the story of the second writing of the ten commandments on new tablets, and this too may have been influenced by Deuteronomy. Another common theme between Jer 7:21-28 and the deuteronomic viewpoint centers on God's continuous sending of new prophets to Israel, all of whom are rejected by the people.

Jeremiah claims the commands of God in the desert period did not include laws about sacrifice, but centered above all on the personal relationship and then on the obedience to the kind of law represented by the ten commandments in Exod 20. This fits well the opinions of modern scholars that the materials in the Books of Leviticus and parts of Numbers were only attached to the early covenant traditions at a late date. From the evidence in v. 22, it seems that at the time of Jeremiah, the Exodus and Sinai story still did not have the cult laws joined to it.

Verse 29 quotes a small snatch of poetry to end this treatment of sacrifice versus obedience. It repeats the thought of the last verse of chaps. 2-6 with its call for lamentation at the funeral of the people.

Verses 30-34 tell of an even greater horror. Besides the rebuff and insult to Yahweh involved in setting up the statues of other gods in his very temple, the people have built a second altar and shrine outdoors in the valley of Ben Hinnom just beyond the city walls. Here they practice human sacrifice. The name Tophet stems from a word that means "fireplace," and the name fits well. From our knowledge of child sacrifice at Carthage in North Africa during Roman times, we can suppose that parents brought a first-born child to be placed in the arms of the statue of the god Baal-Hammon, from which it would roll or drop into the flames of a furnace below. The bones would then be gathered up and buried, often in a pottery vase. Since Carthage had been settled by Phoenicians from the coast of modern Lebanon, presumably the custom originated in the homeland. The Bible itself makes note of child sacrifice in at least two other passages. In 2 Kgs 3:27, Mesha, king of Moab, sacrifices a son on the walls of his city to stop an

Israelite attack. It so horrified the attackers that they withdrew. In 2 Kgs 21:6, king Manasseh of Israel sacrificed a son on an altar. King Josiah tore down the Tophet during his reform to prevent any more human sacrifices. The practice was unknown among the Assyrians and Babylonians, and condemned by the Law of Lev 20:3-5, but seemingly accepted by the Moabites and Phoenicians, although actual references are rare and the actual occurrences may have been few. The sacrifice seemed confined entirely to first-born children, usually males, and stemmed from the belief that the first-born must be consecrated to the gods, just as the first fruits of each crop must be. By giving back to god the first of his gifts of life, even more life-giving blessing will be secured. Israel shared in this belief, but stressed the ransoming of the son rather than the taking of his ife. The story of Abraham's sacrifice of Isaac can be understood as explaining the origin of why Israel does not take the life of first-born sons—it is God's direct command. Exod 34:19-20 and Num 18:15-17 specify that the first-born must be bought back.

The judgment of Yahweh will turn this sacred shrine of child murder into a slaughterground in which the bodies will be so numerous that many cannot even find burial.

> 32Therefore, behold, the days are coming, says the LORD, when it will no more be called Topheth, or the valley of the son of Hinnom, but the valley of Slaughter: for they will bury in Topheth, because there is no room elsewhere. 33And the dead bodies of this people will be food for the birds of the air, and for the beasts of the earth; and none will frighten them away. 34And I will make to cease from the cities of Judah and from the streets of Jerusalem the voice of mirth and the voice of gladness, the voice of the bridegroom and the voice of the bride; for the land shall become a waste.

Jeremiah found very appropriate the phrase, "food for the birds of the air and beasts of the earth"; he repeats it in 15:3; 16:4; 19:7; and 34:20. He also liked the expression, "the voice of the bridegroom and the voice of the bride"; these recur in 16:9; 25:10; and 33:11.

The final passage of this section in 8:1-3 enlarges the theme of the Tophet speech:

> **8** "At that time, says the LORD, the bones of the kings of Judah, the bones of its princes, the bones of the priests, the bones of the prophets, and the bones of the inhabitants of Jerusalem shall be brought out of their tombs; ²and they shall be spread before the sun and the moon and all the host of heaven, which they have loved and served, which they have gone after, and which they have sought and worshiped; and they shall not be gathered or buried; they shall be as dung on the surface of the ground. ³Death shall be preferred to life by all the remnant that remains of this evil family in all the places where I have driven them, says the LORD of hosts."

A century earlier, Amos 2:1 hurled judgment at the king of Moab because he had scattered the bones of the dead kings of Edom on the ground to deny them peace in the afterlife. The pagan nations always considered a proper burial to be very important, and directives to sons to see to the funeral and care of the grave of their parents show up in the Gilgamesh story, in the Ugaritic legend of King Keret and in Egyptian wisdom literature, all written long before Israel's own existence. Most Ancient Near Eastern peoples believed in some sort of land of the dead where individuals would have different fates according to either the kind of lives they had led or the manner of death they had suffered. Few were as optimistic as the Egyptians who pictured a life much like the one on earth, only better. A famous passage from the Epic of Gilgamesh, dating to the 18th century or earlier, gives a Babylonian view in which the hero Enkidu comes from the Underworld and reports to Gilgamesh:

"He who had one son, have you seen him?"
"I have seen. He lies fallen at the wall and weeps
    bitterly."

"He who had two sons, have you seen him?"
"I have seen. He dwells in a brickhouse and eats bread."
"He who has three sons, have you seen him?"
"I have seen. He drinks water from the waterskins
    of the deep."

The narrative goes on to relate how those who died from different causes have fared. The one slain in battle has his mother and wife to hold his head and cry for him, while the unburied person's spirit "does not rest in the underworld" (Gilgamesh XII: 102-153).

Israel shared some of these ideas in its concept of Sheol as a shadowland where the dead exist but have no living force. The vivid description in Ezek 32 shows the bodies lying inert side by side in its darkness. Nevertheless, a passage such as this text of Jeremiah suggests that even Israel was concerned about proper burial and the possible results it would have in the life to come. The real irony in Jeremiah's thought derives from the contrast of these pagan worshippers of the sun, moon and stars, who worked so hard to win a place in the afterlife, now lying out on the ground, denied burial and happiness, but free to continue worshipping their gods in full view.

In the light of the devastation that was coming, even this end would be better than to be part of the remnant that survives. Jeremiah turned later to a more positive hope for the remnant (see chaps. 30-32), but at this stage of his career he still looked on the idea of a remnant in a purely neutral way. When God punishes, if anyone survives that is his or her luck. The actual state of things will be almost as terrible for the survivors as for the dead. In this he agrees with Amos 3:12 where the survivors of Samaria are compared to the piece of an ear or parts of a leg that a shepherd recovers from a lamb attacked by a lion.

VI. ISRAEL'S LACK OF WISDOM
JEREMIAH 8:4-10:25

Chaps. 8-10 have less of a unified theme than chaps. 2-7. If we want to find one word that seems to capture the mood of these three chapters it is *wisdom*. Not that Jeremiah praises Israel for her insight. Far from it! The Israelites lack wisdom and their foolishness can be shown again and again. It leads the prophet to despair whether the people's wounds can be healed, it leads him to wailing and lamenting in grief because he can do nothing to persuade his people to change their ways. Jeremiah mixes his criticism of the so-called "wise" in Israel with a return to his theme of the invading foe and to lurid descriptions of the destruction that will follow.

FOOLISHNESS INSTEAD OF WISDOM
8:4-12

4"You shall say to them, Thus says the LORD:
When men fall, do they not rise again?
    If one turns away, does he not return?
5Why then has this people turned away
    in perpetual backsliding?
They hold fast to deceit,
    they refuse to return.

⁶I have given heed and listened,
　　but they have not spoken aright;
no man repents of his wickedness,
　　saying, 'What have I done?'
Every one turns to his own course,
　　like a horse plunging headlong into battle.
⁷Even the stork in the heavens
　　knows her times;
and the turtledove, swallow, and crane
　　keep the time of their coming;
but my people know not
　　the ordinance of the LORD.
⁸"How can you say, 'We are wise,
　　and the law of the LORD is with us'?
But behold, the false pen of the scribes
　　has made it into a lie.
⁹The wise men shall be put to shame,
　　they shall be dismayed and taken;
lo, they have rejected the word of the LORD,
　　and what wisdom is in them?"

8:4-12 falls into the category of a disputation, in which the accusation consists of a series of questions and answers. Chap. 3:1-5 was similar in form, and such dialogues are a particular mark of the prophetic books, being common in all the major prophets and in such minor prophets as Amos, Hosea and Micah. The questions belong to a prosecutor cross-examining a witness on the stand. The witness has the information and knows the answers, but often does not realize the importance of what is locked up inside, or else refuses to divulge anything for fear of self-incrimination. A skillful attorney can coax forgotten truths, or snag unseen truths, or confront hidden truths and bring them into the open. The questions are usually rhetorical in fact, since Jeremiah's audience knows well what he seeks to bring out.

Verses 4-7 throb with action. The Hebrew verb for turning, *shub*, always signifies moving in some direction. RSV captures some of the play on the different forms of this verb used by Jeremiah with the words "turn away," "return," and "backsliding." The prophet repeats the word root 5 times in vv. 4-5. The people hold fast to only one thing: their deceit. What they might do—speak aright or repent, both favorite words in Jeremiah—they don't. In sharp contrast to Israel's rushing about on her evil ways, the other creatures in nature all know their place and their times. Animals keep the ordinances of God which he has established in creation. But humans, made into the very image of the creator, do not know their place and their ordinances in creation (see also Isa 1:3). We cannot miss the reminder here about how the first couple ate the fruit from the tree of good and evil in order to be like gods, with the result that they came to know evil well, but lost the personal relationship they had with Yahweh in the garden.

The story of Adam and Eve in the garden of Eden is often considered to be the reflections of professional wisdom writers with their interest in the geography of the garden and the many "whys" it explores: why snakes crawl on the ground, why men and women are alike but different, why they are sexually attracted, why they feel shame about their genitals, why women have pain in childbirth, why we have to work for a living, why we die. Jeremiah turns the questions right back on the wise of Israel. In v. 8, he associates the custody of the Law and the work of scribes with the role of wise people. This suggests that he has priests in mind. Teaching the law was a major function of the priestly and scribal office. In chap. 9 of the Book of Nehemiah, Ezra, the great reformer after the Exile, is called both priest and scribe when he has the law read to the people and demands that they obey it. We must see some distinction between the Hebrew word law (*torah*) in v. 8 and ordinance (*mishpat*) in v. 7. The *torah* includes the entire tradition about the covenant and is a way of life for Israel. The *mishpatim*, the rules, judgments or ordinances, are the particular demands contained in this covenant law or that flow from the work of priests, scribes and wise people in interpreting the covenant way of life.

Jeremiah accuses these wise teachers of perverting the law they guard. What should reveal the directives of God for human life and for covenant fidelity have been turned around into a lie. In v. 9 he puts the *word* of the Lord up against the *law* of the Lord, the prophetic challenge against priestly failure. Because the wise act against their own duty, they will be shamed. The word "shame" may seem to be weak to us, but in ancient thought it meant total failure and degradation (*cf.*, Isa 41:11 and Ezek 32:16-30).

These few verses reveal more to us about the practice of writing down official materials than almost any other passage in the Old Testament. Many scholars have denied that Israel put much into writing before the time of the Exile. They point to the poetic nature of many prophetic oracles and to the variations in the historical traditions as evidence that most information depended on oral narration and memorization. These verses hint that a class of scribes did write down laws and judicial decisions for official use as well as keep such historical records as the Chronicles of the kings of Israel and the Chronicles of the kings of Judah which are mentioned frequently in the Books of Kings (*cf.*, 1 Kgs 11:41; 14:19,29; 2 Kgs 20:20). Jeremiah himself resorts to writing his words down both in letter form (chap. 29) and in book form (chap. 36) for others to read aloud.

This first oracle on the theme of wisdom closes in vv.10-12:

> [10]Therefore I will give their wives to others
>   and their fields to conquerors,
> because from the least to the greatest
>   every one is greedy for unjust gain;

from prophet to priest
 every one deals falsely.
11They have healed the wound of my people lightly,
 saying, 'Peace, peace,'
 when there is no peace.
12Were they ashamed when they committed
 abomination?
 No, they were not at all ashamed;
 they did not know how to blush.
Therefore they shall fall among the fallen;
 when I punish them, they shall be overthrown,
                                        says the LORD.

These lines echo the same words found in 6:12-15 except for a few changes here or there. It must have seemed highly appropriate to either Jeremiah or his editor to repeat them at this point since the passage mentions both the evil of the priests and prophets and their callous insensitivity to shame.

The Hebrew notion of *shalom*, "peace," means much more than silence or tranquility, nor is it a negative condition without friction or disturbance. *Shalom* reflects a state of prosperity, completeness and well being in which blessing flows on everyone. The idea of wholeness underlies genuine peace. Only Yahweh can give such peace and the prayer of Israel asks for it often (see Pss 34:27; 122:6; Num 6:26). Peace brings many blessings of bread and good harvests, rains and security, victory over enemies and rest (Lev 26); but as Ps 85:10-11 says so well, peace embraces mercy, faithfulness and righteousness. Thus above all else, the prophets were peacemakers, striving to reestablish justice, uprightness, covenant fidelity and mercy among the people. To charge that the priests and false prophets proclaimed "peace, peace," but neglected these moral foundations of true peace, struck at the heart of the problem. They tried to bandage over the gaping wound to hide the corruption and death working within and never tried to heal the

injured nation. The true prophet always stands against
those who only try to reduce tensions on the surface of social
evil and will not face the deeper rooted causes that come
from the very center of society and its structures of power
and leadership that exclude some members or groups from
sharing the blessing God gives for all to enjoy. He stands
against those who rule for their benefit while reducing
others to subservience and powerlessness. No peace can be
declared until these issues are faced.

THE INCURABLE WOUND
8:13 - 9:1

> [18]My grief is beyond healing,
>   my heart is sick within me.
> [19]Hark, the cry of the daughter of my people
>   from the length and breadth of the land:
> "Is the LORD not in Zion?
>   Is her King not in her?"
> "Why have they provoked me to anger with their
>   graven images,
>   and with their foreign idols?"
> [20]"The harvest is past, the summer is ended,
>   and we are not saved."
> [21]For the wound of the daughter of my people
>   is my heart wounded,
>   I mourn, and dismay has taken hold on me.
> [22]Is there no balm in Gilead?
>   Is there no physician there?
> Why then has the health of the daughter of my people
>   not been restored?
> **9**   O that my head were waters,
>   and my eyes a fountain of tears,
> that I might weep day and night
>   for the slain of the daughter of my people!

The rest of chap. 8 continues the dialogue begun in
the disputation of vv. 4-12. In v. 13 God speaks; in vv. 14-16,

the people respond; in v. 17, God speaks again, and in vv. 18-23, the prophet offers up a psalm of lament.

The section opens with a third use of the vineyard imagery (see 2:21 and 6:9).

> 13"When I would gather them, says the LORD,
>   there are no grapes on the vine,
>   nor figs on the fig tree;
> even the leaves are withered,
>   and what I gave them has passed away from them."

Israelite economic life centered on agriculture and any failure of the crops spelled disaster for the whole nation. God finds no grapes to rescue in the present harvest year. There is some difficulty with the end of v. 13. The translation of the RSV does not make much sense, but with a slight change of letters the original text may have read "and I gave them a barren woods." The joint mention of grapes and figs in v. 13 reminds us of Hosea's imagery of Israel in Hos 9:10-16 where the two fruits also appear together. Jeremiah builds on Hosea's insight.

The decision of the people of the land to seek refuge in the cities from poisoned waters and to die there rather than on their farms probably refers to the effects of famine after a bad harvest. But it could also describe the conditions of desperate starvation and thirst in the time of enemy siege when all supplies have been cut off. Possibly the oracle plays on both meanings. In any case, v. 15 expresses their disappointment that Yahweh did not automatically answer their hopes. Peace and healing—isn't that what a god is for? Instead, he sends the terror of an enemy attack that is so close and so vivid one can hear the heavy breathing of the horses. The divine judgment can be compared to poisonous serpents that can't be stopped or distracted by the snake charmers. The old remedies and magical practices no longer work against the evil that now comes, not from demonic sources, but from the Lord of Israel himself.

The stark reality of the disaster ahead for his own people causes Jeremiah to cry out in grief in 8:13-9:1. Who speaks here, Yahweh or the prophet? The interlocking of spirits is so close that the two cannot be separated. Yahweh calls the people his daughter, they provoke him to anger, yet Jeremiah feels the wound and the sickness grab hold of his own heart and fill him with anguish and even weeping for what he sees ahead. Few passages among the prophetic books express the vitality of the prophet's role as a mediator between God and Israel so sharply as this. Four times in six verses, the prophet calls out the affectionate name, "O daughter, my people," and understands the fear and loss in their question: "Is the Lord not in Zion?" Though he knows that no healing medicines will do any good at this point, he wants desperately to find one that will work. Perhaps among the famed spices and gums of Gilead (Gen 37:25), something might be chanced upon. But even as he prays, his plea turns gradually to a funeral song for those who are or will be slain. This whole episode may actually come from a time about 597 when the Babylonian armies laid city after city waste in their march on Jerusalem. It certainly reels with the trauma of an eyewitness experience. The very name, "daughter, my people," carries a deep sadness with it. Only two books use it extensively, Jeremiah and Lamentations, the latter certainly reflecting the tragedy of the Babylonian destruction of Judah, and attempting to give voice to the despair that the survivors felt when everything was torn down and destroyed. The title points to the tenderness of Yahweh in the moments after the punishment was past. He had not forgotten that they were still his people, his own children.

A FUNERAL LAMENT FOR ISRAEL
9:2-26

> [10]"Take up weeping and wailing for the mountains,
>   and a lamentation for the pastures of the wilderness,

because they are laid waste so that no one passes through,
   and the lowing of cattle is not heard;
both the birds of the air and the beasts
   have fled and are gone.
[11]I will make Jerusalem a heap of ruins,
   a lair of jackals;
and I will make the cities of Judah a desolation,
   without inhabitant."

[12]Who is the man so wise that he can understand this? To whom has the mouth of the LORD spoken, that he may declare it? Why is the land ruined and laid waste like a wilderness, so that no one passes through? [13]And the LORD says: "Because they have forsaken my law which I set before them, and have not obeyed my voice, or walked in accord with it, [14]but have stubbornly followed their own hearts and have gone after the Baals, as their fathers taught them. [15]Therefore thus says the LORD of hosts, the God of Israel: Behold, I will feed this people with wormwood, and give them poisonous water to drink. [16]I will scatter them among the nations whom neither they nor their fathers have known; and I will send the sword after them, until I have consumed them."

Chap. 9 can be divided into several oracles: vv. 2-9 on the depth of Israel's evil bent; vv. 10-11 on God's abandonment of the land; vv. 12-16 on the reasons for exile; vv. 17-22 a funeral lament over Zion; and vv. 23-26 on right virtues and their lack in Israel.

Very much like the last oracle in chap. 8, the first unit of chap. 9 is a dialogue which moves back and forth between Yahweh and the prophet. The intense emotion stems from Jeremiah's total identification with the wrong done to his God. He wants to hide, to leave the land, to be alone: "O that I had in the desert a wayfarers' lodging place"—to go away from such evil and deceitful living. The wicked cannot let a faithful or a truthful person dwell side by side with them. They must destroy anyone who would expose their deeds. Thus words become weapons to tear down, ruin and get rid of honest people. Neighbors, even brothers and sisters, cannot trust one another; it has become so bad that their tongues have forgotten how to tell the truth, and they cannot even find time to learn the difference between falsehood and honesty. Twice Jeremiah links this to their failure, or really their refusal, to know their own Lord. The passage almost bursts with words for evil, slander, deceit, treachery. Interestingly, v. 4 puns on the name of Jacob and his story from the old national epic traditions (*cf.* Gen 27 and 31). Where RSV reads "every brother is a supplanter," we could as easily see in the Hebrew words: "every brother deceives (or slanders) as Jacob." Again dependent on Hosea's thought (Hos 12:2-4), Jeremiah does not praise Jacob as the great father of the nation, but hints none too subtly that the children have the same bad qualities as their ancestor. John Bright, in his commentary on Jeremiah, calls them "as crafty as Jacob." Jeremiah's wish that he could be alone in the desert sums up the only safety possible.

Verses 3 and 8 compare the evil of the people to deadly arrows shot out of ambush at the innocent. But God will call them to double judgment here. First, in v. 7, he will refine them by fire, searching for something valuable to save (*cf.*, 6:27-30). If taken as a prediction, the image foretells the burning down of Israel's cities in the attacks from the northern foe. Second, in v. 9, he will take proper vengeance, giving them what they have deserved by their deeds. Jeremiah has already used this frightening refrain before in chap. 5, where he repeats it in vv. 9 and 29. An Israelite would have heard the threat with much more fear than it comes across to us in English. In the phrase, "a nation such as this," the word for "nation," *goy*, normally refers only to pagan peoples, and God must treat Israel as such because they worship and act like pagans. The covenant cannot save those who refuse to live by it.

The next section, vv. 10 and 11, may have been two small fragments or poems originally, but now share a common thought, a funeral song for the deserted and abandoned land. The description of ruins in which only wild animals will roam does not originate with Jeremiah, although it certainly found favor with him (*cf.*, 10:22; 49:33; 50:39; 51:37). Other prophets used it, especially Isaiah (Isa 13:19-20; 17:1-2; 27:10; 32:14; Zeph 2:13-15; Ezek 25:5), and many ancient Near Eastern treaties contained similar figures as part of the curses against anyone who violated the terms of the agreement. King Esarhaddon of Assyria described one ruined city by saying, "foxes and hyenas made their home there." The treaty from Sefire between two Syrian kings of the 8th century contains a curse against Arpad if her king breaks his side: "May Arpad become a mound for . . . gazelle and fox and hare and wildcat and owl." In the Bible, most examples are aimed at foreign nations, as was the original intention of a treaty curse, because the gods of each nation also bound themselves to the human treaties as witnesses and guarantors of the terms. If one party betrayed the solemn oaths, then the gods must intervene to punish through divine acts of judgment upon the guilty land. But more than once, the prophets turn the tables on Israel itself. Jeremiah does so in this passage and in 10:22, Isaiah does it in Isa 27:10 and 32:14. Part of the genius of the great prophets was their ability to see beyond the surface of established customs and expectations and to detect God working in new ways, sometimes even turning the tables upside down. Always the prophets insist that the only way to know what God plans to do is to know God personally through a life given to covenant fidelity.

Verses 12-16 return to the consideration of true wisdom. To a series of questions asked by a confused and ruined Israel about the reasons for destruction, the Lord gives back a direct answer: because they have forsaken Yahweh's law, his voice, and the paths he gives to follow, and instead have stubbornly followed their own voices and paths to seek out other gods, thus establishing their own *torah*, or law,

God will poison this people, exile them and send enemy swords to slay them. The passage contains many of the key phrases from Deuteronomy: "forsaking the law I have set before them" (Deut 1:8; 30:1,15,19), "obeying his voice" (Deut 4:30; 9:23; 26:17; 30:2,20), "walking in stubbornness" (Deut 29:18); but it also breathes the unique spirit of Jeremiah. The questions to the wise, the threat of wormwood and poisoned water, the menace of sword and exile together, belong to his personal style. Wormwood and poisoned water recur in 23:15, and we have already seen a partial use in 8:14. Only Jeremiah among the Hebrew prophets makes much use of this curse, though it is known elsewhere in Assyrian documents of the same century.

The next section, vv. 17-22, gives a colorful sketch of a funeral service for Jerusalem. Professional mourners must be called quickly for death is near or has already come. They throw dust on their hair, tear their clothes and wail and scream in great shrieks, a scene we know well from Egyptian tomb paintings. The purpose is to help the grieving family and friends to weep and cry freely and assuage their loss, as well as to provide a suitable public expression of the community's sorrow. The realm of death always had a concrete sense of power in ancient thought, and Israel herself often talked about death as a person, as in v. 21. Death himself is coming through the window, snatching the unwary for his kingdom of darkness below the earth. In biblical tradition, death is described as hungry (Isa 5:14; Hab 2:5; Ps 141:7), as shepherd (Ps 49:14), as partner in a covenant (Isa 28:15). Many such personal dimensions of death occur in other passages. Here, Jeremiah's image may well have come to him from the myths of the Canaanite god Mot, whose name means simply "Death." A short section in the Ugaritic myth-epic of Baal describes how Baal wants a palace built when he becomes king of the gods but refuses to allow a window put into it. His advisors finally force him to put one in, and soon enough Death comes stalking Baal to defeat him and bring him to the netherworld. The epic does not state explicitly that Mot came in through the palace window, but many scholars have argued that we can fill in the hole in the Ugaritic tale by using the text of Jer 9:21. Possibly Jeremiah did take up the mythical story to place a strong emphasis on how Israel has turned from serving Yahweh to serving the pagan gods such as Death. On the other hand, the entry of death through windows and into palaces may depict the kind of invisible attack made by a plague or contagious disease as it spreads from house to house. Cecil B. DeMille's movie version of the green fog creeping under doors and through cracks to kill the firstborn of the Egyptians in the Exodus might not be far from the mind of the ancient writers.

Suddenly the text returns to the wise man. Verses 23-24 defends true wisdom not in terms of human learning or power and prosperity, but in light of the three covenant virtues of steadfast love, justice and righteousness. The key to this passage, however, lies in the fact that wisdom comes from imitating Yahweh, who alone truly embodies the full meaning of these virtues and gives the power to live them out to human beings. The Hebrew word for steadfast love, *hesed*, always carries the inner note of loyalty. Family obligations, friendship, duty and mutual agreements bear with them a responsibility of faithful and loving service, even devotion, that must not be broken. And the second Hebrew word, *mishpat*, for justice, also has a very particular coloring: the just decrees and decisions of a judge. Every person has their *mishpat*, their appointed duties and rights, which must be carried out and which must be honored. Yahweh gives Israel the basic social demands through his covenant Torah (which was discussed at chap. 8:7-8), and he is the final judge to whom all these oppressed or suffering people turn for vindication. Finally, the Hebrew word, *sedeqah*, righteousness, stresses the right order of things and the integrity or uprightness of persons. It too stems from the legal world, this time from the role of administration. A king above all must be righteous, keeping order and governing rightly, as in Ps 72:1-2; but above all other kings, Yahweh rules as the righteous one (Pss 7:10; 11:7; 119:137; 145:17; Isa 45:21; Zeph 3:5; *etc.*). For this reason, the word comes to mean divine salvation in later writings such as Ps 24 and Isa 45:8; 46:13; 51:5-6. A century before Jeremiah, the prophet Isaiah had combined justice and righteousness as the key elements in true worship of Yahweh: Isa 1:17,21,26,27; 4:4; 5:7,16,23; 9:6; 10:2,22 among others. In a mere two verses, Jeremiah has given us the heart of the covenant bond between God and Israel. Yahweh, the source and model for the threefold performance of the covenant, delights in and empowers Israel to imitate himself.

Chap. 9 ends with a threat to punish not only Israel but also all the nations around her that also practiced circumcision as a religious rite.

> 25"Behold, the days are coming, says the LORD, when I will punish all those who are circumcised but yet uncircumcised—26Egypt, Judah, Edom, the sons of Ammon, Moab, and all who dwell in the desert that cut the corners of their hair; for all these nations are uncircumcised, and all the house of Israel is uncircumcised in heart."

According to Gen 17, circumcision was to be the sign of the covenant. Fittingly, after describing the ideal of the covenant, Jeremiah must conclude that Israel is no better than other nations. Many think that the list of countries in v. 26 represents a military alliance to oppose the Babylonian takeover of the western peoples. If so, and there is no proof for it, the judgment must go out against them as well—all who claim divine protection by their external rites but whose hearts have long ago forsaken the inner loyalty to justice and integrity demanded by covenant members.

WORSHIP OF FALSE IDOLS
10:1-25

10 Hear the word which the LORD
speaks to you, O house of Israel.
²Thus says the LORD:
"Learn not the way of the nations,
nor be dismayed at the signs of the heavens
because the nations are dismayed at them,
³for the customs of the peoples are false.
A tree from the forest is cut down,
and worked with an axe by the hands of a craftsman.
⁴Men deck it with silver and gold;
they fasten it with hammer and nails
so that it cannot move.
⁵Their idols are like scarecrows in a cucumber field,
and they cannot speak;
they have to be carried,
for they cannot walk.
Be not afraid of them,
for they cannot do evil,
neither is it in them to do good."

⁶There is none like thee, O LORD;
thou art great, and thy name is great in might.
⁷Who would not fear thee, O King of the nations?
For this is thy due;
for among all the wise ones of the nations
and in all their kingdoms
there is none like thee.

Chap. 10 can be divided into two major poems: the first,
vv. 1-16, mocks idol worship and extols the majesty of Yahweh; the second, vv. 17-25, sings a lamentation over the
coming of the foe from the north.

Discussion of the first poem by scholars has been quite
heated. The satire on the making of statues in these verses

resembles the thought of the Second Part of Isaiah, chaps. 40-55, which dates from near the end of the exile. Even the hymnlike praises of God's majesty in vv. 6-7, 10, 12-13 and 16 share more in common with Second Isaiah than they do with Jeremiah's usual manner of expression. We could make a strong case that these verses come from a later hand than that of the prophet himself. An editor may have found the poem in another collection some years after Jeremiah's death, and put it into place here to illustrate the meaning of v. 9:26 in which many pagan nations shall be punished along with Israel. We cannot be altogether certain, however, because the tone of this whole piece has a liturgical ring to it. The alternating verses of mockery and praise could easily have been from a service in which two choirs exchanged singing parts. Most commentators have said as much about the important passages in Second Isaiah, mocking and condemning idols (40:18-20; 44:9-20; 46:5-7), and both prophets may have borrowed their material directly from temple hymnals and adapted it. Pss 115:1-7 and 135:15-18 provide some idea of what the original songs may have been like.

The poem opens with a call to avoid the superstitions and fears of the pagan nations who look to the stars for signs, dread any change in the weather, and build up whole libraries of omens, astrological lore and statistics to warn them of the displeasure of the gods. As v. 3 puts it, the customs of the peoples are an emptiness, a vanity, a nothing (contrary to the RSV's "false"). The same word frequently stands for an idol elsewhere in the Bible. The following description of the workmen building up an idol with the best of gold, silver and ornaments, with strong nails and the best draped clothing, almost recreates the smell of the workshop for us. But for all the labor of love that goes into making the statue, it would still stand silent among the woodchips and dust of the shop if the people hadn't pushed and shoved and dragged and steadied it continually as they moved it into a spot of honor. It is dead and will not speak.

Who can fear its powerful word of judgment, or hope for its blessing? Twice the prophet must repeat how stupid and foolish are those who wait for its teaching (vv. 8, 14). The pagan gods have power over those who cannot resist the costly trappings and surface splendors, but nothing over those who seek teaching and understanding.

In between these spoofs on idols, the composers have spaced the verses of a hymn to Yahweh as warrior and creator. Each section answers the foolish behavior of the peoples with Yahweh's praise. It begins by affirming the power and kingship of Yahweh over the whole earth such that all nations should fear Him (vv. 6-7), while even the physical land with its mountains and valleys tremble before his anger (10). The middle section praises his wisdom as creator and his mastery over all the powers of nature (12-13). Baal was god of the storm in Canaanite religion, and we can detect the Hebrew poet's concern to show that the control of thunder (Yahweh's voice), rain, lightning, and wind belonged only to Israel's God. The poem ends by turning to Yahweh's work for Israel. The "portion" of Jacob reflects a major theme of Israelite hymns, *e.g.,* Deut 32:9; Pss 16:5; 73:26; 119:57. God not only made all things, he owns them and distributes them and has given his inheritance especially to the people of Israel. They are his chosen heirs. The sense of family lies behind this language. The poem on wisdom and creation in chap. 24 of the Book of Sirach shares some of this balance of the universal rule of God with the particular concern for little Israel. Wisdom dwells with God and yet can move through all of creation seeking a place to settle down. Only in Israel does she find a fitting home (Sir 24:1-8). Fittingly, v. 16 closes the poem with the exclamation of God's name: "Yahweh of hosts." The hosts, now an archaic word in English, refer to the heavenly armies that Yahweh commands. They are sometimes called "gods" (Ps 82:1), sometimes "angels" or "messengers" (Josh 5:13-14; Zech 14:13), and sometimes they appear to be personified as the stars (Jgs 5:20). It becomes a shout of victory to declare God's name this way. A similar spirit fills the old victory hymn of the Exodus in which Yahweh triumphs over the Egyptians. Exod 15:3 proclaims, "The Lord is a man of war; the Lord is his name!"

One last comment is in order on vv. 1-16. Verse 11 stands apart from the rest of the poem, both because it sounds more like prose than poetry, and above all because it is not Hebrew but Aramaic.

> [11]Thus shall you say to them: "The gods who did not make the heavens and the earth shall perish from the earth and from under the heavens."

Note that the thought draws obvious conclusions from what has been said in the preceding lines. Some reader, official or not, wrote in his words what he thought vv. 1-10, or perhaps only vv. 8-10, really meant. He almost certainly placed his comment in the margin of the page, but at some point many years later, even centuries later, when the scroll had to be recopied, the new scribe assumed that this line was actually part of the original prophecy but had been accidentally left out; so he neatly copied it into the new text where it best belonged. The Scriptures possess many such small additions, but few can be identified so easily as this one.

The second poem in chap. 10 returns to the vivid use of images for an enemy invasion. In vv. 17-22, they follow after each other quickly, hardly letting one sink into our imagination before the prophet shifts to a new one. Verses 17-18 paint the Israelites being herded together with their meager belongings and force-marched out of the land into exile. RSV's "sling" expresses both the speed and the compulsion. The verb refers to soldiers hurling their slingstones against an attacking army, a scene frequently shown on Assyrian battle reliefs. Verse 19 finds the prophet badly wounded, maybe even fatally so, but he must go on or he will surely die. Verse 20 depicts either a terrible desert windstorm or a raid on a nomad camp. The survivor can only cry in despair because his tents are ruined, his children taken away, and he has nothing left. In v. 21, the scene shifts again, this time to the shepherd in the field who cannot read signs of bad weather or foresee danger or even make preparations for watching the flock at night. Soon the flock disappears, some victims of the wolves, some lost, some wandered off on their own. Judah's leaders were like this. Finally, in v. 22, he returns to the battlefield and its terror when the dust and noise of the invading army come into sight.

At the end, Jeremiah returns to the reflection on Wisdom. Putting himself in the shoes of the whole people, he asks for whatever mercy Yahweh might still give at such a late moment. He knows the punishment must come and cannot be avoided, but perhaps the smallness of human power, the lack of control over so much of what we do, might move the Lord to lessen his wrath and be sparing in his punishment. He closes by quoting the hopes of Israel through the ages that God will not let foreign nations totally destroy his portion and special inheritance, but that these cruel nations shall also receive their punishment. Jeremiah's preaching has mostly opposed such a naive and careless dream, as have all the prophets from Amos on (*cf.* Amos 5:18-20), and he often seems to be a very pessimistic individual, but in small places such as vv. 23-25, his ultimate trust in the mercy and promise of God peeks through the painful mission that has been given to him.

Book II
Stories From the Prophet's Life
Jeremiah 11-20

In turning to chapter 11, a major change appears in the text. Chaps. 11-20 differ from the first ten chapters because of the large amounts of prose that fill the pages. Many of these prose sections relate stories that serve as illustrations or examples of the message of the prophet. Mixed in with these stories are five important poems of personal lament by the prophet concerning the difficulty and the grief he experiences in his prophetic task. These so-called "confessions" of Jeremiah can be found in 11:18 - 12:6; 15:10-21; 17:12-18; 18:19-23; and 20:7-20. They make up the heart of this section, and the remaining accounts of his symbolic actions, such as the loin cloth burial in chap. 13, the breaking of the pot in chap. 19, the story of his encounter with the potter in chap. 18 or his confrontation with the priest Pashhur in chap. 20, all help us to understand better God's action by means of which Jeremiah received the word of Yahweh. We also witness how much God demanded of him in the way of personal sacrifice. Thus we might describe this second large division of the Book of Jeremiah as an explanation of his personal ministry.

But at the same time, it never forgets that the message was for the people. We can roughly break chaps. 11-20 into three parts, chaps. 11-13, 14-16, and 17-20. The first unit centers on the breaking of the covenant, the second weaves oracles against Judah into a theme of drought and rejection which ends with the prophet's own call to celibacy, a living out of the rejection and broken union. The third begins with the idea of a heart so corrupted it will have to be replaced (17:1-4). The oracles and scenes that follow accent the complete shattering of the present Israel. The confessions in this section also draw strong contrasts between Jeremiah's human emotions and his forced announcements of total destruction for his own people. God does it all, not Jeremiah; the prophet's will has been overwhelmed by Yahweh, and he only announced what he must.

I. THE BROKEN COVENANT
JEREMIAH 11:1-13:27

These three chapters form a mixed collection of sayings and stories from the prophet and about the prophet which center on the key command in 11:14 that Jeremiah is not to intercede on behalf of the people. The whole three chapters continue the dialogue between God and prophet over the seriousness of Israel's rejection of the covenant and the difficult position that Jeremiah finds himself in as part of Israel and yet forced to stand against it.

DEFENSE OF THE COVENANT
11:1-17

11 The word that came to Jeremiah from the LORD: ²"Hear the words of this covenant, and speak to the men of Judah and the inhabitants of Jerusalem. ³You shall say to them, Thus says the LORD, the God of Israel: Cursed be the man who does not heed the words of this covenant ⁴which I commanded your fathers when I brought them out of the land of Egypt, from the iron furnace, saying, Listen to my voice, and do all that I command you. So shall you be my people, and I will be your God, ⁵that I may perform the oath which I swore to your fathers, to give them a land flowing with milk and honey, as at this day." Then I answered, "So be it, LORD."

⁶And the LORD said to me, "Proclaim all these words in the cities of Judah, and in the streets of Jerusalem: Hear the words of this covenant and do them."

Chap. 11:1-17 stands as a prose introduction to the material which will come in the chapters ahead. Most of the subjects have been used before by Jeremiah in chaps. 1-10. The one feature that stands out new is the explicit language about a covenant. The mention of curses for those who don't keep it, the answer of "Amen" to its terms, the solemn oath that binds it, the listing of what Yahweh has done for the ancestors, all resemble the standard parts of a Near Eastern treaty as they were drawn up in the Assyrian empire of the 7th century. In the Bible, the nearest document in form to such international contracts is Deuteronomy, whose very shape follows the proper treaty format. It opens with the declaration of the historical relations between Yahweh and Israel, leads into the terms of the laws, ends with solemn oaths on the part of Israel, a threat of curses and a promise of blessings, and a call for the permanent remembrance of the agreement. The language of 11:1-17 indeed sounds very much like that of Deuteronomy throughout and must be understood in light of the theology of the covenant proposed by Deuteronomy. Its heart consists of a conditional promise. God has given the covenant and the land to Israel as his gift, but only if the people keep their freely said "amen" to obey him. If they do obey, God will bless them, truly making the land flow "with milk and honey" (v. 5, and Deut 6:3; 11:9; 26:15), but if they disobey, he will curse them and give their land over to their enemies and drive them from it (v. 11; and Deut 8:11-20; 30:17-18).

Jeremiah is commanded to preach in Jerusalem and in all the cities of Judah. We know he spoke often in the temple (see chaps. 7, 26, 28, 36), but we know little about any effect he may have had outside the city itself. But this does not matter greatly, since the prophetic warning must by its nature include automatically the whole people of the covenant bond. Whether the outposts knew much about the person Jeremiah will probably remain a mystery, but he would touch many, if not most, of those who directed the affairs of the nation: the leaders, the priests, the prophets, the king. One intriguing tablet was found in the burned-out ruins of Lachish, a major fortress of Judah leveled by the Babylonians in their attack of 597 B.C. On it a military commander makes what must have been his final report back to headquarters and mentions a letter from a certain Tobiah, who was a royal official, which came through a prophet with a warning to "beware." The prophet is not named, but how intriguing that it might have been Jeremiah himself! Certainly the message in 11:14-17 has the urgency and the dire warning to be a last ditch attempt to wake Israel to the coming divine anger.

JEREMIAH'S FIRST CONFESSION
11:18-12:17

> 18The LORD made it known to me and I knew;
>   then thou didst show me their evil deeds.
> 19But I was like a gentle lamb
>   led to the slaughter.
> I did not know it was against me
>   they devised schemes, saying,
> "Let us destroy the tree with its fruit,
>   let us cut him off from the land of the living,
>   that his name be remembered no more."
> 20But, O LORD of hosts, who judgest righteously,
>   who triest the heart and the mind,
> let me see thy vengeance upon them,
>   for to thee have I committed my cause.
> 21Therefore thus says the LORD concerning the men of Anathoth, who seek your life, and say, "Do not

prophesy in the name of the LORD, or you will die by
our hand"—22therefore thus says the LORD of hosts:
"Behold, I will punish them; the young men shall die by
the sword; their sons and their daughters shall die by
famine; 23and none of them shall be left. For I will
bring evil upon the men of Anathoth, the year of their
punishment."

12   Righteous art thou, O LORD,
     when I complain to thee;
yet I would plead my case before thee.
     Why does the way of the wicked prosper?
     Why do all who are treacherous thrive?
2Thou plantest them, and they take root;
     they grow and bring forth fruit;
thou art near in their mouth
     and far from their heart.
3But thou, O LORD, knowest me;
     thou seest me, and triest my mind toward thee.
Pull them out like sheep for the slaughter,
     and set them apart for the day of slaughter.
4How long will the land mourn,
     and the grass of every field wither?
For the wickedness of those who dwell in it
     the beasts and the birds are swept away,
     because men said, "He will not see our latter end."

5"If you have raced with men on foot,
     and they have wearied you,
     how will you compete with horses?
And if in a safe land you fall down,
     how will you do in the jungle of the Jordan?
6For even your brothers and the house of your father,
     even they have dealt treacherously with you;
     they are in full cry after you;
believe them not,
     though they speak fair words to you."

Verses 11:18-23 and 12:1-6 are often set off by them-selves as the first of Jeremiah's five great "confessions." 15:10-21; 17:12-18; 18:18-23 and 20:7-18 make up the rest. All share a highly personal description of Jeremiah's own sufferings and moments of despair mixed with a trust in God that reaches out in the dark for help. No other prophetic passage comes close to the intensity of these confessions except perhaps the feelings expressed by Hosea about his experiences with Gomer—if they are in fact based on his own marriage, and are not merely an inspired parable (see Hos 1-3). We can hardly doubt here, however, that the emotion of Jeremiah wells up from his own spiritual anguish. It fits too well the story of his ministry so movingly portrayed in chaps. 36-44, and in the pressures put upon him in a number of other isolated incidents, such as the clash with Hananiah in chap. 28.

Nevertheless, we must not separate this confession in 11:18 - 12:6 (or any of the others) apart from its context in the whole book, as though we have found a true gem buried in a mass of ordinary prophetic rhetoric. Much of the language even of these highly passionate outbursts can be found regularly in psalms of lament or in the complaints of the Book of Job. Unlike modern authors who glory in writing novels that barely mask their own personal story in the fictional plot, ancient writers hid behind their work and preferred to use common phrases and well-loved forms to express their ideas. Jeremiah shared this practice, and it is not the borrowed line of a psalmist or wisdom writer that should surprise us, but rather the presence of any personal feelings or thoughts at all.

In this first confessional section, many scholars have been struck by a certain lack of logical order. This had led to different suggestions for reordering the verses. The most popular option places 12:1-6 before 11:18-23 and sees the whole scene as Jeremiah's discovery of a plot against his life by his own fellow villagers in Anathoth (11:21). His grief and shock led to the present lament and prayer.

The arguments for making prophets logical, however, come from modern minds that refuse to accept the chapter after chapter of prophets and the numerous poems of psalmists which jump here and there, shift topics, and even change the person or persons whom they address from one line to the next. It is still best to take the text as it stands and make something out of it. At least we know that this reflects what the editors understood the book to mean thousands of years ago.

The whole of 11:18 to 12:17 can be divided into four units: 11:18-23; 12:1-6; 12:7-13 and 12:14-17. Each unit leads into the following one with a certain orderliness, much as a conversation moves ahead. A person answers some of the points raised by the other party and adds one or two new ideas that pop into the mind. Like much of the material in chaps. 1-11, this too can be best understood as a dialogue between God and the prophet, even if many diverse oracles and poems have been joined to create it.

11:18-23 has two sides of the first conversation. Jeremiah prays in the words of a psalm of trust (vv. 18-20). This genre always begins with the evil that has befallen someone and ends with a burst of confidence that God will take sides with his or her just cause and punish the wicked enemies. Usually it is very difficult to know exactly what the wicked have done. Sickness, slander, personal vengeance may all play a part in such typical psalms as Pss 22, 56, 57, or 58. In our example, however, the prophet describes the evil in detail. They schemed to take his life. They hid their plot and led him like a lamb to slaughter. But God let Jeremiah discover the plot and so now he prays that God may turn their wickedness against them and punish them. The language of the whole prayer resembles the words spoken about the suffering servant in Isa 53:7-8. The vocabulary in Hebrew is very close but not exactly the same for the two passages. Perhaps the imagery was traditional and used by both prophets separately, or perhaps the later author of Isa 53 knew Jeremiah's verses and freely used them while making his own personal changes.

Jeremiah's distress would have been felt by every Israelite. For somebody to die without children and have no one to carry on the family name was a terrible curse in a nation that put little hope in an afterlife. See the story of Jephthah's daughter in Judg 11:30-40 for a poignant example. But as we discover in vv. 21-23, the situation was more terrible yet. Jeremiah's enemies were his own townspeople. He places his case in God's hands because God will decide justly. Justice will involve punishment for the crime. The word "vengeance" in v. 20 does not carry any sense of personal spite or revenge. It signifies an official court sentence against a criminal.

The plot described in vv. 21-23 hopes to stop the preaching of Jeremiah. We do not know why the people of Anathoth turned against their own son. Was it because they considered his call to accept the Babylonians as God's instrument, and even his further call to surrender (Jer 27:1-11), as treason? Or was it because he condemned Israel so dramatically and hit too close to home too often? We shall never know; but the divine judgment that Jeremiah had so many times proclaimed against Jerusalem and Judah now comes against his home town. They shall not escape the sword or the famine destined for the rest of Judah. The prose layout of this judgment makes it different from the poem of lament and trust that precedes it in 18-20 and from a second poem that follows in 12:1-6. Possibly the two lament poems were put on each side expressly to make sense out of Jeremiah's terrible experience of rejection by his own.

Certainly the prayer in 12:1-6 continues the major theme of the story. Jeremiah hands his case over to Yahweh, the totally just and upright one (vv. 1-4), and God answers boldly (vv. 5-6). In a very rich opening sentence, Jeremiah not only declares his trust that God's decision will be absolutely right, but has the rashness to challenge it a bit. He wants to bring up one more argument in the case: How can the wicked do so well! God blesses them with position and influence, and they turn their good fortune to evil.

They praise God in voice but betray him in action. In his affliction, Job had uttered the same cry (Job 9:24). The problem of a just God who allowed the sinner to prosper and the faithful to suffer bothered Israelite thinkers a great deal. The usual response denied that such appearances were correct. God will take care of those who turn to him, and will punish the doer of evil even if it does not seem to be happening that way at this moment! Pss 1, 37, 73, the friend Eliphaz in Job 15:17-35, the prophet Habakkuk in Hab 1:2-4, all affirm that God shall return punishment for wickedness. But the prophet wants an answer quickly. He has been faithful. God can test his heart and find the true silver there that was missing in Israel (6:27-30), and he has borne great grief for God's cause. Only rightly should the Lord show his justice soon and bring down on the heads of his enemies their deserved fate.

God's answer proves less than the prophet hoped for. "If you can bear no more than this, you are in sorry shape, for worse is coming." Failure in ordinary foot races and stumbling on the sidewalk describe what God gives Jeremiah for everyday burdens. He plans worse. The text lists rejection and even betrayal by his own family still to come; and lurking in the backdrop are the repeated threats of foreign invasion. All this reaches beyond the imagining of the prophet. The mention of the "house" of his brothers and father leads into the fate of the "house of Israel" in vv. 7-13. For this reason, the remainder of chap. 12 must be read together with the confession of vv. 1-6. Both parts stress the symbolic meaning of the words used more than the personal feelings of Jeremiah himself. The idea of testing hearts and of the sheep marked for slaughter in vv. 1-6 echo still earlier themes. The listing of all kinds of terms for God's chosen people in vv. 7-13 which alternate with words of destruction reinforces the constant proclamation by Jeremiah of the tragic nature of the situation.

Israel is Yahweh's *house* (Joel 2:17), his *inheritance* (Ps 78:71; Deut 32:1), his *beloved* (Isa 5:1), his *vineyard*

(Hos 10:1; Ezek 19:10), his *portion* (Pss 16:5; 73:26), and his *land*. The listing leads up to the twice-repeated *land* in vv. 11-12. Both of these verses have strong alliteration. *Shamah, shemamah, shememah, nashammah, ish, sham* captures some of the Hebrew sound in v. 11 alone. Like a Bach fugue, the counter melody runs alongside the tender names giving the horrors of destruction: *forsaken, abandoned, given to enemies, hated, devoured, destroyed, trampled down, desolated*. All that someone might think could never happen to a beloved shall come on Israel. Jeremiah stands the two opposites against each other to shock us into the realization of what is happening. At one point, in vv. 8-9, he even reverses the metaphors of the wild animals. Israel has become like a lion and a bird of prey who attack unsuspecting and innocent victims. But the opposite shall really take place—her enemies will come as lions and hawks against her land.

Finally, the chapter ends with an appendix of consolation. Verses 14-17 involve another of Jeremiah's play on words. This time he refers back to the opening oracle when Yahweh commissions him to pluck up nations, pull down, destroy, overthrow, build and plant (Jer 1:10). God will pluck up the neighboring lands, which must include those that border the Holy Land: Moab, Edom, Ammon, Damascus, Tyre and Sidon (modern Lebanon), Philistia and Egypt. He will also pluck up Israel. But then he will have compassion. The sense of the "plucking up" best fits exile because the compassion includes giving people back to their own lands and their own inheritance. The added condition that the pagan nations must learn the ways of Yahweh's covenant is unusual in the pre-exilic period, and most closely resembles the language of the post-exilic chapters of Isaiah (Isa 56:6-8; 60:11-14). But Jeremiah's hopes often enough for the restoration of Judah (23:3; 24:6; 30:3; 33:10f) and the punning fits his style well. Possibly this small paragraph in 14-17 was a summary of Jeremiah thought by a disciple. It was attached here because of the natural connection to the subject of what will happen to Yahweh's inheritance.

THE ROTTEN LOINCLOTH
13:1-27

13   Thus said the LORD to me, "Go and buy a linen waistcloth, and put it on your loins, and do not dip it in water." ²So I bought a waistcloth according to the word of the LORD, and put it on my loins. ³And the word of the LORD came to me a second time, ⁴"Take the waistcloth which you have bought, which is upon your loins, and arise, go to the Euphrates, and hide it there in a cleft of the rock." ⁵So I went, and hid it by the Euphrates, as the LORD commanded me. ⁶And after many days the LORD said to me, "Arise, go to the Euphrates, and take from there the waistcloth which I commanded you to hide there." ⁷Then I went to the Euphrates, and dug, and I took the waistcloth from the place where I had hidden it. And behold, the waistcloth was spoiled; it was good for nothing.

⁸Then the word of the LORD came to me: ⁹"Thus says the LORD: Even so will I spoil the pride of Judah and the great pride of Jerusalem. ¹⁰This evil people, who refuse to hear my words, who stubbornly follow their own heart and have gone after other gods to serve them and worship them, shall be like this waistcloth, which is good for nothing. ¹¹For as the waistcloth clings to the loins of a man, so I made the whole house of Israel and the whole house of Judah cling to me, says the LORD, that they might be for me a people, a name, a praise, and a glory, but they would not listen.

Chapter 13 contains several different items: a symbolic action and interpretation in vv. 1-11; a parable of wine jars in vv. 12-14; several short oracles on punishment and exile in vv. 15-17, 18-19, and 20-27. Their variety of images adds fresh color but the message remains unchanged.

The symbolic action of the loincloth must be read on several different levels. The picture presents a clear and

forceful action whose point would not easily be missed by
the people of Judah. But to capture what Jeremiah actually
did proves much more difficult. The text says that he
traveled to the Euphrates river, which lay 700 miles or
more east of Judah and formed the traditional western
border of Babylon and Assyria. Such a trip ordinarily
took nearly two months each way and few believe that
Jeremiah ever had the opportunity to make this journey.
A second problem stems from the translation of "waistcloth." In certain texts a belt or girdle for a long robe fits
the sense best (Ezek 23:15), as it is traditionally understood.
But here the intimacy of the garment to the wearer requires
it to be an undergarment, probably a cloth wrapped directly
around the waist and covering the body down to the thighs.
Above this, a person would wear a long tunic from
shoulders to ankles, and if needed, a cape to serve as an
outer coat. And naturally, if we say that the prophet did
not actually go to the Euphrates river, then we must ask
what kind of symbolic action did happen. A vision? A
dream? A journey to a nearby stream? Or is the entire
story a literary parable with no external performance at all?

Commentators have proposed all these answers and
more. Perhaps the key lies in identification of the "Euphrates" as a river or stream closer to home. About four
miles above Jeremiah's hometown of Anathoth the spring
of Ain Farah bubbles out its waters into a brook. In Hebrew, the name *Perath* could well stand for such a stream
as well as for the mighty Euphrates hundreds of miles
away. If we accept this possibility, the symbolism becomes
even greater. Jeremiah does a series of simple actions close
to home, but the meaning can be found far away in a foreign
land. He receives the command to buy a new linen cloth
and wear it as his underwear in its totally unspoiled and
untouched state. This reveals the close and very personal
love that Yahweh had for Israel when He first chose her.
But then God commands Jeremiah to take off that cloth
and carry it far away and bury it by the "Euphrates" in a

hole. The distance, whether four miles or four hundred, matters less than its role of pointing to Babylon where Israel will be buried far from the presence of Yahweh. But the words carry several nuances. Isaiah 2 describes the people hiding among the caves and rocks of the mountains in fear from Yahweh's anger on the Day of his wrath. The darkness of burial and holes in the dirt recall the blindness and darkness of the people's apostasy from their Lord. Thus it signifies their rejection of Yahweh, their helplessness and fear when the punishment comes, and God's exiling of them to Babylon. Next, God has Jeremiah dig up the cloth from the soil and discover that it is too spoiled, rotting and repulsive to ever consider wearing against his body again. Yahweh will not take back his people into the intimacy of the covenant.

The final stage of the action is interpretation. Four times the word of the Lord comes to Jeremiah to direct each step of the drama. Actually, the whole inspiration may have come to the prophet at one time through vision or reflection, but then he carefully acted out the stages over a period of time to attract more attention with each new gesture. The climax would be the proclamation of an oracle of judgment explaining the entire sequence. Its message would be simple: God shall humble the pride of his people. In prophetic language, pride was nothing less than rejecting God because of our own wills and our own stubborn hearts. In Ezek 17:24; Hos 5:5,7; Amos 8:7; and Ps 59:12, God will bring down the proud by punishment and destruction.

Verses 10-11 develop the judgment of v. 9 that God will spoil the pride of Jerusalem and Judah. These verses are often seen as an appendix added by the school of Deuteronomy to spell out the exact meaning of the allegory, especially the charge that the people went after other gods. But the whole description from v. 1 right through v. 11 may belong to the prophet's original edition. If Jeremiah has in mind the combination of God's rejection together with the role of the Babylonians in punishing Israel, it could easily date to the period between 605-598 when Babylon's threat grew stronger. The references to the exile are too vague to know whether they date from after 598 or merely list a common fear that followed upon any attack by a foreign power.

The second unit in chap. 13 tells a parable of the wine jars. The message comes in the storytelling talent of the preacher and requires no actions. Everyone can picture in the imagination a room full of wine pots leaning against one another; as the party goes on and the people get more and more drunk, they knock one brittle pot against another, spilling the wine, cracking the clay, making a mess and finally in the spirit of the melee, throwing the pots at one another or at the wall, as if a rowdy group today hurled each emptied glass of scotch against the fireplace. In some way, the opening dialogue of v. 12 supposes that everyone knew the saying about "all the wine jars will be filled with wine." No doubt it was a favorite Israelite proverb to assure themselves that God would take care of them in the end. From king to commoner they all delude themselves into thinking that God will spare his chosen land, but in the blind drunkenness of their sin they miss the important theological point that the destruction not only comes quickly but they themselves hasten and cause it.

The following two short oracles in 13:15-17 and 18-19 both speak of the agonies of the exile. The first uses the image of night falling on the hills until it becomes so dark that no one can move without danger of stumbling and being lost.

> 15Hear and give ear; be not proud,
>   for the LORD has spoken.
> 16Give glory to the LORD your God
>   before he brings darkness,
> before your feet stumble
>   on the twilight mountains,

and while you look for light
he turns it into gloom
and makes it deep darkness.
¹⁷But if you will not listen,
my soul will weep in secret for your pride;
my eyes will weep bitterly and run down with tears,
because the LORD'S flock has been taken captive.

The message stresses the value of the last light of the day and the thankfulness we should have for it. Verse 17 states clearly that the flock has been taken captive. This suggests that the short poem belongs to the period right after the fall of Jerusalem for the first time in 598-97, a time when King Jehoiachin and many leading citizens were exiled but when the nation as a whole was allowed to continue under the uncle of the king, Zedekiah, who acted as regent with full powers, but subject to the Babylonian overlords.

The same can be said for the second little poem, vv. 18-19. Mention of the king and queen-mother humbled and exiled along with all of Judah—a prophetic exaggeration for effect—puts this poem in the first days after the events of 598-97. Jehoiakim had rebelled against Babylon just about the year 600 or a little earlier. It took several years for the new Babylonian king Nebuchadnezzar to settle his problems at home, but eventually he marched west to force the small western states into line. Judah's turn came in 598 when the Babylonian army began the siege of the city. In the worst hour, Jehoiakim died, leaving his 18 year old son Jehoiachin to take the throne. After only three months as king, the young man surrendered; and he, his mother and his leading officials with about 10,000 other citizens were taken off to Babylon as prisoners of war. 2 Kgs 24 mentions the exile of the king and queen-mother no less than three times. It must have been considered a very important event!

The last oracle in the chapter, vv. 20-27, takes the form of a warning addressed by Yahweh to Jerusalem personified as a woman. She shepherds her flock, the people

of Judah, but cannot protect them from the enemy coming
from the north. She had tried so hard to win them over
by her charms, but now they take charge and throw her off
(v.21). She will suffer the pains of labor, and the shame of a
woman raped on the side of the road—all of the indignities
and hardships that could befall a woman. Verse 23 gives the
answer to her question, why tragedy should happen to her.
The image shifts from Jerusalem the mother to Jerusalem
the guilty people. Her question is insincere, because only
her stubbornness and blindness would make her fail to see.
And that provides Jeremiah with his key response. "Can a
leopard change its spots?" sums up the pessimism of Jeremiah.
Israel has become so hardened in its way of evil that it
can no more hope to convert or learn to do good than a
man can change his race or a woman her height or an
animal its species. Apparently an old proverb stands
behind the remark about the skin of an Ethiopian, for even
in Egypt the saying was current in the *Wisdom of Onch-
sheshonqy*, "There is no negro who lays off his skin."

Because they refuse to respond, Yahweh himself will
cause their exile and shame. They hoped for great things
because they were the Lord's inheritance and portion and
house. But what they will actually receive is far different.
The portion left to them brings only punishment, for they
served only a Lie with a capital L. They remembered all the
promises but forgot all the obligations (v. 25). Yahweh has
little room for the self-satisfied who trust in their own
desires and rationalizations, follow their own course of
action, and pay scant attention to any call from God until
disaster strikes. At that moment, they ask very piously and
even with faint shock, never letting the mask of their
false ways slip for a second, "Why did this happen to us?"
But we cannot fool God: the list of abominations in v. 27
refers to the public and orgiastic rites of the cult of Baal
and his goddess wives, performed on hills and in fields all
across the land. Yet the last verse almost hopes some
break in the pattern of sin and divine punishment might
happen before the end comes.

> [27]I have seen your abominations,
>   your adulteries and neighings, your lewd harlotries,
>   on the hills in the field.
> Woe to you, O Jerusalem!
>   How long will it be
>   before you are made clean?"

Despite the many oracles which announce the total destruction of Judah and Jerusalem in words just as strong as these verses in chap. 13 contain, Jeremiah never completely stops hoping for conversion.

II. FURTHER LAMENTS OVER JUDAH'S SIN JEREMIAH 14:1 - 16:21

Like chaps. 11-13, this unit gathers together many different oracles. All of them can be traced to Jeremiah himself, even if some have been reworked by editors to fit more smoothly into the present arrangement. It begins with an extended treatment of the ravages of the drought and moves through a number of poetic and prose passages that deal with Israel's serious guilt, the justification for the severe punishment that is to come, and the prophet's own suffering. It carries on the basic themes begun in chaps. 11-13 of drought, sword and famine, of Jeremiah's "confessions." A second round intensifies the pathos and the sense of inevitable loss created by the earlier chapters.

A DROUGHT SENT IN PUNISHMENT
14:1-16

> [7]"Though our iniquities testify against us,
>   act, O LORD, for thy name's sake;
> for our backslidings are many,
>   we have sinned against thee.

⁸O thou hope of Israel,
   its saviour in time of trouble,
why shouldst thou be like a stranger in the land,
   like a wayfarer who turns aside to tarry for a night?
⁹Why shouldst thou be like a man confused,
   like a mighty man who cannot save?
Yet thou, O LORD, art in the midst of us,
   and we are called by thy name;
      leave us not."

¹⁰Thus says the LORD concerning this people:
"They have loved to wander thus,
   they have not restrained their feet;
therefore the LORD does not accept them,
   now he will remember their iniquity
      and punish their sins."

Chapter 14 opens with the label that the following sayings concern a drought. How far the subject continues is hard to say. Only 14:1-10 explicitly treat the drought itself, but probably everything in chap. 14 and in 15:1-4 belong under this theme. We can diagram the structure of the whole section as follows:

I. Lamentation over the drought (14:1-16)
   a) Description of the drought (vv. 2-6)
   b) People's prayer for mercy (vv. 7-9)
   c) Yahweh's rejection of their plea (vv. 10-12)
   d) Condemnation of the false prophets (vv. 13-16)

II. Lamentation over defeat and famine (14:17-15:4)
   a) Jeremiah's description of the disaster (vv. 17-18)
   b) People's second plea for mercy (vv. 19-22)
   c) Yahweh's rejection of their plea (vv. 15:1-4)

The discussion of the drought serves as a platform to attract a number of Jeremiah's sayings about famine and the disasters that follow upon defeat. The whole has been united by the editors who inserted much of the material now found in the prose verses of 14:13-16 and 15:1-4 to round off and give an historical viewpoint to God's refusal to accept Israel's prayers for mercy and help. Because of this un-usually strong interest in her unbroken history of rebelling against God and because of the striking mention of Manas-seh as the major cause of the people's apostasy in much the same words as the Deuteronomic passages in 2 Kgs 23:26-27 and 24:3, most critics see the hand of the Deuteronomic editors in these prose parts.

The description of the drought in vv. 1-6 shows that no one can escape such natural disasters no matter how high the position he or she holds. It engulfs everybody from the nobles in the city who have money and power and leisure but cannot find even a bucket of water to drink, to the farmers scratching out a living in the dry fields, down to the animals who are driven to unnatural acts, such as the doe who abandons her fawn to starve because she cannot find any grass. In vv. 7-9, Jeremiah intercedes for his people by admitting the evils of the past. He follows the classic penitential service by beginning with a confession of sin and then turning to ask for help. Jeremiah appeals to God's pride. He must act for the sake of his name lest foreigners mock and deride his power as the God of Israel. Israelite prayer argued this way frequently in the Psalms (Ps 23:3; 25:11; 79:9; 143:11) and in the later prophets (Ezek 20:9; 20:22; Isa 48:9-11), insisting that God must uphold his honor. The setting for this kind of appeal can be found in the developed sense of the covenant as a treaty between God as sovereign of the world and Israel as his chosen vassal state. It would not do for an overlord, a great king, to be shown up by the princes and kinglets of the earthly world created by him.

The plea moves forward quickly, tugging every string that might change the Lord's mind or embarrass him into saving Israel. A deep pathos fills the questions, recalling all the loving deeds God has done in the past. Does He really want pagans to say that Yahweh never really knew this people, that he was a stranger only visiting for a while? Does he want them to mock his power and laugh at the claims of Israelite praise that God had rescued this people from the mighty Egyptians with an outstretched arm and mighty acts of judgment (Exod 6:6)? Or does he want other nations to deny that this Yahweh is truly in their midst? How can God not respond to the needs of those to whom he has tied himself in solemn agreement?

God answers in terms of the covenant in vv. 10-12, but not as Israel had hoped. When Exod 34:6-7 proclaimed the essence of the covenant, it had Yahweh declare that he was "merciful and gracious, slow to anger and abounding in steadfast love (*hesed*) and faithfulness, keeping steadfast love for thousands, forgiving iniquity and transgression and sin." Israel put faith in the divine word, but conveniently forgot the second part of the declaration in 34:7 "but who by no means clears the guilty, visiting the iniquity of the parents upon the children and the children's children to the third and fourth generation." The two statements appear to stand at opposite ends from one another, but they must stand together. The link in a relationship of trust can never be merely a personality feeling deeply and forgiving easily on one side only. That becomes instead paternalistic or maternalistic. The parties must treat each other as equals, rely on one another to do their parts, bear the responsibility of their actions. Israel's refusal of responsibility for the covenant blocks the mutual love from flowing to them; and until that block has been broken up, chopped down and destroyed, the covenant suffers. The iniquity of the parents must be purged for Yahweh to restore the fullness of the covenant blessing. God commands Jeremiah not to intercede for this people as Moses had done so often in the Sinai wilderness. He rejects the value of their sacrifices in changing his mind. Jeremiah knows now that no repentance will come and the end must be near.

The following prose section in vv. 13-16 may have been tacked on to continue the description of the coming sword and famine mentioned at the end of v. 12.

> [13]Then I said: "Ah, Lord GOD, behold, the prophets say to them, 'You shall not see the sword, nor shall you have famine, but I will give you assured peace in this place.'" [14]And the LORD said to me: "The prophets are prophesying lies in my name; I did not send them, nor did I command them or speak to them. They are prophesying . . . the deceit of their own minds. [15]Therefore thus says the LORD concerning the prophets who prophesy in my name although I did not send them, and who say, 'Sword and famine shall not come on this land': By sword and famine those prophets shall be consumed.

One of the chief reasons proposed for God's rejection of the prayers of the people centers on the work of the prophets. By now, we have seen how little respect Jeremiah has for many others who consider themselves prophets. How many men or women this represents is difficult to say. The repeated warnings of Jeremiah to pay no heed to their words and actions hints at a fairly large number. The scholars argue over whether prophets took part in the temple staffs or participated in advisory boards for government decisions. The story of King Ahab and his confrontation with the prophet Micaiah ben Imlah in 1 Kgs 22 implies that prophets did take a role in political functions; and the argument between the priest Amaziah and the prophet Amos in Amos 7:10-17 implies certain prophets received temple employment. Certainly Jeremiah fears the influence of such prophets, and unleashes some of his strongest language against them. The repeated threats of sword and famine which will come over the whole land in v. 12 especially addresses these servants of the great lie—preachers of a covenant where we can do what we want but God will protect us from facing the consequences. The sword and famine they deny will eat them up first.

LAMENT OVER DEFEAT AND FAMINE
14:17 - 15:4

15 Then the LORD said to me, "Though Moses and Samuel stood before me, yet my heart would not turn toward this people. Send them out of my sight, and let them go! ²And when they ask you, 'Where shall we go?' you shall say to them, 'Thus says the LORD:

"Those who are for pestilence, to pestilence,
    and those who are for the sword, to the sword;
those who are for famine, to famine,
    and those who are for captivity, to captivity."'

³"I will appoint over them four kinds of destroyers, says the LORD: the sword to slay, the dogs to tear, and the birds of the air and the beasts of the earth to devour and destroy. ⁴And I will make them a horror to all the kingdoms of the earth because of what Manasseh the son of Hezekiah, king of Judah, did in Jerusalem."

The development of 14:17-15:4 follows that of the first part of chap. 14. In vv. 17-18, the prophet's eyewitness account of the disaster is deeply colored by his own personal anguish. Judah has received a terrible blow, a gaping wound, but it does not result from the drought in the previous section. The sequence of murdered victims and then of a raging famine better follows the pattern of war and siege. Could Jeremiah have given this oracle at some time after the Babylonian army had already conquered many outlying cities but before they came up against Jerusalem itself? The note at the end of v. 18 about the priest and prophet still performing without understanding what these plagues signified implies that they probably still clung to some hope that Yahweh would intervene to save them.

The plea in vv. 19-22 also begs God to act mercifully because of his covenant bonds. Unlike the first prayer in v. 7-9, which argued from God's honor as Lord of the world, this prayer cites his love for Zion where he has made his dwelling and where he has placed his throne above the lid of the Ark of the Covenant. In Hebrew practice, people flocked to the temple courtyards to offer up their sacrifices and to celebrate great feastdays; but only the priests went within the temple itself to place the showbreads before God and to offer incense in the Holy Place (Lev 10:1-2; 24:5-9), and no one went into the last chamber, the Holy of Holies, where the Ark rested between the outstretched wings of two golden cherubim figures, except one day a year, when the high priest entered on the Day of Atonement (Yom Kippur) to sprinkle blood on the lid and to bring incense. There in the darkness and silence, God's glory, his numinous and awesome presence, stayed, often described as though it sat on the cover of the Ark as on a throne. The scene resembles the throne rooms of ancient Near Eastern palaces. On the sarcophagus of Ahiram, a 10th century Phoenician king of Byblos, the sculptor carved the king seated on a throne whose sides and arms are the bodies of lions with eagle wings and human heads. Israel believed that Yahweh too deserved his royal throne. This quality of holiness and awe that surrounded the Holy of Holies can be found in the great vision of Isaiah in Isa 6 when the prophet received his call to prophesy.

Verse 22 adds one additional motive for God to come to the rescue. He alone can bring rain on the earth. No other god can do that. It demonstrates that the God of Israel's personal covenant nevertheless rules all nations and all of nature. This cry expresses their deepest faith discovery and Israel's greatest contribution to world religion. Divine power is not in the conflict and tension among different gods and forces of the world; it is one, it is ordered, and it is personal. "It" can never express the divine relationship to the world. God loves his creation and is present to it in the intimacy that only knowledge and love can give. If said with sincerity, the prayers of chap. 14 would express the true heart of the covenant genius. Israel waits for God's answer.

When it comes in 15:1-4, the answer has the same cold rejection already seen in vv. 10-12. Yahweh will not relent and allow his heart to show mercy towards them. The finality of the moment is summed up in the reference to Moses and Samuel. Both had been God's close friends who could intercede for the people and turn God's anger away even when the penalty was well deserved (see Exod 32:11-14; Num 14:13-19 and 1 Sam 12:19-25). If Moses and Samuel could not melt God's heart now, certainly neither Jeremiah nor the prophets and priests of his day could hope to. In fact, Moses may well represent the best of *priestly* mediation and Samuel of *prophetic* intercession in this passage. Thus all the channels of communication between God and his people have been cut off. If these few verses come from the hands of the Deuteronomic editors, as many believe, then the implications point directly to Jeremiah's own mission. In his call in 1:4-10, his ministry is described in terms of the prophetic offices of Moses and Samuel. Now the Lord absolves Jeremiah of continuing their task of intercession.

The short poem in v. 2 may be the heart of Jeremiah's own words which have been later expanded by reflection on his prophetic experiences. Four fates of war have been allotted to destroy the land and each person will receive his appointed share. The continued listing in v. 3 shifts to the gory picture of the mangled corpses lying unburied and rotting while the wild animals feast on them. The final verse centers the blame for God's rejection on the shoulders of King Manasseh who ruled from 687-642 and who brought peace to the kingdom of Judah by introducing many of the pagan cults and religions into the land to keep the Assyrian overlords at bay and contented. This is an editorial reflection for sure since Jeremiah unrelentingly puts the responsibility on the shoulders of the whole people, but with special fault on the parts of the secular and religious leaders of his own time. See the Deuteronomistic school's similar views in 2 Kgs 23:26-27.

JEREMIAH'S ANGUISH OVER JERUSALEM; HIS SECOND CONFESSION
15:5-21

5"Who will have pity on you, O Jerusalem,
   or who will bemoan you?
Who will turn aside
   to ask about your welfare?
6You have rejected me, says the LORD,
   you keep going backward;
so I have stretched out my hand against you
   and destroyed you;—
   I am weary of relenting . . . .
8I have made their widows more in number
   than the sand of the seas;
9She who bore seven has languished;
   she has swooned away;
her sun went down while it was yet day;
   she has been shamed and disgraced.
And the rest of them I will give to the sword
   before their enemies,

                                        says the LORD."

10Woe is me, my mother, that you bore me, a man of strife and contention to the whole land! I have not lent, nor have I borrowed, yet all of them curse me. 11So let it be, O LORD, if I have not entreated thee for their good, if I have not pleaded with thee on behalf of the enemy in the time of trouble and in the time of distress! 12Can one break iron, iron from the north, and bronze?. . .

¹⁵O LORD, thou knowest;
  remember me and visit me,
  and take vengeance for me on my persecutors.
In thy forbearance take me not away;
  know that for thy sake I bear reproach.
¹⁶Thy words were found, and I ate them,
  and thy words became to me a joy
  and the delight of my heart;
for I am called by thy name,
  O LORD, God of hosts.
¹⁷I did not sit in the company of merrymakers,
  nor did I rejoice;
I sat alone, because thy hand was upon me,
  for thou hadst filled me with indignation.
¹⁸Why is my pain unceasing,
  my wound incurable,
  refusing to be healed?
Wilt thou be to me like a deceitful brook,
  like waters that fail?

¹⁹Therefore thus says the LORD:
  "If you return, I will restore you,
  and you shall stand before me.
If you utter what is precious, and not what is worthless,
  you shall be as my mouth.
They shall turn to you,
  but you shall not turn to them.
²⁰And I will make you to this people
  a fortified wall of bronze;
they will fight against you,
  but they shall not prevail over you,
for I am with you
  to save you and deliver you,

                    says the LORD.

We can divide 15:5-21 into two parts. The first, vv. 5-9,
sings a lament against Jerusalem for her rejection of

Yahweh; the second, vv. 10-21, forms the second confession passage of Jeremiah.

The lament continues the theme of chap. 14 in explaining why calamities have already fallen upon the land. War would be the most natural cause for destruction, the increased number of widows, and the swooning of mothers. The mother of seven of v. 9 expresses the greatest honor accorded a woman in Israelite literature: Job's wife bore seven sons and three daughters (Job 42:13); the Song of Hannah in 1 Sam 2:15 praises the woman with seven children; Ruth is called better than seven sons to the honor of her mother (Ruth 4:15). Thus the image in vv. 8-9 refers not to the death of the women but to the loss of their sons in battle. If the capital has not already fallen, at least the initial armed resistance has failed, leaving many dead and the enemy at the gate. A date in the early stages of the Babylonian conquest of 598 seems best. The attacking army may well have arrived much sooner than anyone expected. The language about a destroyer at noonday, or night falling in the middle of the day accents the suddenness of the defeat.

The confessional passage in 15:10-21 has three divisions, 10-14, 15-18, 19-21, in the arrangement of the RSV. The Hebrew text itself has many problems that lead to the somewhat confusing translations of the speech of the prophet in 10-14. Most commentators try to solve the lack of clarity by accepting a reading of the early Greek translation, the Septuagint, which reads at the opening of v. 11, "Amen, Yahweh," for the Hebrew "Yahweh said . . ." The RSV and others who follow this reading as better, do so because they judge that the whole section should be the words of Jeremiah himself as a psalm of complaint. But this makes less sense than taking the Hebrew original at face value. If Jeremiah begins to speak in v. 10 and God answers in vv. 11-14, then we have an exact parallel to the second complaint series in which Jeremiah laments in vv. 15-18 and God replies in vv. 19-21.

Taken in this way, v. 10 expresses the agony of Jeremiah at the failure of his mission. To curse one's birth was probably a customary way to express profound grief and poignant sorrow. Job opens his dialogues with a similar curse after all the tragedies have befallen him (Job 3:1-10). Jeremiah has done what he thought right, and yet everyone stands against him. Yahweh's response does not pat him on the back nor tell him to hold his chin up for a while longer. God himself has pleaded and begged through Jeremiah for his enemies to repent and turn their ways. If they have been against Jeremiah, how much the more against Yahweh. If Jeremiah has suffered, how much more God himself has had to endure. But the time has drawn near to vindicate the word that God has summoned the prophet to carry and speak with so little reward. The "you" of vv. 11-14 refers to the whole people and not to the prophet alone. God speaks past the question of Jeremiah to address the whole people. The sense of vv. 11-12 is something like:

Yahweh said:
Have I not served you well? and pleaded with you in a time of evil and distress with the enemy? Can (your) iron break the iron from the north and its bronze?

The people never heeded God's concern expressed through the prophets. So now the divine response will be to permit foreign conquest with the looting and slavery that follow. Verses 13-14 are almost identical to the opening lines of chap. 17 and may have been repeated here by the editors to underline God's rejection of any mercy for Israel, a theme which has dominated the last two chapters.

Verses 15-18 take up the lament of Jeremiah anew. His complaint provides a keen psychological insight into the mind of the prophet. He is convinced that God knows and looks on everything that happens to him. The call for God to remember the prophet and to know what pain he endures reveals that the Word of the Lord did not always include a feeling of God's intimacy in personal prayer. The message itself which the prophet has eaten has become part of him; he has, so to speak, swallowed it hook, line and sinker. He loves it; it has become one with his own thinking. Since the heart is the seat of reasoning and thought, v. 16 surely claims that God's word and Jeremiah's thoughts have become closely identified. Thus he can even be called by Yahweh's name. The same idea of eating God's words and rejoicing in them as part of one's own way of thinking recurs in Ezekiel's call to be a prophet (Ezek 2:8-3:3). But although this sense of conviction fills these prophets' hearts, they still experience intense loneliness and alienation from their fellow citizens. People cannot understand the harshness and judgment that burns in Jeremiah's preaching; they find him unattractive and unpleasant to be around. Who wants a chronic complainer at a party or a meeting, or even wants to exchange remarks while passing such a person on the street? Because God's message urged him on constantly, because he felt the "hand" of God upon him, pressing him to warn and speak, he could not join the merrymakers, nor would they want him and his constant indignation (v. 17). Jeremiah describes the pain of this rejection by his own people, and the failure of God to comfort him, as an incurable wound. The commission he accepts, he does not try to throw off the word he must speak; but he seeks consolation from Yahweh, support and healing. Rather boldly, he questions God in v. 18, asking whether Yahweh is like a desert wadi that totally dries up in the summer months. In 2:13, God had been living water, fresh springs, to Jeremiah (see 17:13). Was it all a fraud? Was God really behind his prophet? Let God reassure his servant!

But the answer in vv. 19-21 gives little comfort to the desolate prophet. God does not accept such a line of reasoning. Jeremiah has stated the difficulties entirely in terms of his own feelings. Verse 19 picks up the very term that stands at the center of the prophet's preaching, *shub*, "turn back,"

and hurls it back against Jeremiah. Four times in the same
verse it comes: you turn back and then I will turn back to
you (restore you)! They will turn back to (listen to) you,
but you will not turn back (to listen) to them! The Lord has
not sent this prophet to complain about himself as a hard
master nor to seek praise from the very people he is to
preach against. As long as Jeremiah concerns himself with
such worthless words, he cannot speak for God. Integrity
requires that the prophet know what he says is difficult and
painful and to bear the results in silence and persistence.
Verse 20 recalls the promise made at the first summons to
Jeremiah (1:18-19) that God will not necessarily give him
emotional satisfaction, but will give him all the strength
he needs, as good as any iron or bronze wall. Opposition
may wreck his peace of mind and flood him with anguish,
but it will not be more powerful than the word which
he speaks.

The phrase "I am with you" in v. 20 comes from the
standard formula for divine reassurance. It is quoted at
the burning bush to Moses in Exod 3:12, "I will be with
you," and by the prophet Nathan to David when God makes
the covenant with his dynasty in 2 Sam 7:3. It is repeated
in crucial moments of the conquest in the Deuteronomistic
history (Deut 2:7; 31:8,23; Jos 1:5,9; 3:7; Jgs 6:16, etc.),
and used by the Second Isaiah to encourage the exiles to
have faith in Yahweh's power to deliver them (Isa 41:10;
43:2). Coupled with the words for saving, delivering and
redeeming, the phrase echoes the great deeds of Yahweh
at the Exodus and conquest, and reminds Jeremiah that
God has the power to do what he promises. Jeremiah has
suffered discouragement, but Yahweh does not coddle him
at this time; the task is too urgent, he must pull himself
together and go on with more confidence.

JEREMIAH'S REJECTION AS WITNESS
16:1-13

   16 The word of the LORD came to me: ²"You shall
   not take a wife, nor shall you have sons or daughters in

this place. ³For thus says the LORD concerning the sons
and daughters who are born in this place, and concerning
the mothers who bore them and the fathers who begot
them in this land: ⁴They shall die of deadly diseases. They
shall not be lamented, nor shall they be buried; they
shall be as dung on the surface of the ground. They
shall perish by the sword and by famine, and their dead
bodies shall be food for the birds of the air and for the
beasts of the earth."

Chap. 16:1-13 continues the listing of the hard demands
made on Jeremiah by his ministry. The chapter opens with
the command that he is not to marry but remain single; it
continues with directions to avoid all mourning customs
and all parties. No wonder then that Jeremiah felt shunned
by those around him!

The failure to marry insured that the name of a man or
woman would not live on after his or her death through
whatever children were born. Ancient thought considered
this to be a great tragedy and a sign of divine curse. The
Yahwist source in the Pentateuch stressed the barrenness
of the wives of Abraham, Isaac and Jacob as a key occasion
to show how God worked out his promises by reversing
their cruel fates. Nothing could be a more dramatic witness
to the urgency of the times, to the disruption and uselessness
of all normal hopes and joys, than the sign of celibacy lived
out by the prophet to the derision and curiosity of his
friends and neighbors.

How did Jeremiah himself see the meaning of this sign?
Other prophets often wrote about striking symbolic actions
in their own private lives. We can think of the unfortunate
marriage of Hosea, or Ezekiel's refusal to show any sign
of grief for the death of his wife (Ezek 24). We presume that
these passages reflect the actual events of the prophets' lives,
but cannot always be sure. Scholars continue to argue
whether Hosea's story is a parable or fact, and some ask
whether the reference to "this place" in Jeremiah's direc-
tive of v. 2 means only that he is not to marry in Anathoth,
his hometown, but could elsewhere. But if the permanence

of the sign cannot be proven absolutely by the historian, the significance of it stands out sharply enough for all to hear. Bearing children for the hope of a lasting name will prove a horror, for they shall all die and no one will mourn or even bury them, especially not the parents who had such great hopes for the future. The gruesome details in v. 4 take up the same refrain we saw already in 14:12 and 15:3. They portray the aftermaths of war.

Verses 5-9 give two more ordinary activities that the prophet must avoid. First, he cannot take part in the mourning ritual if someone dies. The death of one person will be almost nothing compared to the slaughter of the whole nation. Moreover, the prophet questions whether they deserve to be mourned at all. God's peace, his steadfast love (*hesed*) and his mercy have all been taken away, and the people's corruption makes them no better than the corpses and the dung they will soon become. Verses 6-7 give us some of the common mourning customs: cutting the arms to draw blood, shaving the head, eating bread and sharing a cup of consolation. Lev 19:27-28 (possibly a sixth century law) forbids cutting one's arms and the shaving of the head, but the practices were common at all periods of Israel's history and the prophets often mention them without condemnation: Isa 22:12; Mic 1:16; Ezek 7:18. The Ugaritic myth of Baal also records their use and this pagan association with the cult of the gods may lie behind the law of Leviticus. The "house of mourning" is probably not a place so much as it is the meal that was held in honor of the dead in the family home. The custom existed in Ugarit and in Aramaic areas also. It would have served the function of the wake in the modern world, and if the Ugaritic descriptions of eating and drinking are any guide, it might have rivalled at times any Irish wake created by James Joyce.

The next command forbids Jeremiah from taking part in joyous partying. The reason remains the same. In a time when lamentation, repentance and mourning shall be the rule, the celebration of new marriages, of new families, of confident hopes for the future, have no place.

Naturally, all these austere actions by the prophet mean something. People take note and ask questions, which gives Jeremiah a chance to deliver an oracle of judgment against them. Ezekiel employs the same procedure in Ezek 24:15-24. When he refuses to mourn at his wife's death, people challenge him and he gives a sentence of death against them. Much of the inspiration for his behavior may have come from reflecting on the events of Jeremiah's ministry in chap. 16.

The reason given in vv. 10-13 repeats the basic message of 9:12-16 and other deuteronomic passages in Jeremiah. Indeed, Deut 29:22-28 already states the same charges in similar words. The passage takes the long view of Israelite history. Not just this generation but earlier ones as well have forsaken the Lord. The promise of exile in v. 13 where the people will be physically forced to bow down in service to the gods of pagans has an eyewitness quality to it, whether from Jeremiah after the first attack in 597 or from a later editor.

THE DIVINE HUNTER STALKS THE LAND
16:14-21

> [16]"Behold, I am sending for many fishers, says the LORD, and they shall catch them; and afterwards I will send for many hunters, and they shall hunt them from every mountain and every hill, and out of the clefts of the rocks. [17]For my eyes are upon all their ways; they are not hid from me, nor is their iniquity concealed from my eyes. [18]And I will doubly recompense their iniquity and their sin, because they have polluted my land with the carcasses of their detestable idols, and have filled my inheritance with their abominations."

Skipping vv. 14-15 for a moment, the thought of the preceding section continues in another short oracle in vv. 16-18. Here under the image of the fisher or hunter who stalks the prey and never gives up until it is captured or killed, the text pictures divine justice that will let none of the guilty slip by. God is both the fisher and the hunter, an image that recurs regularly in the Book of Job and the prophets. Ezek 29:3-4 depicts God catching Egypt like a fish in a net and hurling its carcass onto the land to rot in the sun, while Job complains that God hunts down his life like a lion would (Job 10:16). See also Amos 4:2; Hos 7:12; Isa 24:18; Hab 1:14-17; Ezek 12:13; 19:8 and 32:3. The sharp eyes of the divine hunter see the ploys and escape attempts of the victims and pursues them relentlessly. The hunt is not just for sport, Yahweh is deadly serious because of the size of the crime involved. The "detestable idols" and the "abominations" litter the land, corpselike reminders of the gods whom the people actually worshipped. Death defiled the people of a house and made them unclean so that both they and any open jars had to be purified according to Israelite law (Num 19:11-16); in the same way, the idols had polluted God's land, his inheritance, and forced him to purify it through punishment.

Chap. 16 contains two final small oracles of hope in vv. 14-15 and 19-21. They really do not belong in the midst of Jeremiah's most dire threats and roughest statements. Most commentators believe that the editors of the book put them here away from their more appropriate location in chaps. 30-32 in order to soften the words of Jeremiah in chaps. 14-16. He leaves no hope at this stage of his preaching, and the placement of some of his later words of hopefulness at this point show that the grim oracles did not represent the last word of the prophet.

The first of these, in vv. 14-15, also occurs in 23:7-8 where it stands with several other oracles of hope. Both versions probably come from a well-known saying of the prophet that some day even the solemn confession praising Yahweh as the deliverer of the Exodus, which was used in standard oaths, would be changed to refer to a new and greater rescue from Babylon. In this form, then, it must date to well after the first group of exiles went to Babylon, perhaps around the time of the letter to those exiles in chap. 29.

The last oracle in the chapter contains a short psalm of trust looking to a better day when the pagans themselves will come to Yahweh to acknowledge the worthless idolatry they have practiced. They will humbly confess the very stupidity to which Israel has been blind all along despite the words of her prophets (*cf.*, Jer 10:1-5 and Isa 44:9-20). It ends with God's response that he will reveal his power to the nations so that they will know the name Yahweh. This thought is later picked up by Ezekiel and becomes the key concept in his preaching. God always acts so that Israel or the pagan nations will be awed by the power that he shows and will turn to him in worship. Ezekiel ends nearly every oracle with the same kind of expression "so that they (you) will know that I am Yahweh." Sometimes called the "Recognition formula," it forms the central point of the exilic prophets' insistence on a strict and radical confession of the sole existence and rule of one God and one God only. Jeremiah sees it in the same terms as his successors Ezekiel and Second Isaiah: pagan gods can neither show what is going to happen nor effect what does happen. If you are looking for a divine plan or divine action in the world, only faith in Yahweh will show you what God has done, is doing now, and will do in the future. In this way, the stress on monotheism grounds both the judgment and the hope for future salvation in the one unbroken and consistent will of God.

III. THE COMPLAINTS OF
THE PROPHET
JEREMIAH 17:1 - 20:18

This third and final grouping of material in Jer 11-20, like the earlier sections, contains different types of oracles. Among these are found three of the so-called "confession" passages. But all the selections generally share the concerns of wisdom thinking. Along with Law and Prophecy, Wisdom played an essential role in Israel's religious writing. The nation possessed a tradition of its wise who were trained to explore the questions of life. They learned how to be good government administrators, how to observe nature and its phenomena for signs and lessons, and how to evaluate the range of human experience. They particularly devoted themselves to probe the mystery of the almost unanswerable questions of why things happen: why death? why sickness? why don't justice and fairness prevail? Wisdom in the ancient world stressed reflection on the problems of living; Israelite sages for their part scrutinized the particular relationship between God's power to carry out his plans for the world and our human inability to understand. The major wisdom books, Job, Qoheleth,

Proverbs and Sirach, explore these questions persistently, but they also appear now and again in the prophets. Jer 17-20 collects oracles that ask about mixed human motives. God's justice, the role of obedience, the lessons of nature, the place of suffering, and the problem of deceptive appearances in God's dealings with his people. Jeremiah raises some of the knottiest problems of his ministry here; and both he and his editors provide us with a profound handbook for modern meditation on the ways of divine and human relations.

WISDOM REFLECTIONS OF THE PROPHET; THE THIRD CONFESSION
17:1-18

17 "The sin of Judah is written with a pen of iron; with a point of diamond it is engraved on the tablet of their heart, and on the horns of their altars, ²while their children remember their altars and their Asherim, beside every green tree, and on the high hills, ³on the mountains in the open country. Your wealth and all your treasures I will give for spoil as the price of your sin throughout all your territory. ⁴You shall loosen your hand from your heritage which I gave to you, and I will make you serve your enemies in a land which you do not know, for in my anger a fire is kindled which shall burn for ever."

⁵Thus says the LORD:
"Cursed is the man who trusts in man
    and makes flesh his arm,
    whose heart turns away from the LORD.
⁶He is like a shrub in the desert,
    and shall not see any good come.
He shall dwell in the parched places of the wilderness,
    in an uninhabited salt land.

⁷"Blessed is the man who trusts in the LORD,
     whose trust is the LORD.
⁸He is like a tree planted by water,
     that sends out its roots by the stream,
and does not fear when heat comes,
     for its leaves remain green,
and is not anxious in the year of drought,
     for it does not cease to bear fruit."

King Darius I of Persia (522-486 B.C.) carved an account of his victories over enemies who challenged his throne high on a mountain cliff in Bisutun, Iran. Deeply etched into the face of the rock, the inscription can still be read today some 2500 years later. Jeremiah lived too early to see this great open book some 200 feet above the ground, but he would have appreciated the feat. For Judah's sin has been carved with the same permanence into her way of thinking. Nothing can loosen it or erase it from her heart. The choice of the heart as a tablet signifies an evil deeply rooted in the conviction of the people. They have a stubborn will which Yahweh cannot move to conversion. Yet indeed, this small metaphor prepares us for the great oracle of restoration that Jeremiah would later utter when the disaster had come in full force. In 31:33 he announces that God will make a new covenant by writing it on the hearts of Israel. It will be unlike the old covenant. They had written sin and not *hesed*, rebellion and not faithfulness; now instead God will engrave his law and the knowledge of himself deep into their hearts once and for all. They shall not write down what *they* want, but the *Lord* will fill them. The additional mention of their sin cut into the horns of the altar in 17:1 expresses the same hardened way of sin. The horns were the raised corners of the altar top that stuck up like sharp points. They formed part of both the altar of sacrifice and the altar of incense within the Holy Place of the temple. For the sin offerings required by

Leviticus 4, in which a bull or sheep or goat had to be sacrificed to atone for the inadvertent breaking of a law, some of the blood of the animal was smeared on the horns of the altar of incense or on the altar of sacrifice. But Jeremiah sees the insincerity behind this ritual. The blood could not wipe away the clearly engraved list of their sinful ways. All the sacrificial blood in the land cannot erase what was chiselled on stone.

Verses 3-4 were used before in 15:13-14 but belong here originally. The act of remembering plays an important role in the Judaeo-Christian faith. We remember in liturgy and prayer the saving works which God performed for the generations before us. But Jeremiah charges the unfaithful Israel of his day with remembering only the celebrations of Baal and Asherah and their sacred poles and the groves of holy trees where their altars stood. The punishment will be the loss of the land they treasured, an inheritance which belonged to Yahweh—as the sacred act of remembering proclaimed again and again (Exod 3:8-10; 6:8; 23:28-33; 15:17, etc.). In their sin they had given over his gift to the gods of the Canaanites.

After the opening oracle in 17:1-4, the rest of the chapter gathers together a number of different sayings. The only segment that can be safely identified as Jeremiah's own words comes in vv. 14-18, his third confession passage. The material before that, in vv. 5-13, consists of a series of wisdom reflections and psalms, possibly all composed by Jeremiah, but mostly sounding like well-known and popular verses that the prophet may have borrowed for points that he wished to make. In this case, they stand as comments on the confession in vv. 14-18 which draws the distinction between the innocent and upright heart of Jeremiah and the evil aims and thoughts of the wicked who oppose him. This contrast between the two kinds of heart sums up the whole of 17:1-18, each in its own way.

The poem in vv. 5-8 resembles Psalm 1 to a striking degree. The theme of the two ways, the way of the wicked and the way of the just, recurs often in Wisdom literature. Its two opposing portraits gave teaching models for the moral education of young people and offered points for meditation among the wise.

The comparison of the desert shrub that dries up and blows across the landscape as tumbleweed to a stable tree rooted by the side of a stream proved a favorite image for ancient writers. Jeremiah uses it here, while the editors of the Book of Psalms place their version at the head of the entire song collection to alert readers to the role of the psalter as a guidebook for faithful living. It even appears in Egyptian wisdom writings in the *Instruction of Amenemope(t)*:

> "As for the passionate man in the temple, he is a tree growing in the open. Suddenly comes its loss of foliage and its end is reached in the shipyards, (for) it is floated far from its place and a flame is its burial shroud. But the truly silent man holds himself apart. He is like a tree growing in a garden; it doubles its fruit, it flourishes, it (stands) before its lord; its fruit is sweet; its shade is pleasant, and its end is reached in the garden." (ANET 421-24)

Amenemope(t) teaches the virtue of the silent and reserved person, Psalm 1 the virtue of obedience to the covenant law, but Jeremiah stresses the need for trust in Yahweh and not in ourselves. The heart of rebellious Israel has exalted itself but now the people cannot save themselves; only turning back to Yahweh offers hope of any kind. Yet as the preceding oracles make clear, at this point Yahweh promises very little.

Verses 9-10 build on the thought of the two ways of the heart. This saying and v. 11 sound like proverbs turned into meditations. The intentions and plans of a person cannot be known very easily. Our words and actions often conceal our real aims and desires, but God reaches past the surface to see what really controls our thinking (the heart) and our desires (the kidneys). RSV translates mind and heart to capture this sense, but the physical organs were actually seen as a source or at least as a storehouse of the human ideas and emotions (see the comments on 3:11-4:4, p. 38).

Verse 11 has a simple message. Stealing or dishonesty in order to pile up wealth gains nothing. The metaphor, however, causes some trouble. What the RSV calls a "partridge," the Hebrew names "A calling bird," which could fit the cry of the partridge species. But the image of "gathering" eggs does not fit the habits of this bird. It presupposes the partridge robs the eggs from other birds' nests, which it doesn't, although a popular superstition to this effect may have existed. In such an understanding of the line, the bird sits on a heap of eggs which she did not lay herself. When they do finally hatch, they leave her anyway. The translation offered by the RSV depends on the Greek Septuagint version which seems to have taken the Hebrew verb, *dagar*, which usually means to "heap up," in the sense of "hatch." Another possibility would fit the picture of the ill-gotten wealth more closely. The partridge sits contentedly on her eggs, full of the dreams of a large family to come, but none ever hatch at all. The purpose of this comparison in chap. 17 eludes nearly everybody. The best that can be said for it is that it continues the series of contrast proverbs which point out the foolishness of relying on one's own thoughts and promptings rather than on Yahweh's.

Verses 12-13 summon up the image of the temple as God's throne over Israel (see above p. 115 on 14:17-15:4). He lives in their midst as the source of their national strength and purpose. The Israelite sees the temple and remembers the promises of Yahweh. Each of the faithful recalls the Law and the great acts of divine rescue and takes hope in the value of the ancestral faith. But those who turn away from Yahweh are put to shame, *i.e.*, revealed in their weakness, disgrace and punishment (*cf.* above p. 74

on 8:4-12). In v. 13, the "earth" means literally "under the earth" in the land of the dead. Instead of being alive and inscribed on the temple lists among the people of the covenant, they will be enrolled on the lists of the dead in Sheol, that musty land of death where spirits abide listlessly (see above, p. 70 on 7:1-8:3). Only the living presence of Yahweh enthroned in his temple gives a secure source of hope. As in vv. 1-10, this small poetic fragment reminds us of the need to trust in Yahweh.

The actual confession of Jeremiah in vv. 14-18 puts these thoughts into autobiographical form.

> ¹⁴Heal me, O LORD, and I shall be healed;
>   save me, and I shall be saved;
>   for thou art my praise.
> ¹⁵Behold, they say to me,
>   "Where is the word of the LORD?
>   Let it come!"
> ¹⁶I have not pressed thee to send evil,
>   nor have I desired the day of disaster,
>   thou knowest;
> that which came out of my lips
>   was before thy face.
> ¹⁷Be not a terror to me;
>   thou art my refuge in the day of evil.
> ¹⁸Let those be put to shame who persecute me,
>   but let me not be put to shame;
> let them be dismayed,
>   but let me not be dismayed;
> bring upon them the day of evil;
>   destroy them with double destruction!

Jeremiah is pleading for Yahweh's mercy to heal the wound that will not heal (15:18), *i.e.*, the burden of preaching an unpopular message. The previous confession in 15:15-18 came near to despair. But it never became Jeremiah's last word. Now he can pray in trust that God will stand by him through all the dangers, threats, and shame. For too long he has been taunted that he always preaches doom and destruction but none of it ever happened. This might describe any time in the years before the Babylonian attack of 593, but would really have force in the period after Jehoiakim stopped sending the tribute money to Nebuchadnezzar (shortly before 600) but before the Babylonian ruler could free himself to send an army west in the summer of 598 to punish such open defiance and rebellion on the part of a vassal state.

The call for God to punish his enemies and bring down evil on their head plays a large part in the traditional psalm of lament, and Jeremiah returns to this theme often in his confessions (see 15:15; 11:20; 20:12). It should be read in the context of ancient thought which was not so peace-loving as modern religious sentiment would demand. Moreover, the language is really traditional and formal. How much Jeremiah would have rejoiced at watching the slow torture of his opponents cannot be decided just because he says it harshly. His willingness to plead for restoration for the people later on shows a ready disposition to forgive. The whole of the confession bears a strong likeness to a classic lament psalm like Psalm 17 and may even imitate it.

OBSERVING THE SABBATH
17:19-27

19Thus said the LORD to me: "Go and stand in the Benjamin Gate, by which the kings of Judah enter and by which they go out, and in all the gates of Jerusalem, 20and say: 'Hear the word of the LORD, you kings of Judah, and all Judah, and all the inhabitants of Jerusalem, who enter by these gates. 21Thus says the LORD: Take heed for the sake of your lives, and do not bear a burden on the sabbath day or bring it in by the gates of Jerusalem. 22And do not carry a burden out of your houses on the sabbath or do any work, but keep the

sabbath day holy, as I commanded your fathers. [23]Yet
they did not listen or incline their ear, but stiffened their
neck, that they might not hear and receive instruction.'"

The last section of chap. 17 has been written in the prose
style of the so-called "deuteronomic editors." At least the
basic demand that Israel listen to the commands of the Lord
follows the patterns of the Book of Deuteronomy, although
other topics such as the Sabbath observance and the
references to the princes and kings of Judah, to the various
towns and regions, do not reflect the particular style and
interests of the deuteronomic school of thought. The
present passage continues the collection of sayings on the
two ways of good and evil that fill chap. 17; and that would
explain its present position in the text even though the
Sabbath law itself has not entered into the argument until
this point. Probably the oracle contains Jeremiah's own
strong denunciation of those who did not observe the
Sabbath regulations demanded by both versions of the
Ten Commandments in Exod 20:8-11 and Deut 5:12. But it
has been written down and edited by the same hands that
gave the distinctive tone to the rest of the prose narrative,
whether Baruch or the deuteronomic priestly school.

To complicate matters further, Jeremiah's chief complaint centers on bringing loads into the city on the Sabbath,
presumably for commercial business and selling. This
duplicates a problem dealt with by the governor Nehemiah
in the mid-fifth century, some one hundred years after the
exile, which has been recorded in Neh 13:15-22. The two
accounts have so much in common that many critics believe
the present oracle in Jeremiah has been inserted by a very
late source that knew the situation of Nehemiah in order
to tie Jeremiah's message to a post-exilic reform program
involving better observance of the Sabbath. On the other
hand, the reforms of Ezra and Nehemiah themselves
undoubtedly drew on the authority of both Deuteronomy
and the prophetic collections, including Jeremiah's works,

to establish their programs. The references to kings and princes in power suit the period of Jeremiah better than that of the 400's when no leadership other than the Persian governor and the High priest were functioning in Judah. But even though this reasoning supports Jeremiah's authorship, it does not make us certain, since vv. 25-26 may well express a hope for a return of the kings as Yahweh had promised to David in 2 Sam 7; namely, that his descendants would sit on this throne "forever." Likewise, the limited vision of the people flowing to the city of Jerusalem from the neighboring regions could describe the very narrow boundaries of post-exilic Judaism, hardly larger than the city itself.

In most examples, when later texts have been inserted into an earlier prophetic book, the reasoning of ancient editors differs from our modern mentality. They associated any developments which stemmed from the influence of a prophet with the original message itself. By combining a series of original oracles with what they saw as the natural consequences of the word, they could show how God effected what he had promised. The most famous example of this way of thinking comes in the Book of Isaiah where a whole collection of an anonymous exilic prophet, now found in chaps. 40-55, have been tacked onto the writings and speeches of the 8th century Isaiah, and the whole book now goes by his name even though it contains sections that were written over a 250 year span.

THE ALLEGORY OF THE POTTER
18:1-17

18 The word that came to Jeremiah from the LORD: ²"Arise, and go down to the potter's house, and there I will let you hear my words." ³So I went down to the potter's house, and there he was working at his wheel. ⁴And the vessel he was making of clay was spoiled in the potter's hand, and he reworked it into another vessel, as it seemed good to the potter to do.

⁵Then the word of the LORD came to me: ⁶"O house of Israel, can I not do with you as this potter has done? says the LORD. Behold, like the clay in the potter's hand, so are you in my hand, O house of Israel. ⁷If at any time I declare concerning a nation or a kingdom, that I will pluck up and break down and destroy it, ⁸and if that nation, concerning which I have spoken, turns from its evil, I will repent of the evil that I intended to do to it. ⁹And if at any time I declare concerning a nation or a kingdom that I will build and plant it, ¹⁰and if it does evil in my sight, not listening to my voice, then I will repent of the good which I had intended to do to it. ¹¹Now, therefore, say to the men of Judah and the inhabitants of Jerusalem: 'Thus says the LORD, Behold, I am shaping evil against you and devising a plan against you. Return, every one from his evil way, and amend your ways and your doings.'

¹²"But they say, 'That is in vain! We will follow our own plans, and will every one act according to the stubbornness of his evil heart.'"

Chap. 18 consists of three separate passages which have been tied together: (1) a divine offer of mercy that is rejected by the people (vv. 1-12); (2) a decree of judgment in response (vv. 13-17); plus (3) Jeremiah's fourth "confession" (vv. 18-23).

The opening unit builds on an incident from the life of Jeremiah. He goes on divine impulse to the potter's shop and watches while the craftsman works, turning small lumps of clay into attractive ceramic vessels by the deft movement of his hands while he spins the clay as fast as possible by kicking a wheel around with his feet. A good potter can turn out a well-formed dish or pitcher in seconds if his hand remains steady, nothing distracts him from maintaining even pressure and speed on the footwheel, and no hard knots or impurities appear in the clay he uses. This latter problem seems to be what Jeremiah observed. The clay proved bad and the potter had to ball up the half-turned piece of clay and work the impurities out before trying again. Maybe the clay had been too thin to make a large vessel whose sides would not collapse, or maybe it had become too dry to do fine detail work. In any case, what the potter wanted and what the clay would do did not blend together. The key to the illustration does not lie in the potter's patient reuse of the raw clay but in the implied threat that God may change his attitude toward Israel. If the nation has not worked out as a "covenant-of-Moses vase," for example, he may have to do something else with it. The image ends in v. 6 with the simple application that Israel is the clay in the hands of Yahweh. No more really needs to be said. The idea of a God who creates humans from clay can be found in some of the oldest myths of the Near East. In Egypt the ram god Khnum appears on reliefs shaping little humans on a potter's wheel, and the Babylonian *Atra Hasis* epic describes a creation in which Mami, the mother goddess, nips off lumps of clay (made up of the flesh and blood of a god) and has gods and goddesses fashion them into human shape (*Atra Hasis* I: 189-290). Israel knew this kind of myth and used its language for the account of creation in Gen 2:7. But Jeremiah warns that God can just as readily begin again.

Verses 7-12 use much of the same deuteronomic language in order to apply the meaning of the potter's story to the choice that lies before Israel. Citing Jeremiah's own prophetic commission in 1:10 to pluck up and break down, to build and to plant, these verses proclaim that God will threaten the first option; but if people repent, he will change his mind and not destroy them. So too, he also promises to build and to plant, and if the people refuse to follow him in this, turning instead to evil, he can change his mind the other way and give punishment instead. The story ends with a warning that the latter option is very close, yet the people spurn the threat and determine to continue on their own way.

Jeremiah has done his best to convince them of the need to reform and of the possibility of God's mercy, but nothing seemed to work. So now a sentence of judgment must be delivered. The poem in vv. 13-17 serves as a divine answer to the total refusal found in v. 12. Not even the pagan nations would reject their gods the way Israel has rejected Yahweh.

> [13]"Therefore thus says the LORD:
> Ask among the nations,
>   who has heard the like of this?
> The virgin Israel
>   has done a very horrible thing.
> [14]Does the snow of Lebanon leave
>   the crags of Sirion?
> Do the mountain waters run dry,
>   the cold flowing streams?
> [15]But my people have forgotten me,
>   they burn incense to false gods;
> they have stumbled in their ways,
>   in the ancient roads,
> and have gone into bypaths,
>   not the highway,
> [16]making their land a horror,
>   a thing to be hissed at for ever.
> Every one who passes by it is horrified
>   and shakes his head.
> [17]Like the east wind I will scatter them
>   before the enemy.
> I will show them my back, not my face,
>   in the day of their calamity."

Jeremiah challenges Israel to inquire among the pagan nations, to see if they reject their gods in the way that Yahweh is rejected by his own people. Loyalty to the chief god of the country sets each nation apart; and when a king conquered a neighboring state, his first act was to order the statues of the local gods carried back to the home country to be placed in the temples of the conqueror where they would wait upon and serve his own supreme deity. Isa 46:1-2 gives a vivid picture of the conquered divinities of Babylon marching off to captivity and exile.

Israel's desertion of her god shocked even pagans. She did not even maintain the fidelity of nature. The next image in v. 14 has caused difficulty for all translators, although everyone knows what the prophet is trying to say. The 9000 feet of Mt. Hermon in the Lebanon mountains hold snow all year round and the springs and streams that come from these high mountains never run dry as a result. Yet Israel acts more like the desert *wadis*, or stream beds, that rush with torrents in a sudden winter thunderstorm, but stand dry and cracked much of the year. They prove unpredictable and dangerous places to be caught unawares for often the storm water has fallen unseen well upstream and suddenly, hours later, roars down a narrow gully like a wall upon unsuspecting campers or hikers. Such behavior in the moral sphere horrifies even hardened nations. The Israelites abandoned its main highways to walk around in side paths, the prophet says, and we can well believe he means this metaphorically. They deserted the way of the just and the upright for the way of evil. God will turn his back on his own people and not listen to their cries when the disaster befalls them for their behavior. Like the dreaded sirocco, the hot East Wind from the Syrian desert which brings torrid temperatures and gagging sand to later Summer and Fall days, God will overwhelm them with his anger. They will desperately seek for shelter but find nowhere to hide from the penetrating heat and sand particles, the withering ability of God to reach into even the most hidden places of our lives and expose our guilt.

JEREMIAH'S FOURTH "CONFESSION"
18:18-23

¹⁸Then they said, "Come, let us make plots against Jeremiah, for the law shall not perish from the priest, nor counsel from the wise, nor the word from the prophet. Come, let us smite him with the tongue, and let us not heed any of his words."

¹⁹Give heed to me, O LORD,
    and hearken to my plea.
²⁰Is evil a recompense for good?
    Yet they have dug a pit for my life.
Remember how I stood before thee to speak good
    for them,
    to turn away thy wrath from them.
²¹Therefore deliver up their children to famine;
    give them over to the power of the sword,
let their wives become childless and widowed.
    May their men meet death by pestilence,
    their youths be slain by the sword in battle.
²²May a cry be heard from their houses,
    when thou bringest the marauder suddenly upon them!
For they have dug a pit to take me,
    and laid snares for my feet.
²³Yet, thou, O LORD, knowest
    all their plotting to slay me.
Forgive not their iniquity,
    nor blot out their sin from thy sight.
Let them be overthrown before thee;
    deal with them in the time of thine anger.

    The fourth of Jeremiah's confessional passages is built around another plot on his life as in 11:18-12:6. We do not know whether the same people are involved or not, although we may guess that this comes from a Jerusalem group. Later chapters (36-45) describe strong opposition against the prophet in Jerusalem itself and report more than one attempt to have him killed (*cf.*, chaps. 37 and 38). His enemies could be from any number of different groups. As the opening lines in 18:18 indicate, he had antagonized priests, wise men and prophets alike in his opposition to their words, at other times he antagonized the king (chap. 36) or leading nobles (chap. 38). From the emphasis in v. 18 on the type of words that he spoke, we can guess that the plotters wanted to silence his attacks on their professional career and slander him personally. Thus they would take away any respect for his position, and finally would convince the people that his prophetic word had less authority and reliability than their own teaching did. In short, these are the same people to whom he has addressed himself all along, the priest and prophet who speak comfort when they should be warning the people.

The lament prayer opens in v. 19 with Jeremiah's defense of his own cause. If they plan to bring charges against him, he will answer in the divine law court. He has spoken only good, he has interceded as the prophet should, he has tried to plead for their cause, all of which suggests that Jeremiah was indeed sensitive to the charges that he preached only doom and destruction. It also explains why his oracles stress so definitely that God ordered him not to intercede any longer, and has explicitly refused to hear the people's pleas. Jeremiah does not necessarily abandon hope for Israel's turning back to Yahweh, even though he now seeks revenge and hates them for the hatred they show him. If he holds out no chance for mercy in these oracles—the time of the Babylonian invasion is very near—it is because God himself has commanded it. Despite the unswerving duty that he has performed for his own nation, they have turned on him and tried to kill him.

We can understand Jeremiah's anger and emotional feelings. We have seen how passionate he can be when something big is on his mind, but many readers are unprepared for the almost outright hatred that seems to fill

the words of his curse in vv. 21-23. We must recall that
Jeremiah's whole self is tied up in the words he speaks even
if they do belong first of all to Yahweh. Rather than condemn the shortcomings of the prophet, we should learn
more deeply the painful struggle that individuals must go
through to separate their feelings from their message. For
modern apostles as well as for ancient ones, the task never
becomes easy, but requires a lifelong process of growth and
learning. But more than just emotion enters the picture
here. Jeremiah knows Yahweh as a friend and trusts that
Yahweh knows him too. The guilt of the people and their
rejection of their God wounds Jeremiah deeply because he
knows what terrible consequences will befall. And we
should not forget the remarks made earlier about the other
confession passages, that much of the language is exaggerated and formal, chosen because of the traditional
curses and the power of the words (see chaps. 15:15-18 and
17:14-17).

SMASHING ISRAEL LIKE A POT
19:1-15

[10]"Then you shall break the flask in the sight of the
men who go with you, [11]and shall say to them, 'Thus says
the LORD of hosts: So will I break this people and this
city, as one breaks a potter's vessel, so that it can never
be mended. Men shall bury in Topheth because there will
be no place else to bury. [12]Thus will I do to this place,
says the LORD, and to its inhabitants, making this city
like Topheth. [13]The houses of Jerusalem and the houses
of the kings of Judah—all the houses upon whose roofs
incense has been burned to all the host of heaven, and
drink offerings have been poured out to other gods—
shall be defiled like the place of Topheth.'"

Chap. 19 records a second symbolic action performed
by Jeremiah with a pottery vase. After chap. 17's strong

condemnations, chaps. 18-20 form a loose series of examples built around the two stories of the pots and the sufferings of Jeremiah when he did deliver such dire warnings. Although the entire bloc of material in chap. 19 and in 20:1-6 deals with the oracle that Jeremiah delivered upon smashing the pot, there is good reason to believe that this is not all one piece. One need only notice the slight contradictions present in the story to discover why most commentators believe that two separate oracles have been stitched together here. In v. 1, Jeremiah speaks to elders and priests but in v. 3 addresses instead the kings and people. In v. 2 he goes to the Potsherd gate area but in vv. 6, 11 and 12 he seems to be standing in the Topheth shrine area. Because of these small changes, the text may have originated as two parts. The first is a short action and word in 19:1-2 plus 19:10-11, in which Jeremiah goes out to the gate of the Hinnom valley and smashes the pot before some elders and priests and then announces that Yahweh will do the same to this people. This incident continues in vv. 14-15 and in 20:1-6 when Jeremiah returns into the city and is arrested for repeating the message in the temple area.

Second, inserted into the middle of this simple story is either an editorial explanation or another speech of Jeremiah reported by the deuteronomic editors. This fills vv. 3-9 and the last sentence of v. 11 ("Men shall bury in Topheth because there will be no place else to bury"), and vv. 12-13. This second oracle has great similarities to the judgment against the Topheth in Jer 7:31-34, and may belong with it to a collection of his words against child sacrifice. In putting the book of Jeremiah together, the editors took parts from a number of collections of Jeremiah's words and recombined them where they thought best. The point of this oracle at this particular place comes from the need to explain why Yahweh plans to smash Israel like a pot. The reason remains the same old story: the people burn incense to pagan gods, offer child sacrifice to

Baal, kill innocent victims (vv. 4-5). Divine judgment will make this place the scene of carnage when the enemy troops storm the city and hurl the bodies of the slain from the city walls. The Topheth, and the Valley of Ben-Hinnom generally, served as the city garbage dump and the fire of garbage and the wild packs of dogs scavenging must have made a scene worthy of Dante's Inferno. No wonder that *Gehenna*, the shortened form of the name, became the image of the fiery punishment of the Afterlife in Jesus' preaching. Jeremiah pictures no less of a hell on earth, when the starvation caused by a long siege leads people to eat the flesh of their own children who have died in order to keep alive themselves.

If this describes Topheth, it also describes the city as a whole. The incense burns on every roof in honor of the divine stars, and the city itself shall become as burning garbage like the Topheth. While two separate accounts may have been combined in this chapter, the union is almost complete. The dramatic nature of the present dialogue creates suspense as Jeremiah holds the pot in his hand and lists the curses that shall come upon the people and the places of the city. While the word covenant does not occur, no one can doubt that the charges involve violations of the covenant. Three times in v. 5 Yahweh solemnly announces that these abominable actions were not part of his law or commandments: "I did not command, nor speak this, nor did it ever enter my mind." This makes the curses worse, for Israel was sworn to the covenant and the people called down the curses on themselves if they violated their part in it.

The mention of people hissing at the land of Israel and thinking of it as a horror (see also 18:13-17) reminds the hearers that no ancient nation, no matter how cruel or barbaric, could conceive of any nation rejecting its god and getting away with it. A terrible curse would be on that people and disaster was surely to follow. The climactic moment arrives when Jeremiah announces that God would shatter the people; he then hurls down his pot to shatter into hundreds of fragments on the ground. We can imagine the shock wave through his circle of listeners. Actions and words were not just clever illustrations; they possessed the power to let loose forces contained in their meaning and began the process which would lead to their fulfillment.

The last two verses of the chapter bring Jeremiah back into the city and into the temple courtyard where he repeats the basic message of doom. These provide a transition to the following story of his arrest.

JEREMIAH IN THE STOCKS
20:1-6

> **20** Now Pashhur the priest, the son of Immer, who was chief officer in the house of the LORD, heard Jeremiah prophesying these things. ²Then Pashhur beat Jeremiah the prophet, and put him in the stocks that were in the upper Benjamin Gate of the house of the LORD. ³On the morrow, when Pashhur released Jeremiah from the stocks, Jeremiah said to him, "The LORD does not call your name Pashhur, but Terror on every side. ⁴For thus says the LORD: Behold, I will make you a terror to yourself and to all your friends. They shall fall by the sword of their enemies while you look on. And I will give all Judah into the hand of the king of Babylon; he shall carry them captive to Babylon, and shall slay them with the sword. ⁵Moreover, I will give all the wealth of the city, all its gains, all its prized belongings, and all the treasures of the kings of Judah into the hand of their enemies, who shall plunder them, and seize them, and carry them to Babylon. ⁶And you, Pashhur, and all who dwell in your house, shall go into captivity; to Babylon you shall go; and there you shall die, and there you shall be buried, you and all your friends, to whom you have prophesied falsely."

Pashhur seems to have been the chief security officer in the temple charged with keeping order. The text does not tell us what grounds he used to arrest Jeremiah, but one likely excuse would be his disturbing the peace. Ancient penalties were often harsh for small offenses and a beating and one day period in the stocks would not hint at too serious a charge. He likely felt he was doing his duty.

Jeremiah's wrath the following day should not be taken as personal revenge against Pashhur only, even if we can sympathize with Jeremiah's anger at unjust treatment. More to the point, Pashhur had prevented Jeremiah from preaching the message God gave him and thus tried to chain the word of God. As v. 6 notes, the real evil consisted in proclaiming the opposite view, that is, in preaching comfort in a time of warning; and the most flagrant abuse of such false prophecy lay in attempting to silence the true prophetic word of judgment by force and scorn. The fate decreed by Jeremiah's oracle against him made him into an accursed person who would bring down ruin on all who associated with him. The power of the curse intended by the actions of the smashed pot is extended to Pashhur by conferring on him a new name. Given Jeremiah's love for a play on words, everybody is convinced that the name "Terror on every Side" must reverse or explain the meaning of the name "Pashhur." Only nobody can be quite sure what the connection is. Some of the more interesting suggestions include the possibility that the Hebrew for the priest's name itself sounds like "destruction all about." Then Jeremiah extends the range by saying that Pashhur really is going to be the cause of such destruction, "the terror round about" to everyone. Another possibility starts from the sounds of the new Hebrew name, *magor missabib*, which echoes similar sounding words for "terror," "hatred" and "sojourning in exile"; and these in turn stand opposite to the echo heard in Pashhur, which sounds like "be fruitful."

The whole combination announces that Yahweh will reject his covenants with Adam and Noah to be fruitful on the earth, and with Abraham to sojourn in a new land. In some way, Pashhur's priestly role as guardian of the temple and representative of the covenant law has been turned into a curse where instead of bringing the blessing of prosperity and peace, he brings destruction and terror. Since in chap. 29, another priest, Zephaniah, holds the title of chief officer of the Temple after the Babylonian deportation of 598, we can presume that Jeremiah's prediction came true and that Pashhur was among those exiled to Babylon.

The remark that Pashhur was among those who prophesied falsely in v. 6 may be important in confirming that many of the prophets did function as actual working priests on the temple staff. Jer 1:1 tells us that Jeremiah himself was from a priestly family but his book never shows us any indication that he performed particular priestly tasks. Of course, the term may be used here quite loosely to speak about anyone who had a formative role on policy or a teaching office. But not enough information can be found in such a short remark to make any sweeping conclusion.

JEREMIAH'S FIFTH CONFESSION
20:7-18

> [7]O LORD, thou hast deceived me,
>   and I was deceived;
> thou art stronger than I,
>   and thou hast prevailed.
> I have become a laughingstock all the day;
>   every one mocks me.
> [8]For whenever I speak, I cry out,
>   I shout, "Violence and destruction!"
> For the word of the LORD has become for me
>   a reproach and derision all day long.

⁹If I say, "I will not mention him,
    or speak any more in his name,"
there is in my heart as it were a burning fire
    shut up in my bones,
and I am weary with holding it in,
    and I cannot.
¹⁰For I hear many whispering.
    Terror is on every side!
"Denounce him! Let us denounce him!"
    say all my familiar friends,
    watching for my fall.
"Perhaps he will be deceived,
    then we can overcome him,
    and take our revenge on him."
¹¹But the LORD is with me as a dread warrior;
    therefore my persecutors will stumble,
    they will not overcome me.
They will be greatly shamed,
    for they will not succeed.
Their eternal dishonour
    will never be forgotten.
¹²O LORD of hosts, who triest the righteous,
    who seest the heart and the mind,
let me see thy vengeance upon them,
    for to thee have I committed my cause.

The fifth and last of Jeremiah's confessions comes immediately after the story of his beating and imprisonment in the temple guardhouse. Whether he actually composed this lament on that occasion or at another time hardly matters. It expresses well the human dilemma he found himself in. He gave great effort to proclaim loudly and forcefully the message God had put within him, but he got back no applause or appreciation, only hatred and persecution and people's laughing at him. This last may have been the worst trial of all, since Jeremiah was a shy man by nature, who did not consider himself a great speaker (1:6), and who was very sensitive to anything he considered unfair or unjust.

He accuses God of deceiving him with a false word. Some commentators point out that the Hebrew verb, "to deceive," can also mean "to seduce" a young woman (Exod 22:16), but that is not the major point. Like the ancient prophet Micaiah ben Imlah of the time of king Ahab (1 Kgs 22), Jeremiah had a strong conviction that God had given him special knowledge of the divine plan by letting him eavesdrop upon the deliberations of God's heavenly Council. Chap. 23 offers a fuller picture of this contrast between the true message from Yahweh's own mouth and the false word that comes from the promptings of the person's own spirit. In the Micaiah story, God even went so far as to send a "lying spirit" to *deceive* the false prophets (1 Kgs 22:22-23). The word "to deceive" is identical with the verb used in Jeremiah, and the "lying spirit" is the same word that Jeremiah applies to the prophets of his own day: they are both "servants of the Lie."

Jeremiah borders on blasphemy by addressing God this way. But the succeeding verses help us to understand how hard he struggled to understand what was expected of him. Yahweh had overwhelmed him with the divine word and Jeremiah had accepted. He felt compelled to speak judgment. Vigorously he shouted out his warning of the coming judgment, but people mocked him and asked him to prove it. Where was this terror he proclaimed? Very humanly, Jeremiah decided to keep quiet and not play the fool any more. But the compelling power of God still ruled him and he was constantly gnawed by guilt and the knowledge that he had to cry out whatever words God gave him. They left him no peace, but ran through his mind night and day. Yet all over Jerusalem people joked behind his back that old "Terror on Every Side" is preaching again today. They sought to stop his work, get him to make a mistake or to attack something sacred like the temple, so that they could turn him in and possibly murder him without the public being aroused. Even his friends, the very people he trusted, turned on him and derided him, wanting to stop his proclamation. In v. 10, they hope he will be deceived by Yahweh and can be accused. The irony lies in the reversal of roles. He had pointed out the deceptions and hypocrisy in so many areas of their life, now they search for the slightest weakness on his part. No one could be more alone in spirit than Jeremiah at the moment of this prayer.

It is not a cry of despair that finishes Jeremiah's thought. The prophet knows he has nowhere to turn but back to Yahweh in trust. Remembering Israel's moments of rescue from the very jaws of defeat, he recites Yahweh's praise as a warrior. Echoing the great victory hymns of Exod 15, Judg 5, Hab 3 and Psalm 24, he clings to the faithfulness of God and takes his stand against all human odds. Jeremiah has been overwhelmed by Yahweh, and compelled to speak, and so has little choice but to commit his cause to his God. Ultimately, as v. 12 says, God must be trusted because he is the Just One who punishes the wicked and supports the upright. When the prophet's case comes to trial, Yahweh must intervene for him.

The first part of the confession ends in v. 13 with a small hymn of praise, much like many psalms of personal trust (Pss 11, 23, 27, 62 and 63):

> [13]Sing to the LORD;
>   praise the LORD!
> For he has delivered the life of the needy
>   from the hand of evildoers.

It even moves from the passionate direct address of vv. 7-12 to the wider and more universal praise of God who watches over all of the poor of the earth. The prophet does not have in mind the physically needy so much as the humble who look only to God for their support. This sense occurs often in the Psalms where the poor may be identified with the faithful, with those who are more often among the oppressed (rather than among the oppressors), because they seek to do God's will rather than make personal gains.

Verses 14-18 form a separate lament from vv. 7-13 and almost reverse the conclusion of confidence and trust achieved in vv. 11-13. Since the preceding is a complete psalm of lament and trust that moves from the call on God to pay heed to the troubles of the pleader forward to confidence that Yahweh does hear and respond, the bitter poem of total failure that follows was probably composed for another occasion and placed here to underline how deeply Jeremiah experienced the rejection by his own people. Taken alone, it would leave little room for faith in the divine power to support the prophet in difficult times. Put at the end of Jeremiah's confessions it should be understood more as a comment on the collection of oracles that has been gathered together in chaps. 11-20. All can be situated during the years of King Jehoiakim from 609 down to 598, all are full of warning that doom and punishment are not only determined with little hope for reversing the sentence, but all are also filled with the personal pain of the prophet as he finds himself and his word rejected outright.

Jeremiah's confessions conclude on this despondent note:

> [14]Cursed be the day
>   on which I was born!
> The day when my mother bore me,
>   let it not be blessed!
> [15]Cursed be the man
>   who brought the news to my father,
> "A son is born to you,"
>   making him very glad.
> [16]Let that man be like the cities
>   which the LORD overthrew without pity;
> let him hear a cry in the morning
>   and an alarm at noon,

> [17]because he did not kill me in the womb;
>   so my mother would have been my grave,
>   and her womb for ever great.
> [18]Why did I come forth from the womb
>   to see toil and sorrow,
>   and spend my days in shame?

The wish that he had never been born ranks with the most poignant woes of the Scriptures. The only other passage comparable to its grief is Job 3. In both, the sufferer curses the *day* of his birth to avoid cursing parents or Yahweh, a capital offense of blasphemy. Both begin with the joy that a son would bring to a family and end with the wish that instead he had been stillborn. Perhaps it stands as a final comment on the disaster of 598, in which Jeremiah's personal suffering becomes representative of the nation as a whole. He expresses in his life the total identification with the fate of Israel. In many ways he becomes the prototype of the great servant songs found later in the exilic writings of Second Isaiah (Isa 42:1-4; 49:1-6; 50:4-9; 52:13—53:12). It is more than likely that both the Book of Job and Second Isaiah knew and used Jeremiah's work for the development of their own thought.

Book III
Late Oracles from the Time of Zedekiah
Jeremiah 21-25

I. JUDGMENT AGAINST KING AND CITY JEREMIAH 21:1 - 23:8

Where the previous ten chapters collected the oracles of Jeremiah from the times of King Jehoiakim, almost all of the passages in chaps. 21:1-23:8 come from the days of the last King of Judah, Zedekiah. This puts us into the period between the first attack and destruction of Jerusalem in 598-597 B.C., and its final fall in 586 B.C. We glimpse Jeremiah as he wrestles with the questions raised by national policy that continued to oppose and challenge the power of the Babylonians despite the terrible losses in the first siege. Much of his energy is now directed at the chief center of national policy, the king, and the king's place in God's plan for Israel. The prophet reveals his conviction that Yahweh can and will let go of the royal line in its present form and begin again at a later date. He also intends to undermine the blind conviction that God could not and would not allow Jerusalem and the Davidic dynasty to fall. Both the royal policy and the popular opinion clung to this belief even after surviving the attack of 598 and the exile of so many of their leading citizens.

The oracles in this section on kingship are not necessarily in the order in which Jeremiah delivered them. More likely, too, for most of them, we stand near the end of the nation's independence, *i.e.,* during the final Babylonian assault of 586, rather than early in the reign of King Zedekiah. Jeremiah focuses on the history of the recent kings from the time of Josiah to Zedekiah and underlines their failure to do the one essential royal duty of promoting justice in the framework of the covenant. For this reason, God has rejected these shepherds and yet promises to begin again.

ZEDEKIAH'S PLEA FOR A SALVATION ORACLE 21:1-14

21 This is the word which came to Jeremiah from the LORD, when King Zedekiah sent to him Pashhur the son of Malchiah and Zephaniah the priest, the son of Maaseiah, saying, ²"Inquire of the LORD for us, for Nebuchadrezzar king of Babylon is making war against us; perhaps the LORD will deal with us according to all his wonderful deeds, and will make him withdraw from us."

³Then Jeremiah said to them: ⁴"Thus you shall say to Zedekiah, 'Thus says the LORD, the God of Israel: Behold, I will turn back the weapons of war which are in your hands and with which you are fighting against the king of Babylon and against the Chaldeans who are besieging you outside the walls; and I will bring them together into the midst of this city. ⁵I myself will fight against you with outstretched hand and strong arm, in anger, and in fury, and in great wrath. ⁶And I will smite the inhabitants of this city, both man and beast; they shall die of a great pestilence. ⁷Afterward, says the LORD, I will give Zedekiah king of Judah, and his servants, and the people in this city who survive the pestilence, sword, and famine, into the hand of Nebuchadrezzar king of

Babylon and into the hand of their enemies, into the hand of those who seek their lives. He shall smite them with the edge of the sword; he shall not pity them, or spare them, or have compassion.'"

Chap. 21 centers on a story about a request for a hopeful oracle of deliverance that the king made to Jeremiah. Verses 1-10 form the heart of the king's question and the prophet's response, but two brief words of the prophet have been attached in vv. 11-12 and 13-14 that extend the message originally given for Zedekiah to the whole royal dynasty and even to the royal city itself. The addition of these two oracles broadens the object of Jeremiah's word of doom from Zedekiah's failures alone to those of his predecessors as well, including Jehoiakim and his son Jehoiachin. Verses 11-12 suggest the reason for God's rejection of the royal house of Judah, and vv. 13-14 attack the myth of Jerusalem's special protection from harm because it is the site of the temple. Much in this chapter tallies well with the warnings first given in the Temple sermon of chap. 7.

The moment is desperate. Zedekiah, after several years of quiet submission to the Babylonian rule, has openly revolted under the prodding of his advisors, and the Babylonian response has been swifter than expected. Egyptian help has been slow in coming or even already thrown back by the armies of Nebuchadnezzar. Only now, when his military and political options have run low, does the king turn to Yahweh and his prophet for help. He sends high officials to personally request Jeremiah to seek an answer from Yahweh about the outcome of the war. From the tenor of his instructions, it is clear that the king desperately wants Yahweh to work another miracle for Israel as he did at the Red Sea and as he did for King Hezekiah when he spared Jerusalem from the Assyrian invasion of 701 B.C. through the prayer of Isaiah the prophet (*cf.*, 2 Kgs 19:32-34). In his favor, Zedekiah was more pious than Jehoiakim, who had steadily refused to listen to Jeremiah at all. Later chapters record that on more than one occasion Zedekiah either sent for Jeremiah in person (usually secretly) or sent officials to receive an oracle from him (see chaps. 37:3-10, 16-20 and 38:14-26). Thus, despite a reluctance to take the prophet's advice, at least the king listened to his words.

Verses 1-2 sketch the scene briefly. Pashhur and Zephaniah both hold important positions with the king. From 29:25-26, we discover that Zephaniah was the priest in charge of the temple grounds, and from 38:1-5, that Pashhur was a prince and member of the king's inner circle. Their politics differed. Zephaniah seemed to respect Jeremiah and wanted to treat him gently, while Pashhur opposed him and sought to have him executed later on. They bring a royal order to inquire of Yahweh about the divine will. Jeremiah does not refuse to do this, though we might have expected him to refuse in light of the very specific answer that the king almost orders the prophet to give. Zedekiah wants nothing less than a promise that Yahweh will arrange the withdrawal of the enemy's armies from the land.

One reason why Jeremiah probably agreed to do the king's will stems from the long tradition in the Ancient Near East that rulers should always seek divine guidance before major political decisions. The prophetic oracles from 18th century Mari, a town very near to Babylon itself, often dealt with decisions about war. One of them even reassures the king of Mari, Zimri-Lim, that he will be successful if he goes to battle against Hammurabi, the king of Babylon! The story of the prophet Micaiah ben Imlah in 1 Kgs 22 centers on a request by King Ahab for prophetic oracles about his upcoming war with the Aramaeans. Other means were also common, especially divination by which the omens could be read. Specially trained priests studied the unusual signs in the livers of sheep or the entrails of birds in order to foretell the pleasure of the gods before important events. The letters of the Assyrian kings frequently mention how the gods blessed one campaign or another with favorable omens. The presence of large numbers of prophets in the royal palace during the reign of Ahab and his successors suggests that being available for consultation on state policy was an expected duty for anyone claiming prophetic authority. Even Amos ran up against the anger of the priestly staff of the shrine of Bethel because he preached *against* the king's policy in the king's own temple (Amos 7:10-13).

Like Amos, Jeremiah did not consider himself a servant of the king, paid to give back the hoped-for answers on cue. His response in vv. 3-10 could hardly have cheered the king's heart in the midst of a losing war. Jeremiah announces that Yahweh himself will weaken the fighting forces of Judah in the battle, forcing them back inside the walls of Jerusalem where they will be trapped, and then he will even fight for the Babylonians against them. The image of God's outstretched hand and strong arm occurs in both the priestly tradition of the Exodus (Exod 6:6) and in Deuteronomy in reference to God's great deliverance of Israel from slavery. Here, Jeremiah turns it around against the people. Yahweh will not give victory, but only a fearful end, ravaged by pestilence (v. 6), or by pestilence, sword and famine (v. 7). These three terms became somewhat of a catchword for Jeremiah in the later years of Jehoiakim's reign and in Zedekiah's years. He returns to them again and again in chaps. 14, 15, 16, 18, and 38. Verse 7 reaches a crescendo like cymbals in the final movements of a symphony. Every sector is repeated three times: the king, his officials, and the people; the pestilence, the sword and the famine; Nebuchadrezzar, their enemies, and those who seek their life; he shall not pity them, spare them, nor have compassion.

The spelling of the Babylonian king's name varies throughout Hebrew tradition. Ezekiel favors the more accurate spelling, Nebuchadrezzar, which can be derived from *Nabu-kudurri-usur* ("May the god Nabu protect the boundary," or "May Nabu protect the son") in Akkadian, the language of the Babylonians. The Book of Daniel regularly uses the form Nebuchadnezzar; and Jeremiah has both. In chaps. 21-25, Nebuchadrezzar occurs several times, while in chaps. 27-29, the name is spelled Nebuchadnezzar. The form with "n" probably stems from an attempt by Hebrew speakers to pronounce the foreign word in their own language. Such linguistic variations are common everywhere.

Verses 8-10 set out an option for the king to follow:

> 8"And to this people you shall say: 'Thus says the LORD: Behold, I set before you the way of life and the way of death. 9He who stays in this city shall die by the sword, by famine, and by pestilence; but he who goes out and surrenders to the Chaldeans who are besieging you shall live and shall have his life as a prize of war. 10For I have set my face against this city for evil and not for good, says the LORD: it shall be given into the hand of the king of Babylon, and he shall burn it with fire.'"

Baldly stated, Jeremiah's oracle proposes surrender. In almost any age this would come under the category of high treason if preached publicly against the policy of the government. From the tone of his earlier oracles we can guess that Jeremiah never consented at any time in his ministry to keep his advice private for the king's ears only. There is even an account of his treason trial in chap. 38. But Jeremiah certainly never intended to betray Israel or to gain personally from underhanded behavior. He did not flee when he had the chance after the city was captured (40:1-6), and even encouraged the people to stay in the land rather than go down to Egypt because God would turn against the Babylonians (42:7-12). Jeremiah was no pro-Babylonian. He did not admire their superior culture and military achievements nor did he want to bring them into Israel. But he did see submission to the Babylonian rule as part of Yahweh's plan for Israel.

The prophets from Isaiah until the exile constantly stressed how Yahweh could use foreign powers as instruments in his hand. This does not mean that Isaiah or Jeremiah glorified the high moral virtue and noble intentions of Assyrian and Babylonian kings. Far from it. Isa 10:5-19 clearly states that God used King Tiglath Pileser III of Assyria as a rod to punish Israel and Judah, but the Assyrian king himself had other plans—nothing less than the total conquest and destruction of the chosen people. Because this went far beyond God's plan, Isaiah promised that Assyria would itself be severely punished and destroyed in turn. In the same way, Jeremiah understands the role of King Nebuchadnezzar as a tool of God's wrath against a sinful Israel, but when the work of punishment has been completed, the Babylonians must back off. If they don't, God will act against them as Jeremiah makes clear in chap. 42.

From another angle, Jeremiah did not stand entirely alone. Despite the attempt of many important leaders such as Pashhur to have him removed because of his political advice, he found other highly placed officials to save his life. These may have actually accepted his message of surrender as good strategy in a hopeless war without giving much heed to his religious demands that went along with the political message. Jeremiah promised that the Babylonians would spare the lives of those who surrendered. Knowing the ferocity of conquerors in the ancient world toward cities that resisted, to get out of the war with "your life as your prize" would be fortunate enough for anyone.

The short oracle in vv. 11-12 addresses the entire line of Judah's kings who have put so much stock in their direct descent from King David and have been so confident that Yahweh would stand by them in every situation no matter how grim. Jeremiah makes a little pun: "Go down to the house (=palace) and speak to the house (=dynasty) of David." The word of the Lord itself has a classic prophetic simplicity to it: three short lines demanding justice; three short lines warning of punishment. It stands here as a transition to the long speech on royal justice that follows in chap. 22.

The last two verses of the chapter are less clear.

> 13"Behold, I am against you, O inhabitant of the valley,
>   O rock of the plain,
>
>   says the LORD;
>   you who say, 'Who shall come down against us,
>   or who shall enter our habitations?'
> 14I will punish you according to the fruit of your doings,
>   says the LORD;
>   I will kindle a fire in her forest,
>   and it shall devour all that is round about her."

Who are the inhabitants of the valley and what is the rock of the plain? From the context of Jeremiah's message so far and from the position of this oracle in the midst of a section directed at the royal palace in Jerusalem, we must presume that the prophet is describing the city Jerusalem as though a person. The Hebrew grammar of v. 13 certainly permits the interpretation offered by the RSV translation, but it hardly captures the actual location of the city high on the ridge of mountains between two steep valleys. Moreover, cities were intentionally placed on raised and difficult points of land to prevent an enemy from easily gaining a way into the city. If situated in a valley or on a plain, a city would be vulnerable to such a siege. Thus another possible translation for v. 13 would suit the situation better:

"Behold, I am against you who sit over the valley,
O rock fastness with your leveled top, says the Lord."

The forest can then refer to either the wooded hills surrounding the city, or even in metaphor to the throne room of the king's palace, which Solomon had named "The Forest of Lebanon" (1 Kgs 7:2). Because the capital city is synonymous with the king's power, this brief word of doom against it has been inserted into the book at this point.

THE KING'S DUTY TOWARDS JUSTICE
22:1-9

22 Thus says the LORD: "Go down to the house of the king of Judah, and speak there this word, ²and say, 'Hear the word of the LORD, O King of Judah, who sit on the throne of David, you, and your servants, and your people who enter these gates. ³Thus says the LORD: Do justice and righteousness, and deliver from the hand of the oppressor him who has been robbed. And do no wrong or violence to the alien, the fatherless, and the widow, nor shed innocent blood in this place. ⁴For if you will indeed obey this word, then there shall enter the gates of this house kings who sit on the throne of David, riding in chariots and on horses, they, and their servants, and their people. ⁵But if you will not heed these words, I swear by myself, says the LORD, that this house shall become a desolation.'"

Chap. 22 opens with a strong plea for the kings to consider justice as their most important task in office. If they neglect it for some other concern, then for that reason alone, the royal line and the royal city will be destroyed. Jermiah makes no mention of the king's duties to preserve the temple or to lead worship, only to act justly. He intentionally delivers his word in the entrance to the palace where justice is dispensed. And he aims at a wider audience than the king. Through these gates pass the officials ("servants") and the important citizens doing business with the government. Because the covenant involves the whole nation, the king and people must be one in the obligation of justice. But the king must *lead* the way. He stands as the *shepherd* of the flock (*cf.*, 23:1-8), the *son* of God (Ps 2:7), *anointed* by Yahweh above his fellows (Ps 45:7), *seated* at God's right hand (Ps 110:1), and given *blessing* and long *life* (Ps 21:3-4). But he must also excel in justice. Isa 11:3-4 demands of the righteous king that "he shall not judge by what his eyes see nor decide by what his ears hear; but with righteousness he shall judge the poor and decide with equity for the meek of the earth." Ps 72:4 prays that "he defend the cause of the poor of the people, give deliverance to the needy, and crush the oppressor." In this concept of office, the kings of Israel stand in a long Near Eastern tradition. In the 18th century B.C., Hammurabi of Babylon prefaced his famous law code with a lengthy prologue explaining how the sun god Shamash had appointed him to administer justice in the land (ANET 164-165).

The unique aspect of Israelite kingship was the conviction that the kings themselves were subject to a covenant with the people given by Yahweh at Mt. Sinai. They did not stand above the law as sacred persons, but were to excel in the same covenant fidelity expected of every Israelite. The two words, "justice and righteousness," with which Jeremiah opens his list of obligations recurs throughout the Old Testament as a key phrase of covenantal responsibility. Amos 5:7 from the North and Isa 1:21 from the South, Ps 72 from the North and Ps 89 from the South, all agree on the king's duty towards these two primary obligations. Many of the specifics in Jeremiah's list—caring for the alien, the orphan and the widow—come straight from the major collections of covenant law: Exod 22:21-26, Lev 19:33-34, and Deut 10:18-19. The category of those robbed by oppressors probably refers to people cheated or defrauded from their land or wages by large employers, landowners, and moneylenders. This too covered by the same covenant law under directions for just weights and lending without interest (Exod 22:25; Lev 19:35-36). The Book of Deuteronomy, whose thought stands so close to Jeremiah's on all covenant issues, sums up the same message when it defines the king's role:

> And when he sits on the throne of his kingdom, he shall write for himself in a book a copy of this law, from that which is in the charge of the Levitical priests, and it shall

be with him, and he shall read it all the days of his life, that he may learn to fear the Lord his God, by keeping all the words of this law, and these statutes, and doing them; that his heart may not be lifted up above his brethren, and that he may not turn aside from the commandment either to the right hand or to the left (Deut 17:18-20).

Verses 4-5 lay down a choice. If the people obey, then God will continue to guarantee the dynasty of David upon the throne in peace and prosperity (riding on their chariots); but if they do not listen, God himself will bring down the royal house (both the building and the family). A certain tension had always existed between the equality inherent in the national covenant and the place of a king over the people. Its roots extend back before the time of David into the period of the Judges, when tribal independence resisted the appointment of a single ruler for the twelve tribes. The people remembered that the covenant given them on Mt. Sinai had been with the whole nation as one voice (Exod 24:3-8), and could be summed up in the beautiful words of Exod 19:6: "You shall be to me a kingdom of priests and a holy nation." Only when the danger from the Philistines became so acute in the time of Samuel did Israel pull together and agree on a king, Saul. But even this came about only over some very strong objections (1 Sam 8).

When the prophet Nathan announced a *personal* covenant from Yahweh to Saul's successor, David, one which promised a lasting dynasty on the throne of Jerusalem as the sign of divine favor, it set the stage for trouble. Such a covenant with the king threatened the democratic roots of the Sinai covenant and the traditions of the twelve tribes. At Solomon's death, the split between Judah and the northern ten tribes can be directly traced to the excessive claims of the king over the tribes. This resulted in both sides opposing their ideas of the covenant to one

FAMILY CHART OF KING JOSIAH
THE LAST KINGS OF THE HOUSE OF JUDAH

JOSIAH[1]
born 648, king 640, died 609

JOHANAN[2]
1st born
(1 Chr 3:15)

JEHOIAKIM
(Eliakim)[3]
born: 634
king: 609
died: 598
reign: 11 years

JEHOAHAZ
(Shallum)
born: 632
king: 609
died: ?
reign: 3 months

ZEDEKIAH[4]
(Mattaniah)
born: 619
king: 597
died: 585?
reign: 11 years

ZEDEKIAH[4]
(2 Chr 36:10)

JEHOIACHIN[5]
(Coniah)
born: 616
king: 598
died: ?
reign: 3 months
in 598-597

¹If the dates are correct, Josiah married young. His first child, Johanan, was born before he was 14.

²Johanan never lived to succeed his father as first-born. He is mentioned only in the list of sons in I Chr 3:15.

³Each of the kings has a personal given name which was changed when he succeeded to the kingship for a throne name.

⁴A confusion exists over the identity of Zedekiah, who succeeds as the last of the kings of Judah. 2 Chr 36:10 claims that he is the son of Jehoiakim and the brother of Jehoiachin, while 2 Kgs 24:18 notes that he is the uncle of Jehoiachin and full brother of Jehoahaz by the wife of Josiah, Hamutal. This would also be part of the list in I Chr 3:15.

⁵The reign of Jehoiachin is listed as three months in 598. But some evidence exists to suggest that even in captivity in Babylon, Jehoiachin was considered the real king and Zedekiah only a regent in his place. Ezekiel 1:2 is dated from the exile of Jehoiachin, and the Weidner tablets, a group of Babylonian documents listing administrative details of the royal palace in Babylon, lists provisions for the family of king Jehoiachin of Judah.

another. In Judah, the royal family and the temple liturgy extolled the unconditional promise to David's line (2 Sam 7 and Ps 89); in the North, the kings took steps to prevent the local people from having anything to do with the Jerusalem temple (1 Kgs 12:25-29), and the people themselves took to heart the tenet of no lasting dynasty. The history of assassinations and palace intrigues in the two hundred years of the northern kingdom makes that clear (1 Kgs 15:27; 16:10, 16-18; 2 Kgs 9:14-28; 15:10,14,25,30).

Only after the fall of the northern state in 722 do we find prophetic writings that reunite the concepts of the Sinai covenant with the Davidic covenant. Hosea and Amos preaching in the north had never mentioned the promises to David; Isaiah working in the South, had never referred to Sinai. But in Jeremiah, Ezekiel, Second Isaiah and Deuteronomy a century later, a synthesis develops that stresses the primary role of the Sinai covenant with a *conditional* and secondary promise to king David (1 Kgs 9:4-9; Jer 22:4-5; Ezek 34:23-25; Isa 55:3-4; Ps 132:12). Jeremiah stresses the conditional side strongly. Verses 6-8 put it into the form of a judgment oracle. The opening lines in poetry compare the king to the almost mythical greatness of the cedar trees that covered Lebanon and Gilead. The cedar was a divine tree, but God could still cut it down and burn it to nothing (*cf.*, a similar line of thought in Ezek 31). There may also be present here, as in 21:14, a reference to the destruction of the royal palace and its "Forest of Lebanon." The questions put by the passersby explain in deuteronomic terms the punishment that God sends. Note the similarity of Jer 22:1-9 to the covenantal description in 1 Kgs 9:1-9. The prohibition against worshipping and serving other gods appears often in Deuteronomy (Deut 6:14; 7:4; 8:19; 11:16). Because of the strong resemblance of this passage to the thought of the school of Deuteronomy, many commentators believe that the best solution would be to think of a short word of Jeremiah that has been expanded by the editors of his book to summarize the prophet's teaching on the role of the king.

THE ROYAL FAILURES
22:10-30

Chap. 22 continues with three examples of the failure of the kings during Jeremiah's own lifetime. *Shallum*, in vv. 10-12, is none other than Jehoahaz, the son of Josiah who succeeded his father to the throne in 609 B.C.; *Jehoiakim*, in vv. 13-19, was another son of Josiah, but by a different wife, who replaced his half-brother after only a few short months and reigned from 609 until his death in 598 B.C.; and *Coniah*, in vv. 20-30, was the young son of Jehoiakim who became king under the name Jehoiachin at his father's death in the middle of the Babylonian attack of 598, and was sent into exile shortly afterwards. Jeremiah does not hold much respect for any of them, and in fact compares the first two quite unfavorably with their father Josiah. There may even be some irony intended by the choice of names. Shallum and Coniah represent the personal names of the kings, what they were called as children growing up. Upon becoming king they received a more official royal name, often called a throne name, much as the pope today assumes a new name when elected. The use of the childhood names for the two kings who barely got a chance to be crowned before they were deposed, suggests that Jeremiah did not consider them as responsible and mature leaders. He saves a much harsher judgment for his oracle against Jehoiakim in vv. 13-19.

Jehoahaz, the first of the kings, appears fourth in the list of the sons of Josiah (1 Chr 3:15), and would not normally become king ahead of his brothers. But the rule that the firstborn son succeeds to the throne had been set aside before in Israelite history, most notably in the case of Solomon, the son of David (1 Kgs 1:15-40). Jehoahaz may have shown more ability than his brothers; or his mother, Hamutal, may have been the queen, the chief wife, of Josiah. He may also have been appointed king by the royal advisors and men of importance in Josiah's government. Since Josiah had died prematurely in battle trying to prevent the spread of Egyptian power north, we can guess that his officials wanted a son that could carry on this anti-Egyptian policy. Naturally, too, the Egyptians, once they had secured their victory in Palestine, quickly removed the young king in favor of a more tractable and cooperative brother, Jehoiakim. Jeremiah mentions no personal criticism of Jehoahaz; he may even have thought well of him personally. But he does strongly challenge those who hope for his return from captivity in Egypt. Jehoahaz will not come back, his policies will not again take effect. Rather, the people should stop their funeral mourning for Josiah and wail instead for Jehoahaz, for he is just as surely dead and gone.

The second oracle in this section bluntly describes the next king, Jehoiakim, as a man who enslaves his own people and oppresses them cruelly for his own pleasures and vain ego.

> [13]"Woe to him who builds his house by unrighteousness,
>   and his upper rooms by injustice;
> who makes his neighbor serve him for nothing,
>   and does not give him his wages;
> [14]who says, 'I will build myself a great house
>   with spacious upper rooms,'
> and cuts out windows for it,
>   paneling it with cedar,
>   and painting it with vermilion.
> [15]Do you think you are a king
>   because you compete in cedar?
> Did not your father eat and drink
>   and do justice and righteousness?
>   Then it was well with him.
> [16]He judged the cause of the poor and needy;
>   then it was well.
> Is not this to know me?
>
>   says the LORD.

17But you have eyes and heart
   only for your dishonest gain,
for shedding innocent blood,
   and for practicing oppression and violence."
18Therefore thus says the LORD concerning Jehoiakim
the son of Josiah, king of Judah:
"They shall not lament for him, saying,
   'Ah my brother!' or 'Ah sister!'
They shall not lament for him, saying,
   'Ah lord!' or 'Ah his majesty!'
19With the burial of an ass he shall be buried,
   dragged and cast forth beyond the gates of Jerusalem."

In a small nation, with barely enough resources to survive and paying heavy tribute to foreign conquerors, he builds like Solomon in the heyday of the Israelite empire in the 10th century. The burden was too much for even the wealth of Solomon and it caused the breakup of that empire when the northern tribes refused to continue to bear the taxes and labor gangs (1 Kgs 11-12). Jeremiah has nothing but scorn for this small-minded man who needs a huge palace to prove he is a king. The prophet sees only one thing that will make a king great: his love for justice and righteousness (*mishpat* and *sedeqah*), the two pillars of the covenant (see the comments on vv. 1-9 above). But Jehoiakim does neither. His acts contrast completely with those of his father, Josiah, who not only lived in as high and regal a style as Jehoiakim ever would, but did justice and righteousness all his days. The key to Jeremiah's thought lies in v. 16. Josiah knew Yahweh, and therefore he kept Yahweh's covenant faithfully. To know the Lord comes down to obeying his will, and Josiah had responded fully and piously to the demands presented to him by the Lawbook found in the Temple early in his reign. In just the opposite manner, Jehoiakim had thought only of his own gain, stopping at nothing to achieve it. Verse 17 lists a terrible trio that sums up the lengths to which this king went: murdering the innocent, oppression, and violence (*cf.*, 2 Kgs 24:4).

Jeremiah ends his accusations against Jehoiakim with a sentence of judgment. He will be denied burial, and will be thrown out like the dead carcass of an ass, an unclean animal (Lev 11:3) which the Israelites are forbidden to touch because it would defile them (Deut 14:8). Jeremiah repeats this threat a second time in chap. 36:30 (unless it represents two accounts of the same oracle). But it seems to contradict the report of 2 Kgs 24:6, that Jehoiakim "slept with his fathers." This expression may be only a frozen formula used over and over in the Books of Kings to mean simply "he died." If so, then various options for his burial or lack of it during the Babylonian siege can be proposed. Some have suggested that the king was buried peacefully but had to be disinterred and thrown outside the city walls to prove to the Babylonians that he really had died before they would consider making peace with his son Jehoiachin. But this is pure fancy. We just do not know if Jeremiah's prediction came true or not.

Verses 20-23 interrupt the sequence of oracles against kings at this point to insert a lament over the fall of Jerusalem. Funeral customs in the ancient world often employed professional mourning women who would wail and beat their heads and breasts and perform all the proper rituals to insure a good burial and reception of the deceased into the afterlife. Egyptian tombs picture many such scenes, and Ezekiel gives a mocking view of their performance in his oracles against Egypt in Ezek 32:16 and 32:17-32. Jeremiah calls upon the women to go to the nations all around the Holy Land and announce the death of the city. All her friends will be found far away now—in exile, flight or slavery. The sudden shift of reference to Jerusalem as a cedar of Lebanon is another use of the same metaphor of the divinely favored status and greatness of the almost-mythical tree that we have seen in 22:6-7. The inclusion of this oracle in the middle of the description of royal failures may help us to date it to the year 598, at the very time of the fall of Jerusalem and the reign of three kings in one year (*cf.*, the shepherds carried away by the wind in v. 22).

The oracles mentioning Coniah or Jehoiachin in vv. 24-30 can be put in the same year.

> 24"As I live, says the LORD, though Coniah the son of Jehoiakim, king of Judah, were the signet ring on my right hand, yet I would tear you off 25and give you into the hand of those who seek your life, into the hand of those of whom you are afraid, even into the hand of Nebuchadrezzar king of Babylon and into the hand of the Chaldeans. 26I will hurl you and the mother who bore you into another country, where you were not born, and there you shall die. 27But to the land to which they will long to return, there they shall not return."
> 28Is this man Coniah a despised, broken pot,
>   a vessel no one cares for?
> Why are he and his children hurled and cast
>   into a land which they do not know?
> 29O land, land, land,
>   hear the word of the LORD!
> 30Thus says the LORD:
> "Write this man down as childless,
>   a man who shall not succeed in his days;
> for none of his offspring shall succeed
>   in sitting on the throne of David,
>   and ruling again in Judah."

The image of the king as God's signet ring has been interpreted as a mark of special favor for this young son of Jehoiakim. But from Jeremiah's words here, we have little reason to think that the prophet saw much in him to admire.

Ezek 28:12 calls the king of Tyre a signet ring who has betrayed his role as God's subordinate. Several examples of royal signet rings worn or carried by high officials of the king are known. The most famous is that of Shema, a royal officer of Jeroboam II, the king in northern Israel from 786-746. The ring was found in the excavation of the ruins of Samaria, the capital of the northern state, and had the imprint of a lion on it with the words, "Shema, servant of Jeroboam." The prophet Haggai refers to Jehoiachin's grandson, Zerubbabel, the governor of Judah after the exile, as a signet ring for Yahweh (Hag 2:23). The religious meaning of the title undoubtedly stresses the authority of the ruler to act in the name of Yahweh, the true king of Israel. It signifies not so much intimacy as delegated authority.

Jehoiachin's capture and exile are recorded in 2 Kgs 24:10-12 and 25:27-29 (Jer 52:31-34). It lasted a minimum of 37 years, long after the deaths of Zedekiah, his successor, and of Jeremiah himself. He died in Babylon presumably, as did his children after him. 1 Chr 3:17-19 gives the names of seven sons and two grandsons, one of whom, Zerubbabel, came back as the governor of the Persian province of Judah sometime before 520 B.C. (see Ezra 1-3). Both Haggai and Zechariah speak hopefully of him as God's chosen (Hag 2:20-23 and Zech 4:1-14), but he disappears from history shortly after; whether dead or recalled by a watchful Persian government wary of revolts, no one knows. But the statement of Jeremiah that no descendant of Jehoiachin would again rule in Judah, proved true. Jeremiah did not intend it, however, merely as a notice of coming events, but as a sentence of judgment. Israelites believed that someone lived on only in the children they left behind them. Jehoiachin's name as king would be cut off by the failure of any of his sons or grandsons to succeed him. See similar thoughts in Ps 72:17; Isa 66:22; 1 Kgs 1:47-48.

A TRUE SHEPHERD AND RIGHTEOUS BRANCH
23:1-8

23 "Woe to the shepherds who destroy and scatter the sheep of my pasture!" says the LORD. ²Therefore thus says the LORD, the God of Israel, concerning the shepherds who care for my people: "You have scattered my flock, and have driven them away, and you have not attended to them. Behold, I will attend to you for your evil doings, says the LORD. ³Then I will gather the remnant of my flock out of all the countries where I have driven them, and I will bring them back to their fold, and they shall be fruitful and multiply. ⁴I will set shepherds over them who will care for them, and they shall fear no more, nor be dismayed, neither shall any be missing, says the LORD.

⁵"Behold, the days are coming, says the LORD, when I will raise up for David a righteous Branch, and he shall reign as king and deal wisely, and shall execute justice and righteousness in the land. ⁶In his days Judah will be saved, and Israel will dwell securely. And this is the name by which he will be called: 'The LORD is our righteousness.'"

The final section of Jeremiah's treatment of kingship turns from the failures of Judah's kings to the promise of a greater care and renewed hope. It consists of three short sayings, vv. 1-4, 5-6, and 7-8. The first and last are generally considered to be prose and form a sandwich around the middle verses, which most commentators (unlike the RSV!) interpret as an original poem of Jeremiah that contrasts a new messianic king to king Zedekiah.

The shepherds condemned en masse in the first saying (vv. 1-4) can only be the kings of the Israelite nation. But whether it refers just to the recent kings of Jeremiah's own day or to the whole line of kings from the time of David on, cannot be absolutely decided. The second poem foresees the restoration of the united kingdom of North and South as it was in David's reign before the following kings, one after another, turned to evil ways, according to the judgment of the Book of Kings. But the hints at exile and scattered sheep in vv. 1 and 3 might more naturally be applied to the fate suffered by Judah at the hands of the Babylonians in 597 and 586. Verses 1-4 would then date to shortly after Zedekiah's collapse in 586-585.

The message looks beyond the fates of the individual kings and even beyond the continuation of the kingship itself. Yahweh will replace the shepherds by his own immediate care of his sheep. In v. 2 the kings are blamed for dispersing the sheep, in v. 3 God is said to have done the dispersal himself. The two contrary explanations of the exile reveal the nature of Israel's understanding of cause and effect. Human actions do bring about good and evil results. People are not slaves, they make choices that effect history. The prophetic language of obedience and disobedience, warning and threat, presupposes this freedom all the time. Jeremiah's call to conversion, so prominent in the early chapters of his work, only makes sense if people can change their minds. But like most of the ancient world, Israelites did not perceive the universe as a vast clockwork that automatically ran on predetermined laws and secondary causes as modern science would. Explanations of gravity, solar systems, or atmospheric inversion layers were not available to them. They could see that the world had order and that experts could predict the patterns in the cosmic events, but they also believed that all things happened by divine choice. The gods personally *willed* that the various parts of the world work and could block it if they were angered or desired to punish human beings. Thus God watched over and caused all things according to his plan at the same time that we choose and act on our level. The two explanations stand side by side but both are needed.

Yahweh promises to bring back the remnant of his sheep. Not all of them, only some. This remnant may include all of those who went into exile in Babylon. Certainly Jeremiah indicates in later chapters that he placed his hopes on the exiles rather than on the people left in the land after the conquest of Nebuchadrezzar was over (24:1-10; 29:1-23). The vision of this remnant in vv. 3-4 bubbles with hope for a new day. It contains several aspects: (1) Yahweh himself will bring it about directly; (2) exiles shall be restored to their own land and homes; (3) a new and better line of rulers will govern the land; (4) there will be peace and freedom from fear; (5) there will be great prosperity. The note that the people "will be fruitful and multiply," recalls the blessings God bestowed on the earth at creation (Gen 1:28; 9:7). Jeremiah hints at a new creation for Israel, a new beginning without bearing the guilt of the past around with them. RSV translated the last phrase in v. 4 as "none of them will be missing." It comes from the same Hebrew word, *paqad*, that appears twice at the end of v. 2 as "pay attention." This verb has many nuances, and can be translated into English by "watch over, guide, punish, govern, call to account," depending on the context. The best overall sense for both vv. 2 and 4 can be expressed by the idea of "render an account." Thus in v. 4, the remnant is not to be afraid ever again of being held accountable for the sins and wickedness of its past.

The theology of the remnant did not begin with Jeremiah. Earlier prophets had already threatened the nation with such divine punishment that only a few would survive, and their fate would not be much better than those who perished by the sword and terror of their enemies. Amos 3:12 and Isa 1:9 both conceive the remnant as little more than those lucky enough to live through disaster. They have no particular virtue or goodness that makes them better than their fellows who perish. But a second and more positive vision of the remnant begins to grow beside the first. This new idea sees a remnant that learns from the punishment and returns wholeheartedly to the Lord and the Lord restores blessing as in the days of the original creation: Isa 10:20-23; 11:1-9; 33:15-20; Mic 4:7; 7:18. Jeremiah stands in the latter tradition (*cf.*, 24:40-43), especially here in 23:4-5 with the explicit reference to the blessings of creation.

Verses 5-6 shift the focus from the remnant of the people to the person of a new king. The expression "the days are coming" avoids too specific a prediction of when God will raise up this new ruler (*cf.*, 7:32 and 9:25). It could happen soon or it could remain a hope for the future. The prophet calls him a "Righteous Branch from David's line." Two other prophetic books, Isaiah and Zechariah, use the same language about a future king that will arise like a budding shoot from David's tree; but in the case of Zech 3:8 and 6:12, the hope seems to be for quick action on God's part, perhaps only a matter of months, while in Isa 11:1, the descriptive language suggests a paradisal future in which lamb and lion will lie down together, a dream for the end of times. In light of Jeremiah's pessimism that any son or grandson of Jehoiachin will succeed to the throne, we must assume that his prophetic vision does not dream of quick fulfillment. The messianic king will have three qualities: he shall rule as a king should, he shall be wise, and he shall fulfill the two covenant requirements of justice and righteousness. He shall also reunite Judah and Israel as one. These sum up the biblical virtues said of David (Ps 89; 1 Chr 28:9-10; 29:14-21); and of Josiah by Jeremiah himself (see 22:15). They lived what the new name for the monarch signified: "The Lord is our righteousness." For all of their faults, they submitted themselves to the demands of the covenant and the rule of Yahweh as the true king of Israel. The word *sedeqah*, "righteousness," has several different meanings, as do so many Hebrew words. The poetry plays on them all: "victorious, righteous, legitimate, true." The king to come will be a true son of David, upright like David, obedient to Yahweh as victor, and legitimate in all senses of the word.

As his name indicates, *yahweh sidqenu* ("Yahweh is our righteousness") he will be the opposite of Zedekiah, whose name, *sidqiyahu*, means "My righteousness is Yahweh." The future ruler shall rule as befits a king, unlike Zedekiah who was technically only regent; he shall be wise, unlike Zedekiah; he shall do justice and righteousness unlike Zedekiah; and he shall rely on Yahweh's righteousness and victory, and not his own, unlike Zedekiah.

The final two verses of this section (vv. 7-8) compare the promised restoration to a new Exodus. The great saving event of Israel's religious faith had been the Exodus. All her faith and obedience to the covenant with Yahweh stood rooted in the conviction that he had indeed chosen this people and delivered them from slavery and given them this land to live in. But if it had been a great miracle to turn the fortunes of the nation around then, it will surely be a greater miracle for the Lord to reverse the destruction and exile coming upon Israel in the sixth century. The people swore by the solemnity of their belief in the first event, now they will just as solemnly swear by the new Exodus. The two historical moments, nearly 700 years apart, can be placed side by side because of the profound conviction of biblical faith, that what God revealed in the first Exodus, and what he reveals in any later moments of salvation, are *expectable*. God is a god of continuing deliverance, and continuing closeness, and unbroken faithfulness to his choice to be present to his people. No one who reads the Scriptures and confesses belief in them can say that our God made the world, set it going according to his rules, and now stands apart from it. He may not tinker with his well-ordered world for every individual request by changing the laws of nature, but he is always present to the one who requests and responds within his *covenant*.

II. JUDGMENT AGAINST
THE PROPHETS
JEREMIAH 23:9-40

This long section addresses the problem of false prophets and together with chap. 28 comprises a mini-handbook on the subject. Jeremiah directs his remarks against the prophets of his day in a great number of oracles but rarely does he expound on the exact distinctions between them and himself. These thirty-two verses contain his most complete statement on the subject. It can be broken into two major sections, vv. 9-22 and vv. 23-40, the latter with two subdivisions, 23-32 and 33-40.

WORSE THAN THE PROPHETS OF BAAL
23:9-22

> [13]In the prophets of Samaria
> I saw an unsavoury thing:
> they prophesied by Baal
> and led my people Israel astray.
> [14]But in the prophets of Jerusalem
> I have seen a horrible thing:
> they commit adultery and walk in lies;
> they strengthen the hands of evildoers,

so that no one turns from his wickedness;
all of them have become like Sodom to me,
   and its inhabitants like Gomorrah."
15Therefore thus says the LORD of hosts concerning
the prophets:
"Behold, I will feed them with wormwood,
and give them poisoned water to drink;
for from the prophets of Jerusalem
   ungodliness has gone forth into all the land."

The first section, vv. 9-22, itself divides into three separate oracles: vv. 9-12, 13-15, and 16-22. Clearly, the editors have gathered many originally independent sayings of Jeremiah together in this one spot to reinforce the often repeated conviction that the prophetic professionals of his day played a major role in the ethical and religious decay of Israel.

Verses 9-12 fall once again into the pattern of a dialogue between prophet and Yahweh. Jeremiah opens with a discouraged and poignant statement about his own anguish and confusion caused by the tension between the word he preaches and the apparently total lack of moral change or improvement in the land. His "broken heart" refers to a loss of mental power. He cannot think straight any longer. He doubts his mental acuity and ordered logic. It has affected him physically in his bones, and mentally and spiritually in his confidence. Not that Jeremiah doubts the value of the ultimate victory of God's message, rather he is shaken by the people's lack of understanding and their unwillingness to listen to what must have seemed obvious to him. The sin, summed up by the charge of adultery, fills the land; at the same time, drought and famine stalk the country. The prophet calls the land cursed, but he means that the people are the curse. The word translated "curse" can with only the slightest change be read as "these": thus, "Because of these, the land mourns." They sound alike: *'alah* (curse) and *'elleh* (these), and so remind us that evil deeds and misused power do not stem from nature but from the prophets and leaders. Jeremiah has indulged himself in yet another pun.

Yahweh responds in vv. 11-12. The cause of disaster in the land can be traced directly to the religious leadership: priest and prophet. And it is not just a case of having weak people holding office and leading scandalous personal lives while doing good work on the job. They celebrate their evil in the very temple. If adultery stands for both personal sexual excesses and for idolatry, then they are the chief celebrants in the liturgy of idolatry. Their fate might not seem so terrible at first glance. Surely after some of the fearsome images Jeremiah has used before, to talk of being driven down a slippery path until one stumbles and falls doesn't sound like much. But we need to remember that this sums up one of the great characteristics of Sheol, the land of the dead. Death opens its mouth to swallow its victims whole (Exod 15:12; Num 16:30,32,34; Deut 11:6; Prov 1:12; and *cf.*, Pss 124:3; 69:16; Jon 1:17; and Jer 51:34) and traps its victims in its slippery throat as in a swamp (Pss 40:3; 69:2; 88:6; Isa 25:8). Jeremiah ironically mocks these devotees of Baal and their false cults. In Canaanite mythology, part of the Ugaritic myth of Baal tells how Baal himself was swallowed up by the god of death, Mot, and had to be rescued by his sister-wife Anat, but not until the earth withered up in drought and famine.

The second oracle, in vv. 13-15, matches the previous one beautifully. The hints at the cult of Baal lead naturally into a comparison of the present evil prophets with those who were responsible for the fall of the northern kingdom in 722. The history of the North involves a ceaseless struggle by prophets who were zealous for Yahweh against the inroads of the cult of Baal. The cycle of Elijah and Elisha legends in 1 Kgs 17—2 Kgs 9 grew up around these battles. But even if those prophets who supported the apostasy to Baal must be held accountable, Yahweh now announces that the Jerusalem prophets have done worse. Presumably even Baal prophets did their prophesying as they thought the pagan god inspired them (see a vivid description of this prophetic frenzy in 1 Kgs 19:25-29), but the prophets in Judah lacked any sincerity about their work at all. They used their position and influence to aid evildoers. Jeremiah has told us often enough that the prophet must warn and challenge the nation to return to the covenant teaching. But Judah's have done the opposite, living a personal example of debauchery and helping others to act even worse. Again, he says of them that they are disciples of the "Lie" (*cf.*, 14:14; 27:15; 29:9, and a slightly different word, "fraud," in 18:15). Given the character of Israelite thought, we might suspect that the "Lie" is intended as a mocking title for a pagan god. Probably Jeremiah intends Baal directly.

Sodom and Gomorrah had become proverbial examples of the perversion of moral behavior. Their story in Gen 18 and 19 details the sexual laxity of the citizens, their lack of respect for even the most fundamental treatment of visitors, and the terrible punishment God exacted as a result. Israel's prophets will receive no less a punishment. Jeremiah has already threatened wormwood and poisoned water in 9:14. No food or water will keep them alive from the wrath of Yahweh. The poison that they have fed the people will come back upon them as destruction.

The third oracle, vv. 16-22, provides the deepest analysis yet of what makes a false prophet. Verse 16 lists three characteristics: they do not speak words that come from Yahweh's mouth; they speak visions and imaginings of their own hearts; they stress vain hopes. In turn, the following verse names their willing audience: those who despise the word of Yahweh, and those who stubbornly follow their own thinking and reject obedience to God's commands. Interestingly, the prophet and the audience fit one another very well. Both want only their own mind and reject any submission to authority or direction from outside, especially from heaven. The false prophets want to give what the people want to hear. A message of complacency suits them perfectly because it means that they will not have to change their evil ways. If they can reassure their supporters that God would only intend peace and welfare, then they will not have to fear the consequences of their current lifestyle. The lesson can be applied in almost any age, but it has a particular relevance to the situation in the twentieth century. Believing Christians, for example, closed their eyes to the growing persecution of the Jews in Germany between World War I and World War II because they wanted only peace. Somehow they complacently thought that Hitler could be contained without nations facing the evil that he was doing. Exhausted from one horrible war, they did not want to face more conflicts. The result was not only another war, but the Holocaust, in which European Judaism was nearly extinguished. In the United States, many complain about pornography, sexually explicit films and T.V. programs, lack of religious or moral training, the rise of crime, and other signs of decay in the social structure, but they want the government to handle the problem rather than risk changing their own way of life or accepting the moral responsibility for fighting for justice and equity in their office or local housing situation.

Jeremiah claims that the false prophets did not receive their message from Yahweh. The reason for this is simple. No false prophet has stood in the council chamber when God makes his decrees and sends forth his word. If they were not there, they cannot be true messengers from Yahweh.

> [18]For who among them has stood in the council
> of the LORD
>   to perceive and to hear his word,
>   or who has given heed to his word and listened?

The language of the divine council chamber appears quite often in the Old Testament. The prophet Micaiah ben Imlah in 1 Kgs 22 describes in detail his presence in God's council as evidence against the false prophets of king Ahab. The setting of Job 1 and 2 takes place in the divine council; Isaiah has a vision of the council during his own call in Isa 6; the Second Isaiah also seems to be part of the divine council meeting when he receives the call in Isa 40:1-11. Even the famous statement in Gen 1:26, in which God says, "let *us* make humans after *our* own image and likeness," may reflect a dialogue between God and his angelic council. In any case, the prophetic examples all point to a certain understanding of their role in which the certitude that God speaks through them comes from an experience of actually being in the heavenly court. Whether this "experience" was a vision, an ecstatic rapture, a dream or a matter of hearing something, we cannot know for sure. Possibly the prophet entered into the divine dialogue in the midst of a profoundly silent meditation. What they heard there, however, made them absolutely sure that the vanities, the complacency, and the self-serving messages of the "false" prophets did not come from Yahweh. Because they themselves were to bring that word from the divine council to Israel, they must preach and proclaim no message but the one given to them in that experience.

Contrary to the false message, God will indeed send destruction.

> ¹⁹Behold, the storm of the LORD!
>   Wrath has gone forth,
> a whirling tempest;
>   it will burst upon the head of the wicked.
> ²⁰The anger of the LORD will not turn back
>   until he has executed and accomplished
>   the intents of his mind.
> In the latter days you will understand it clearly.

> ²¹"I did not send the prophets,
>   yet they ran;
> I did not speak to them,
>   yet they prophesied.
> ²²But if they had stood in my council,
>   then they would have proclaimed my words
>   to my people,
> and they would have turned them from their evil way,
>   and from the evil of their doings."

God's word will be anything but peaceful. Jeremiah compares the coming punishment to a sandstorm that whirls in from the hot eastern deserts of Arabia, bringing choking dust and unsupportable heat. This east wind in biblical thought represents the angry breath of Yahweh's nostrils, in contrast to the gentle spirit he breathes into living beings when he creates them (Gen 2:7). But as v. 20 makes clear, his anger is not fickle or volatile—the rages of a moody deity—but flows solely from the necessity to complete his divine plan for the world. Jeremiah has often affirmed how difficult it is to know the mind of Yahweh clearly. The easiest and surest way is to look back afterwards. Jeremiah himself uses this argument in chap. 28 against the prophet Hananiah, and he uses it here. But, naturally, that only begs the question for anyone who has to make a decision for or against a prophet right now. And it does not represent the heart of Jeremiah's thought on the question. The key element comes in the last verse of this oracle, v. 22, where the message from the divine council is recognized by its challenge to wickedness and sin. If Judah's prophets had been in the divine council, they would preach what Yahweh really wanted and the people needed to hear; but since they had not been there, they had no moral guidance to offer. In no way can they claim the all-important commission that God *sent* them as faithful messengers. Jeremiah has emphasized this before (14:14 and 23:14) and will return to it again (27:15).

THE PROPHETS AND THEIR DREAMS
23:23-32

23"Am I a God at hand, says the LORD, and not a God afar off? 24Can a man hide himself in secret places so that I cannot see him? says the LORD. Do I not fill heaven and earth? says the LORD. 25I have heard what the prophets have said who prophesy lies in my name, saying, 'I have dreamed, I have dreamed!' 26How long shall there be lies in the heart of the prophets who prophesy lies, and who prophesy the deceit of their own heart, 27who think to make my people forget my name by their dreams which they tell one another, even as their fathers forgot my name for Baal? 28Let the prophet who has a dream tell the dream, but let him who has my word speak my word faithfully. What has straw in common with wheat? says the LORD. 29Is not my word like fire, says the LORD, and like a hammer which breaks the rock in pieces? 30Therefore, behold, I am against the prophets, says the LORD, who steal my words from one another. 31Behold, I am against the prophets, says the LORD, who use their tongues and say, 'Says the LORD.' 32Behold, I am against those who prophesy lying dreams, says the LORD, and who tell them and lead my people astray by their lies and their recklessness, when I did not send them or charge them; so they do not profit this people at all, says the LORD."

The final prose section of chap. 23 can be divided into two parts, each of which stresses the solemn nature of a different prophetic formula. Verses 23-32 warn against a light use of the standard phrase "an oracle of Yahweh" (RSV "an oracle of the Lord") which occurs widely in the prophetic books. Verses 33-40 attack those who declare "the burden of Yahweh" at every whim and without authorization from God. Both oracles seem to be from the period of King Zedekiah when Jeremiah felt most strongly the growing chaos of voices raised in the besieged land, all declaring God's will was this, or it was that, or it was both! And although they now appear in prose in our standard translations, both oracles show the repetitions of key phrases and words that suggest they were originally delivered as poetry.

The questions that open the first oracle in v. 23 are naturally rhetorical. God is *not* a deity near at hand; he is indeed far off. This may strike us strangely, for the search to find God nearby characterizes the modern religious mentality. Jeremiah, however, wants to remind his audience that God cannot be grabbed hold of, cannot be treated in human terms, cannot be restricted to this sphere of action or to that part of life. He dwells where the ancients believed all great gods had to dwell—in the far reaches of heaven from where he controlled and directed the universe. Yahweh is no local divinity, but master of creation. The proof for this is that no one can hide from his glance. He sees all things and knows the secrets of every heart. One of the most beautiful expressions of this thought develops in the story of Samuel's choice of David to be king in 1 Sam 16:7. Samuel was sure that God wanted an older son of Jesse, but Yahweh speaks to Samuel, "Do not look on his appearance or on the height of his stature, because I have rejected him; for the Lord sees not as humans see; humans look on the outward appearance, but the Lord looks on the heart." This sense of moral observation by God is found also in Ps 33:13-15: "The Lord looks down from heaven, he sees the entire human family; From where he sits enthroned he looks forth on all the inhabitants of the earth, he who fashions the hearts of them all, and observes all their deeds." Similar beliefs occur throughout the ancient world about high gods. A hymn to Shamash, the sun god, comes from the library of the Assyrian king Asshurbanipal just before the days of Jeremiah. In one passage, the worshipper declares: "The people of the world, all of them, thou dost watch over . . . those endowed with life, thou dost tend; thou indeed art their shepherd both above and below" (ANET 387). Like the pagan gods, Yahweh always maintains his transcendent status. In the wonderful hymn of creation in Genesis 1, Yahweh looks down on what he makes and blesses it. There can be no confusion between God the creator and what is created. The Hebrews protected this distinction zealously. Never did they discuss a wife or consort for Yahweh, and they constantly found ways of avoiding any suggestion that one really saw God in the flesh (even though the language occasionally occurs in such stories as the Garden of Eden in Gen 2-3), using terms like the angel of the Lord, the face of Yahweh, the Name of Yahweh, his spirit, his word, his glory. Where pagan religions declared the gods to be distant while at the same time worshipping them as powers of nature, Israel refused to speak of God in nature. The story of Elijah at Mt. Horeb in 1 Kgs 19:11-13 in which God was not in wind or earthquake or fire, but was in the small still voice that speaks within, represents the best of prophetic tradition.

Yet this God could be near. In Exodus 3, Yahweh tells Moses that he has come down to rescue his people, reveals his own name and promises a lasting bond in the words: "I will be your God and you will be my people." (Exod 6:7 and often). The prophets frequently use the phrase, "Yahweh is with us" (Isa 7:14; Hos 11:9; Amos 5:14). The richest prophetic affirmation of this truth comes in Deut 4:7, when Moses asks "What great nation is there that has a god so near to it as the Lord our God is to us whenever we call upon him?" Jeremiah may stress the transcendent ability of God to know all things, but in his very questioning, he reminds his audience that this same God has promised never to abandon or forget this people.

Verses 25-28 take up the problem of prophetic dreams. Jeremiah clearly does not equate experiences in dreams with the coming of the word of Yahweh to a prophet. Variously he calls these lying dreams, chaff, or deceitfulness of the hearts. Deut 13:1-2 and Zech 10:2 also condemn dreams as inadequate for prophecy. Yet within biblical tradition itself, dreams have an honored history as a means of God's communicating to humans. Jacob received important revelation in dreams at Bethel in Gen 28:10-22, and at Penuel in Gen 32:23-32, Solomon had a dream at Gibeon in which he received the gift of wisdom (1 Kgs 3), and the boy-hero Daniel is included among the prophets in the Western tradition partly because of his revelatory dreams (Dan 1-6). Num 12:6 seems to give authority to dreams as one of the ordinary ways in which Yahweh makes his word known to prophets. The other, and equal, means is the vision. Jeremiah may well object to the dream as a vehicle of communication from God because of its long history of use among pagan religions. We know of dream oracles in the time of Gudea of Lagash (2100 B.C.); and a series of prophecies have been unearthed at Mari in eastern Syria which came to prophets and prophetesses while sleeping (1800 B.C.). Among the tablets found at Ugarit on the coast of Syria, one told the story of king Keret and his dream oracle (1300 B.C.). The charge in v. 27 that the dream-prophets make the people forget God's name and go after Baal would suggest Jeremiah's conviction that both pagan religions and the false prophets twisted the ordinary fancies of their dreams into revelations from God in order to serve their own ends or to make themselves look important. For Jeremiah the dream is like chaff, or as the RSV puts it, like straw—it is inedible, it gives no nourishment. The word of the Lord, on the other hand, feeds and sustains us.

The imagery of Yahweh's word like a fire or a hammer conveys its strength to achieve God's purposes, but also its potentially destructive force. The word can punish. Isa 5:24 develops the same thought at some length when it describes God's anger against the people as a fire that goes forth at God's command to consume them (cf., Nah 1:6 and Ps 89:46). The hammer that smashes the rock into pieces confirms the threat that Jeremiah levels against the false prophets. He feels so strongly about the question of their lack of authority that he repeats his condemnation of vv. 16-22 again in vv. 30-32. These three verses are packed with arguments against his adversaries:

(1) They steal the words they speak from one another; what they say is cut and dried and never new because they have received nothing from Yahweh.

(2) They trip the consecrated formula "oracle of the Lord" (or "says the Lord") off their tongues at the drop of a hat, trying to bolster their position by implying that they are indeed prophets.

(3) They rely on dreams rather than on a true word from Yahweh.

(4) They tell their dreams as guides to how people should live—a guide that leads the hearers into the evil of the lie.

(5) God never sent them as messengers.

(6) God never gave them any commands at all.

The conclusion is hardly surprising: their advice is worthless.

NEVER SAY, "THE BURDEN OF THE LORD!" 23:33-40

> 33"When one of this people, or a prophet, or a priest asks you, 'What is the burden of the LORD?' you shall say to them, 'You are the burden, and I will cast you off, says the LORD'."

The last oracle in chap. 23 deals with the use of the second formula for announcing an oracle of divine origin: "the burden of the Lord." The Hebrew word for "burden," *massa'*, usually means a heavy load that an animal or person must carry. Somehow, as words often do, it became a metaphor for carrying God's word; it expressed the heavy task of proclaiming prophetic oracles. In this latter sense, it does not occur regularly within the sayings of the prophets, but serves quite frequently as a label to introduce an oracle. Examples of this turn up in Isa 13:1; 15:1; 17:1; 19:1; 21:1; 22:1; 23:1; Nah 1:1; Hab 1:1; Zech 9:1; 12:1; Mal 1:1. In one passage, Ezek 12:10, the prophet combines two formulas: "Thus says the Lord God, this *burden* concerns the prince . . .". Some experts have suggested that the choice of "burden" over other more common formulas is determined by the idea that it means a "lifting up of the voice," that is, a public proclamation, and so makes a fitting title for oracles delivered against foreign nations. A look at the examples in the Book of Isaiah reveals how many of the oracles titled this way are indeed addressed to pagan peoples.

Jeremiah himself gives so much attention to the "burden" because it provides him a new opportunity for a pun that will bring out forcefully his basic message that God speaks judgment through his prophets and not peace. Verse 33 summarizes the entire argument. God has no new "burden" to give; instead, it is the nation itself that has become the burden, and Yahweh is about to lay it down; or better, to throw it down. He repeats how priests, prophets and people all seek to give an oracle. Almost anyone thought that they could repeat as divinely inspired their views of what God wanted done. Jeremiah rejects this completely. The proper response of faith must be to listen where God is speaking. A true Israelite must ask "What has the Lord spoken?" The attitude needed in Israel's time of greatest crisis was not more diverse opinions and confusing directions from heaven, but silence. Jeremiah repeats the basic message of the preceding oracle—the words of those who use this formula, like those who tell their dreams, serve nothing more than their own musings and wants. The RSV translates v. 36 as "you *pervert* the words of the living God." "Pervert" comes from a verb that literally means "to overturn." It reverses the very way that God communicates through his chosen messengers, it substitutes for a special message given in the divine council by invitation only a whole grabbag of false ideas and plans. In the cacophony of evaluating and weighing all these so-called "divine messages," people never remember Yahweh's covenant at all. Jeremiah obviously felt strongly enough about this to repeat the entire message a second time in vv. 38-40.

Our own age suffers the claims of multiple voices all speaking with authority. The problem of discernment remains as difficult today as it was in the time of Jeremiah. His approach, from which we can learn, does not demand simply that we hearken to the voice of God spoken in past tradition, nor only seek for the new voices pointing to the future. It has elements of both. The prophet must be known for fidelity to the covenant message and steeped in the tradition of his community's experience of God, but he must also be prepared to preach a new course of action and new ways of responding to changed times. But above all, a true prophet can be recognized because his words build holiness. It first points to God's holiness and transcendence ("A God far" but also near); it leads to love for the covenant and its demands; it is accompanied by both suffering and deep trust in Yahweh (Jeremiah's "confessions"); it leads the prophet and the hearers to "know" Yahweh first as a God of compassion, of promise, of lordship over the world (Yahweh's "plan"); and it summons the hearers to judgment, to accountability, about their choice of actions and their response, especially as a community. These still hold true even for Christian decision-making today.

III. JEREMIAH'S VISION
IN SUMMARY
JEREMIAH 24:1 - 25:38

The three remaining passages in Jer 1-25 function as general reflections or concluding summaries to Jeremiah's collection of judgment oracles. The vision of the two baskets of fruit in chap. 24 sets forth the possibility of a new direction to God's dealings with Israel. The quotation of an earlier oracle from the time of Jehoiakim in 25:1-14 summarizes the history of frustration suffered by Jeremiah in proclaiming his message. The final oracle in 25:15-38 directs our attention ahead to the oracles against foreign nations in chaps. 46-51 and to the broader picture of a new world order directed by divine justice.

THE VISION OF THE BASKETS OF FRUIT
24:1-10

24 After Nebuchadrezzar king of Babylon had taken into exile from Jerusalem Jeconiah the son of Jehoiakim, king of Judah, together with the princes of Judah, the craftsmen, and the smiths, and had brought them to Babylon, the LORD showed me this vision: Behold, two baskets of figs placed before the temple of the LORD.

²One basket had very good figs, like first-ripe figs, but the other basket had very bad figs, so bad that they could not be eaten. ³And the LORD said to me, "What do you see, Jeremiah?" I said, "Figs, the good figs very good, and the bad figs very bad, so bad that they cannot be eaten."

⁴Then the word of the LORD came to me: ⁵"Thus says the LORD, the God of Israel: Like these good figs, so I will regard as good the exiles from Judah, whom I have sent away from this place to the land of the Chaldeans. ⁶I will set my eyes upon them for good, and I will bring them back to this land. I will build them up, and not tear them down; I will plant them, and not uproot them. ⁷I will give them a heart to know that I am the LORD; and they shall be my people and I will be their God, for they shall return to me with their whole heart.

⁸"But thus says the LORD: Like the bad figs which are so bad they cannot be eaten, so will I treat Zedekiah the king of Judah, his princes, the remnant of Jerusalem who remain in this land, and those who dwell in the land of Egypt. ⁹I will make them a horror to all the kingdoms of the earth, to be a reproach, a byword, a taunt, and a curse in all the places where I shall drive them. ¹⁰And I will send sword, famine, and pestilence upon them, until they shall be utterly destroyed from the land which I gave to them and their fathers."

Chap. 24 describes still another vision of the prophet in which he saw two baskets of figs and drew his lessons from the difference between them, one rotten, one good. Whether Jeremiah actually happened upon a table with the two baskets sitting on it and God inspired him with a sudden flash of insight into how these could represent the two groups of Judah's citizens, those left behind and those in exile; or if he received the whole in visionary form, we cannot know. But it certainly occurred at a time when the problem of the two groups was on his mind. Ironically, during the reign of king Jehoiakim from 609 down to 598, Jeremiah received strong support from high officials despite the king's hatred of him and thus avoided any serious threat to his life, but when the first exile engulfed the people in 597, and Zedekiah became king over a new bureaucracy, the reverse happened. Zedekiah personally liked and even respected the role of Jeremiah, but the nobles hated him and plotted to get rid of him. Part of the difficulty lay in the quality of those who were not exiled. As v. 1 makes clear, the best and most talented people were taken away to Babylon (see 2 Kgs 24:14-15). This left a new and more uncertain leadership which did not have the experience needed to deal with defeat at all.

Almost from the beginning of his reign, Zedekiah was under strong pressure to rebel and continue to fight for independence, and he soon succumbed to the temptation. Jeremiah must have felt this as rank blindness and betrayal of Yahweh's message written in the horrors of the first destruction of Jerusalem in 597. How pleased Jeremiah actually felt about the exiles at this point might be debatable —they certainly made up the majority of those he condemned so roundly in all of the preceding oracles! But at some point, as the development of this chapter indicates, he began to see that God could and would in fact reject the land and the covenant as it had been known, and would start again. Possibly even the idea of a new Exodus and new covenant already played a role in this early period by which God would deliver his people from Babylon—the "Egypt" of oppression and slavery—and restore them anew in the Promised Land. With time, this became the standard expectation of Israel's prophets. Jeremiah develops it further in chaps. 31-32, Ezekiel builds on it in Ezek 36-38, Second Isaiah makes it the most explicit in Isa 40-48.

The vision of two baskets, one good and one bad, is reported to be in front of the temple. This curious reference raises the possibility that the two baskets might have been offered there to Yahweh. Verse 2 describes them as "first-ripe" figs, the very fruits that were required to be brought to the temple at the beginning of the harvest to acknowledge Yahweh as the giver of all good blessing. This usually took place at the Feast of Weeks, 7 weeks after Passover. See Exod 34:22; Lev 23:15-22; Deut 16:9-12; and especially Deut 26:2-11, in which the offering is to be made in gratitude for the gift of the land and is to include the recital of Yahweh's great saving acts in the Exodus from Egypt. If Jeremiah was alluding to the First Fruits sacrifice at the temple, then the people gathered in worship are actually the bad figs, unworthy offerings for the land. Jeremiah, therefore, has already written off Zedekiah's reign and begun to place his hopes on a new action of God to save Israel through the ripe figs, the exiles in Babylon.

A second sign of Jeremiah's change of thought comes with the reference to his mission and initial call at 1:10: he was to build up and tear down, plant and uproot. Only this time it is changed: now he shall build up but not tear down, plant but not uproot. It is joined to the promise of a new heart for the exiles by which they shall "know" Yahweh, and through which he will re-establish his covenant so that once again as at Sinai, "they shall be my people and I will be their God" (see Exod 6:7). Thus, vv. 4-7 become a summary of the developed thought of the later Jeremiah, especially as it is found in chap. 31:27-34, the final collection of Jeremiah's message of hope.

Verses 8-10, by contrast, describe the fate of the bad figs. The clear reference not only to the king and the people of the land, but also to some who went down into Egypt, has led many scholars to date this particular oracle to a time after 586 when many citizens fled to Egypt to escape the punishment of the Babylonians for killing the governor Gedaliah (43:1-7). However, this does not have to be the occasion. Several other options are possible. In 609, King Necho of Egypt forced Jehoahaz to Egypt, and many might have gone with him (2 Kgs 23:34); four years later when

Jehoiakim severed his ties to Egypt and joined the Baby-lonians, many pro-Egyptians may have had to flee (2 Kgs 24:1). Jews had gone there at other times as well and formed a sizable colony of foreigners. A considerable library of Aramaic documents was found at Elephantine in the far south of Egypt that described the life of a Jewish mercenary fort which flourished there from at least 520 to 400 B.C. Later in the third century, Alexandria, the new city of the Greeks in Egypt, may have already had the largest Jewish population in the world of its time.

The oracle ends with the characteristic bluntness of Jeremiah. The destruction that he has preached so long against the nation and which everyone thought had come with such force in the Babylonian attack of 598, was still not completed. God would still turn his people into a curse, shame them, and send the sword, the plague and the famine on them—just as Jeremiah had said over and over (15:4 and 21:7) and would say again (29:18 and 34:17).

Much of the contents of this oracle in chap. 24 seems to be highly developed reflections on the importance of the exiles in God's plan and a conviction that he had rejected any who were left in the land. For this reason, commentaries often stress that parts of the oracle must have come from editors who looked back after the final collapse of Jerusalem in 586. Jeremiah's original oracle states the basic message, namely that God would continue to punish Jerusalem if the king and people persisted in their evil, and that God could easily begin anew with the very people that everyone considered gone for good. This same core vision stands at the heart of his letter to the exiles reported in chap. 29. But certain elements were probably added by the editors, such as the references to those who had to flee to Egypt, the quotation of the commissioning text in 1:10 about the purpose of Jeremiah's preaching, and the use of the oracles about the new covenant from chap. 31:27-31.

THE END DRAWS NEAR
25:1-14

25 The word that came to Jeremiah concerning all the people of Judah, in the fourth year of Jehoiakim the son of Josiah, king of Judah (that was the first year of Nebuchadrezzar king of Babylon), ²which Jeremiah the prophet spoke to all the people of Judah and all the inhabitants of Jerusalem: ³"For twenty-three years, from the thirteenth year of Josiah the son of Amon, king of Judah, to this day, the word of the LORD has come to me, and I have spoken persistently to you, but you have not listened. ⁴You have neither listened nor inclined your ears to hear, although the LORD persistently sent to you all his servants the prophets, ⁵saying, 'Turn now, every one of you, from his evil way and wrong doings, and dwell upon the land which the LORD has given to you and your fathers from of old and for ever; ⁶do not go after other gods to serve and worship them, or provoke me to anger with the work of your hands. Then I will do you no harm.' ⁷Yet you have not listened to me, says the LORD, that you might provoke me to anger with the work of your hands to your own harm."

The oracle in 25:1-14 can best be described as a *report* about the words Jeremiah spoke to king Jehoiakim many years before this passage was written down. In many ways it resembles the temple speech of chap. 7, and the editors may have taken parts of that speech and of other oracles and combined them to form a conclusion for chaps. 1-25. Certainly the comment in v. 13 (see below) comes from the hand of an editor who considered the body of oracles to be closed at this point. Even Jeremiah himself is referred to in the 3rd person as someone different from the writer of that verse. The words "everything written in this book," cannot reasonably describe any other body of oracles or stories than those which have gone before, since they mainly speak of judgment against Israel rather than of Jeremiah's life story or of his oracles of hope, most of which follow in chaps. 26-51. Those responsible for putting together and organizing Jeremiah's words selected this one speech to sum up the essential message of the prophet's preaching from the time of Josiah down to the final fall of Jerusalem in 586. Its historical overview of Israel's constant rejection of the true prophets captures the loneliness and frustration of Jeremiah as he tried to make people understand what was happening.

The oracle opens with some specific dates in Jeremiah's career. The fourth year of Jehoiakim, 605 B.C., corresponds to the same year that Jeremiah ordered Baruch to write down all his oracles on a scroll and read them to the king (Jer 36:1-8). As noted in the introduction, most scholars judge that this scroll (rewritten and expanded by Jeremiah himself—*cf.*, 36:27-32) contained the heart of the material found in chaps. 1-25. This scholarly consensus receives indirect corroboration by the date in 25:1. The further reference to Jeremiah's career in v. 3 states he had received and transmitted the word of the Lord for twenty-three years, that is, from 627, the year of his call, up to 605. This statement supports those scholars who continue to hold that Jeremiah was already a young man of 18 or so at the time of his call and that his actual adult ministry lasted well over forty years. It creates more difficulties than help for the other scholars who believe that 627 was the date of Jeremiah's birth and that he gave no oracles until the time of Jehoiakim in 609 B.C. However, since the whole speech in vv. 1-14 has been re-edited, we cannot base a decision on the beginning of Jeremiah's preaching from this text alone. Both sides still have a case to make.

The following vv. 3-7 list the crucial points of Jeremiah's oracles of judgment: (1) God has sent prophets continually to Israel—their mission is not something novel or frivolous; (2) the people have just as continually refused to heed them; (3) the basic message was repentance—"turn back" from your evil, "turn to" Yahweh; (4) the motive for repentance was the hope of living in the land and not to be thrown out of it; (5) the chief evil that the people have committed is idolatry and the making of idols; (6) this has provoked the divine anger and caused the punishment that they shall receive.

Many of these points reflect the message of the Book of Deuteronomy, especially "walking after other gods," hearing his word, turning back to Yahweh, living in the land, and provoking God to anger—as recorded in such passages as Deut 7:4,12; 8:2, 19-20; 11:9; 13:6-8. As a result, this passage too points to deuteronomic influence in the editing of Jeremiah. But like several of the other examples, it does not entirely imitate Deuteronomy's language. For instance, the phrase, "the work of your hands," does appear regularly in Deuteronomy (Deut 2:7; 4:28; 14:29; 16:15; 24:19; 27:15; 28:12; 30:9 and 31:29) but just as often in Isaiah (nine times), the Psalms (eleven times), Job (three times), and at least ten other places, not to mention the seven occurrences in Jeremiah itself (1:16; 10:3; 25:6,7,14; 32:30 and 44:8). We can only conclude that the expression was commonly used as a euphemism for idols and does not belong in any special way to Deuteronomy.

The second part of the oracle, vv. 8-14, announces the punishment God will send.

> 8"Therefore thus says the LORD of hosts: Because you have not obeyed my words, 9behold, I will send for all the tribes of the north, says the LORD, and for Nebuchadrezzar the king of Babylon, my servant, and I will bring them against this land and its inhabitants, and against all these nations round about; I will utterly destroy them, and make them a horror, a hissing, and an everlasting reproach. 10Moreover, I will banish from

them the voice of mirth and the voice of gladness, the voice of the bridegroom and the voice of the bride, the grinding of the millstones and the light of the lamp. [11]This whole land shall become a ruin and a waste, and these nations shall serve the king of Babylon seventy years. [12]Then after seventy years are completed, I will punish the king of Babylon and that nation, the land of the Chaldeans, for their iniquity, says the LORD, making the land an everlasting waste. [13]I will bring upon that land all the words which I have uttered against it, everything written in this book, which Jeremiah prophesied against all the nations. [14]For many nations and great kings shall make slaves even of them: and I will recompense them according to their deeds and the work of their hands."

Even in the RSV translation, these verses sound somewhat awkward with the combination of Nebuchadrezzar, Babylon, and nations of the North. Because the Greek text does not have the reference to the Babylonian king in v. 9, nor again in v. 11, and lacks a whole phrase about the "land of the Chaldeans" in v. 12, Jeremiah may have originally only spoken about the countries of the North in his oracle, while a later copiest or editor added the specific listing of the Babylonians to make sure the audience did not miss the point!

There is a striking reference to Nebuchadrezzar as the servant of Yahweh. Naturally, the Babylonian did not worship, and probably had never even heard of, Yahweh; but he could still serve Yahweh's purposes. The term may stem from the performance of the duties of a vassal king to an overlord. Ancient treaties often mention the obligations of the smaller states to serve the great king, particularly in time of war. Each of the kinglets must provide army units to fight for the overlord; and if they don't, they will be guilty of treason and removed from their thrones. Here Yahweh as the great king, the overlord of all nations, has summoned his vassal states from the North and East to punish Israel. The first punishment confirms this interpretation that the nations are in sacred service to God. They are to perform the *herem*, the "ban," on Israel and its inhabitants as Joshua had done to the Canaanites centuries before (Josh 6:17). A conquest made with divine help and at divine command required the conquered people to be offered as a sacrifice or holocaust to God. It seems barbarous to us. Yet in our own day it was a basically Christian nation that authorized block bombing and even atomic bombing of cities during World War II. We must not forget that the Bible is a living record of people far removed from us in time and often much less sensitive to evil, in whom the spirit of God was working, even if he had not brought them to a complete realization that zeal for God and cruelty do not necessarily go together. Once again the ideal of a sacred campaign or "holy war" for the land may come from the deuteronomic editors. It can be found in Deut 7:1-5, 20:16 and elsewhere.

The remaining punishments come from Jeremiah's usual storehouse of curses. See similar examples in 18:6; 19:8; 23:40; 24:9; 25:38; 42:18. The "voice of the bridegroom and the bride" is among Jeremiah's unique contributions, occurring only in 7:34; 16:9; 33:11 and this passage. The total time of punishment will be seventy years. This period may be just a general statement to indicate an entire generation will pass, or even to stand for a long time without specifying it to the exact month or year. The number 70 does appear to represent a large crowd in Judg 1:7; 1 Sam 6:19 and 2 Sam 24:15, and this seems the best solution here, particularly since no easy combination of events arises to fit exactly 70 years. From the fall of Judah (either 598-97 or 587-86) to the freeing of the exiles in 539 the time span is too short. The only possible combinations that match exactly are the interval from the Fall of the first temple in 586 to its rebuilding in 516, or else from the death of Josiah in 609 to the Persian release from exile in 539. But neither of these seems to be called for in this text.

Later biblical books were fascinated by Jeremiah's prophecy and many use it: Zech 1:2; 2 Chr 36:20-23; and Dan 9:24. Zechariah seems to move from 586 down to his own day, 519-518, approximately 70 years; Second Chronicles quotes Jeremiah to mean only the period from 586 to 539, or 47 years; and Daniel reuses the date to cover from 586 down to the time of Antiochus Epiphanes and after, in the second century, or about 400 years. These mysterious variations and vaguely specified times have been the source of much unwarranted calculations of the coming of the messianic kingdom among both Jews and Christians. It is certain that Jeremiah meant no more than to say that the exile would last a long time, longer than anyone alive would live to see its end, yet it would certainly end.

Verse 14 together with the last part of v. 13 ("all that Jeremiah preached against all the nations") introduces the next oracle in vv. 15-38, and may actually serve as the label or heading for the remaining twenty-seven chapters.

THE LORD'S CUP OF WRATH AGAINST THE NATIONS
25:15-38

15Thus the LORD, the God of Israel, said to me: "Take from my hand this cup of the wine of wrath, and make all the nations to whom I send you drink it. 16They shall drink and stagger and be crazed because of the sword which I am sending among them."

17So I took the cup from the LORD'S hand, and made all the nations to whom the LORD sent me drink it: 18Jerusalem and the cities of Judah, its kings and princes, to make them a desolation and a waste, a hissing and a curse, as at this day; 19Pharaoh king of Egypt, his servants, his princes, all his people, 20and all the foreign folk among them; all the kings of the land of Uz and all the kings of the land of the Philistines (Ashkelon, Gaza, Ekron, and the remnant of Ashdod); 21Edom, Moab, and the sons of Ammon; 22all the kings of Tyre, all the kings of Sidon, and the kings of the coastland across the sea; 23Dedan, Tema, Buz, and all who cut the corners of their hair; 24all the kings of Arabia and all the kings of the mixed tribes that dwell in the desert; 25all the kings of Zimri, all the kings of Elam, and all the kings of Media; 26all the kings of the north, far and near, one after another, and all the kingdoms of the world which are on the face of the earth. And after them the king of Babylon shall drink.

The final unit (in the first half of the Book of Jeremiah) introduces the reader to the universal rule of Yahweh over all nations. The theme centers on God's wrath against nations other than Israel and provides a fine introduction to the oracles against foreign nations found in chaps. 46-51. This connection between the end of chap. 25 and a body of oracles some twenty-one chapters later indicates that the intervening material may derive from a separate source and that the actual oracles against other nations were cut off and put at the end of the book for a special reason, the most likely one being to avoid breaking up the oracles and stories that pertain to Jeremiah's experiences at home. The Greek Septuagint, itself a very old witness to the text of Jeremiah, positions the oracles found in chaps. 46-51 right after chap. 25:13 and includes the present unit of 25:15-38 at their end as a kind of conclusion before continuing with what now is chaps. 26-45.

The highly descriptive "cup of wrath" that Yahweh pours out was a favorite expression in the time of Jeremiah and after. It appears in the oracles of Habakkuk (2:16), Ezekiel (23:32), Second Isaiah (51:17,22), Lamentations (4:21) and Ps 75:7-8, which can be best dated to the same period. Jeremiah uses it against foreign nations in 49:12 and 51:7. The choice of a cup may be influenced by the tradition of an ordeal in which the guilt or innocence of a person is revealed when they drink the special potion. Num 5:11-31 describes this ordeal for a secret case of adultery. If a woman who drinks the "water of bitterness" is guilty, she will have terrible pains and not be able to bear children. In this instance, the nations shall drink the cup and prove themselves guilty. Jeremiah describes the results of the drinking as drunkenness and staggering. From this we may conclude more particularly that their own drunken stupor will bring destruction with it. Isaiah had used this same image to describe Judah's guilty behavior years before (Isa 28:7-13), and Jeremiah borrowed it for the same purpose in 13:12-14. But it can just as well apply to foreign peoples (*e.g.,* Egypt in Isa 19:14).

A list of all the foreign nations who will drink this cup now follows. For the most part it is a standard list including all of the nations against whom Jeremiah actually delivers prophecies in chaps. 46-51, namely Egypt, Ammon, Edom, Moab, Tyre, Sidon, the Philistines, Elam and Babylon. Only Damascus is missing. But some new nations have been included that do not appear in later oracles: Uz, the land of Job (Job 1:1), which seems to be in northern Arabia near Edom (*cf.,* Lam 4:21); Dedan, Tema and Buz, all in northern Arabia, and Zimri, which nobody can identify, but may also refer to an Arabian tribe or area. This list provides a number of side comments that give interesting information. Verse 20 suggests that large colonies of foreigners have already settled in Egypt, perhaps some of them Jews. The five traditional cities of the Philistines have been reduced to three and a half with the loss of Gath and the apparent conquest of Ashdod. Gath probably simply declined to unimportant status since the time of King David; while Herodotus, the Greek Historian, reported that Pharaoh Psammetichus devastated the city of Ashdod in the mid seventh century. Verse 21 hints at a large number of Phoenician colonies when it mentions the kings of the coastlands across the Sea. Known outposts of Phoenician culture existed in Sardinia, Sicily, Spain and along the North African Coast. Verse 23 in the RSV names some Arabian tribes who "cut the corners of their hair." The Hebrew text is somewhat difficult at this point, and most scholars have assumed that it refers to a custom of cutting the hair and beard in honor of the dead, a custom forbidden by Lev 19:27 and 21:5. But as the New English Bible suggests, it may better be rendered as "those who wander the corner of the deserts," *i.e.*, nomads or semi-nomads, which would fit well with the other Arabian tribal references in the same verse. The Medes are mentioned in v. 25, but not the Persians, indicating that Cyrus the Great had not yet broken away from his Median overlords. And finally the reference to Sheshak in the Hebrew reading of v. 26 must be understood as a coded name for Babylon itself. (The RSV drops the word "Sheshak" and simply reads "Babylon.") The Hebrew makes use of the ancient art of *Atbash*, reversing the alphabet. Thus the first letter, *aleph*, is written for the last letter, *tau*. The second letter, *beth*, is written for second last, *shin*, etc. (-A-T-B-SH). The letters for Babylon, b-b-l, become in this code sh-sh-k. There would be no reason for this unless one had to avoid critical remarks about Babylon for security reasons.

Many commentators date this passage to the editors of the book at a fairly late stage. The mention of the devastation to Judah "as at this day" could well mean that the fall of the city in 586 was already an event of the past. On the other hand, the list gives all the nations that fell under Babylonian control during the reign of Nebuchadrezzar and ends with the conqueror itself receiving the cup of punishment. This would fit well sometime in the ministry of Jeremiah after Nebuchadrezzar began his reign in 605 B.C. The prophet warns that each in turn, beginning with Judah, will experience God's punishment by means of the Babylonians, but that they will not escape the same fate in the long run.

The list concludes with the addition of two short poetic oracles in vv. 30-33 and 34-38. These may have been placed here to illustrate the point of universal punishment. The first opens in v. 30 with the famous saying of Amos, the earliest writing prophet, against foreign nations—"the Lord roars from Zion" (Amos 1:2). All the verbs for shouting and roaring create the sense of an impending attack or military invasion. Probably Jeremiah has had a vision of the heavenly army marching at Yahweh's command to fight his battles against all enemies. The mention of the "holy abode" in v. 30 draws on a long history of mythical language about the divine warrior who dwells in his palace on a holy mountain and marches forth to do battle on behalf of his people. Some of Israel's most archaic poetry plays on this theme: Exod 15 and Hab 3, and particularly Judg 5. In Amos 1:2 the holy mountain is Zion; in Hab 3, it is Mount Paran, associated with the Exodus wanderings. The roots of this metaphor lie deep in Canaanite myth. The epic of Baal found at Ugarit and dating to the middle of the second millenium associates the kingship of the god with both his conquest of enemies and his erection of a royal palace on Mt. Saphon, usually located in northern Syria. Jeremiah makes use of this mythical reference to divine lordship over the land to introduce the special prophetic theme of God's lawsuit against Israel. The lawsuit, directed first against Israel in chap. 2, now applies to all nations. God's justice is universal. The penalty will be capital punishment and the executioner according to the warlike vocabulary of v. 32 will be the Babylonian armies. Verse 33 rounds off this short oracle with a prosaic addition, perhaps added by a commentator many years later. It describes a massive slaughter of God's enemies on the day of battle in which the corpses will extend from end to end of the universe. This has more in common with Ezek 38-39 and its vision of the final victory of Yahweh over all the world powers and so belongs more to the post-exilic age than to the time of Jeremiah.

The same message of a universal victory of Yahweh over the rulers of foreign nations is expressed by vv. 34-38 in the portrayal of the shepherds and masters of the herds. The word "lord of the flocks" depicts kings and leaders in biblical usage, and the prophet has powerfully created the fearful scene of a lion on the loose, killing lambs, mauling shepherds, endangering everyone. No pasture is safe and no ruler is secure. The lion may well be Nebuchadrezzar's military advance, but it is also Yahweh, whose fierce anger controls even the Babylonian might.

With this sweeping vision of Yahweh's justice in operation, the first half of the Book of Jeremiah draws to a close with its major collection of warnings and judgment oracles. Chaps. 26-52 continue with more detailed accounts of Jeremiah's work and his reactions to the disaster of Exile.

BIBLIOGRAPHY FOR FURTHER READING

Commentaries:

Andrew W. Blackwood, Jr., Commentary on Jeremiah (Word Books; Waco, Texas; 1977) 326 pp. A detailed commentary from the Conservative Christian tradition. It offers suggestions on a line by line and word by word basis, which makes it an easy book to follow. Its strength lies in the practical applications to the modern world that Blackwood works into every chapter, and his ability to bring out the New Testament value for the Christian reader.

John Bright, *Jeremiah* (Anchor Bible 21; New York, 1965). A very thorough historical treatment of Jeremiah's life and the problems of his ministry.

Guy P. Couturier, C.S.C., "Jeremiah," *Jerome Biblical Commentary* (Prentice-Hall, 1968), ch. 19. Popular commentary close to Jeremiah's historical period and literary style. Careful attention to important Hebrew words. Complete bibliography.

H. Cunliffe-Jones, *Jeremiah: God in History* (Torch Bible Commentaries; SCM Press, 1960). Short explanations of each section in a very readable style.

J. Philip Hyatt, "Jeremiah" in the *Interpreter's Bible* (vol. 5; Abingdon, 1956). A slightly older but easily read commentary that stresses the relevance of the prophet.

E. W. Nicholson, *The Book of the Prophet Jeremiah* (Cambridge Bible Commentary; 2 vols.: Cambridge Press, 1973, 1975). A very compact, readable but critical analysis of the oracles of Jeremiah and their further additions.

J. A. Thompson, *The Book of Jeremiah* (Eerdmans; 1908). The most thorough of modern commentaries; more conservative than Nicholson, yet discusses all critical problems.

W. Rudolph, *Jeremiah* (3rd revised edition in the *Handbuch zum Alten Testament* series; Tübingen, 1968). In German, but the most detailed and scholarly commentary available.

Other Recent Studies:

Sheldon Blank, *Jeremiah: Man and Prophet* (Hebrew Union College Press, 1961). An insightful examination of the message of the prophet from a Jewish and primarily psychological perspective.

James Efird, *Jeremiah: Prophet Under Siege* (Judson Press, 1979). A readable treatment of Jeremiah's personality as prophet.

William Holladay, *Jeremiah: Spokesman out of Time* (Pilgrim Press, 1974). Treats Jeremiah's prophecy from the unique aspect of his self-consciousness and ability to question, thus having much in common with modern thinking.

E. W. Nicholson, *Preaching to the Exiles: A Study of the Prose Tradition in the Book of Jeremiah* (Schocken Books, 1970). The most detailed exploration of the problem of the prose speeches and their relation to Jeremiah himself.

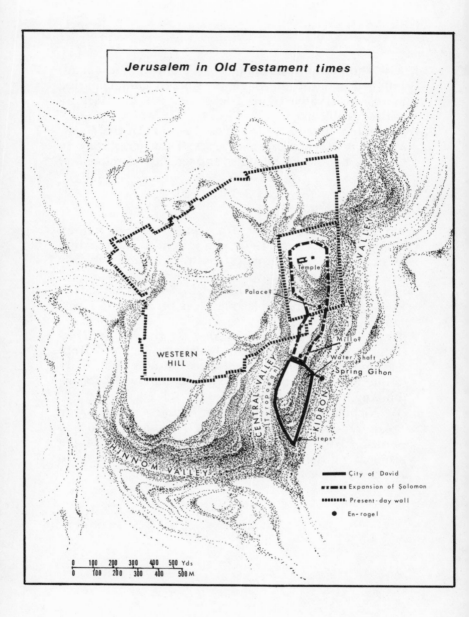

Jerusalem in Old Testament times

Temple

Palace?

WESTERN HILL

CENTRAL VALLEY (Tyropoeon)

KIDRON VALLEY

Millo?
Water Shaft
Spring Gihon

Steps

HINNOM VALLEY

City of David
Expansion of Solomon
Present-day wall
En-rogel

0 100 200 300 400 500 Yds
0 100 200 300 400 500 M

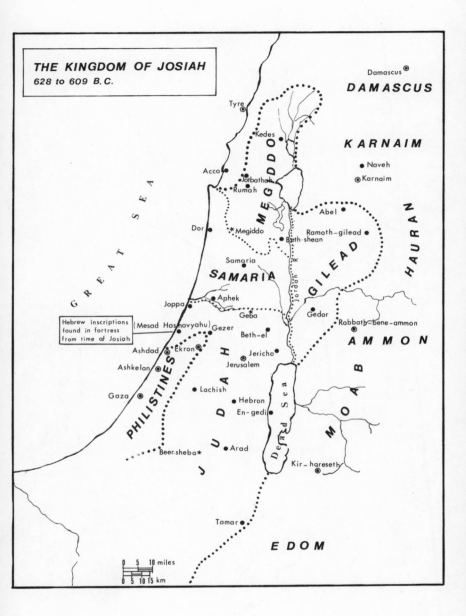

THE KINGDOM OF JOSIAH
628 to 609 B.C.

Damascus ◎
DAMASCUS

KARNAIM

Tyre ◎

Kedes ●

● Naveh
◎ Karnaim

Acco ●

Jotbathah ●
Rumah ●

● Abel

MEGDDO

Dor ●

＊ Megiddo
Beth-shean ●
Ramoth-gilead ●

HAURAN

Samaria ●

SAMARIA

GILEAD

Joppa ●
Aphek ●

Geba ●

Gedor ●

Rabbath-bene-ammon ●

Hebrew inscriptions
found in fortress
from time of Josiah
(Mesad Hasavyahu)
Gezer ●

Beth-el ●

AMMON

Ashdad ◎ Ekron ◎
Ashkelon ◎

Jericho ●

Jerusalem ⊗

J U D A H

Lachish ●

P H I L I S T I N E S

Gaza ◎

Hebron ●
En-gedi ●

M O A B

Beer-sheba ＊

Arad ●

Kir-hareseth ◎

G R E A T   S E A

Dead Sea

Jordan R.

Tamar ●

E D O M

0   5   10 miles
0   5   10 15 km

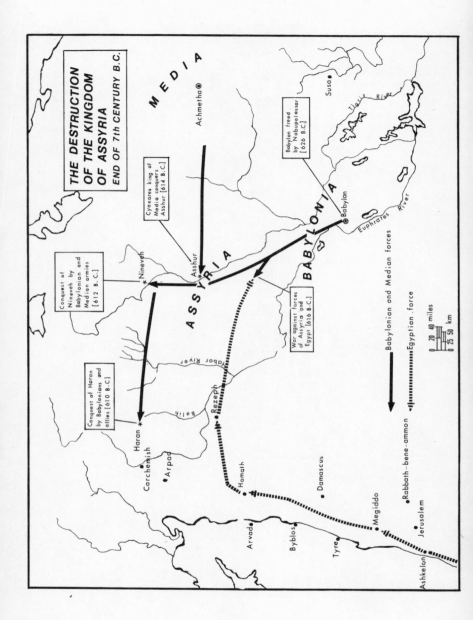

THE DESTRUCTION
OF THE KINGDOM
OF ASSYRIA
END OF 7th CENTURY B.C.

MEDIA

Achmetha ⊙

Susa ●

Tigris River

Cyaxares king of
Media conquers
Asshur [614 B.C.]

Babylon freed
by Nabupolassar
[626 B.C.]

BABYLONIA

Babylon ⊗

Euphrates River

Conquest of
Nineveh by
Babylonian and
Median armies
[612 B.C.]

Nineveh
*

Asshur
*

ASSYRIA

War against forces
of Assyria and
Egypt [616 B.C.]

Conquest of Haran
by Babylonians and
allies [610 B.C.]

Habor River

Haran
*

Balih

Rezeph ●

Babylonian and Median forces

Egyptian force

0   20   40 miles
0   25   50 km

Carchemish ●
● Arpad

Hamath ●

Damascus ●

Arvad ●

Byblos ●

Tyre ●

Megiddo ●

Rabbath-bene-ammon ●

Jerusalem ●

Ashkelon ●

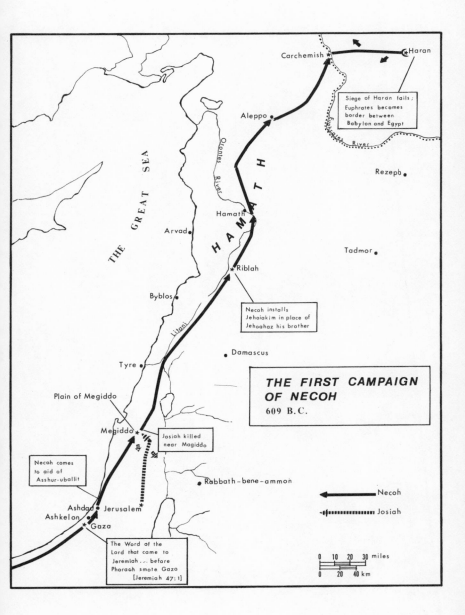

Carchemish ⋆ ✻Haran

Siege of Haran fails;
Euphrates becomes
border between
Babylon and Egypt

Euphrates River

Aleppo ●

Rezeph ●

THE GREAT SEA

Orontes River

H A M A T H

Hamath ●

Tadmor ●

Arvad ●

⋆ Riblah

Byblos ●

Necoh installs
Jehoiakim in place of
Jehoahaz his brother

Litani

● Damascus

Tyre ●

**THE FIRST CAMPAIGN
OF NECOH**

609 B.C.

Plain of Megiddo

Megiddo ⋆

Josiah killed
near Magiddo

Necoh comes
to aid of
Asshur-uballit

● Rabbath-bene-ammon

◀━━━━━ Necoh
◀▪▪▪▪▪▪▪▪▪ Josiah

Ashdod ● Jerusalem ⋆
Ashkelon ●
⋆ Gaza

The Word of the
Lord that came to
Jeremiah ... before
Pharaoh smote Gaza
[Jeremiah 47:1]

0   10   20   30 miles
0   20   40 km